Change

THEORIZING AFRICAN AMERICAN MUSIC

Series Editor: Philip Ewell

Make Rappers Rap Again
Interrogating the Mumble Rap "Crisis"
Heidi R. Lewis

Change
The *New Thing* and Modern Jazz
Kwami Coleman

Being Dope
Hip Hop and Theory through Mixtape Memoir
A. D. Carson

Change

The *New Thing* and Modern Jazz

Kwami Coleman

OXFORD
UNIVERSITY PRESS

Oxford University Press is a department of the University of Oxford.
It furthers the University's objective of excellence in research, scholarship,
and education by publishing worldwide. Oxford is a registered trade mark of
Oxford University Press in the UK and in certain other countries.

Published in the United States of America by Oxford University Press
198 Madison Avenue, New York, NY 10016, United States of America.

CIP data is on file at the Library of Congress

ISBN 9780197780091 (pbk.)
ISBN 9780197780084 (hbk.)

DOI: 10.1093/9780197780121.001.0001

The manufacturer's authorised representative in the EU for product safety is
Oxford University Press España S.A. of El Parque Empresarial San Fernando
de Henares, Avenida de Castilla, 2 – 28830 Madrid (www.oup.es/en or
product.safety@oup.com). OUP España S.A. also acts as importer into Spain
of products made by the manufacturer.

Dedicated to those artists—past, present, and future—forging a path through the unknown.

And to Earl R. Coleman, my first and most important music teacher.

Contents

Closing: Black Power

Figures

Foreword

African American music, with its numerous genres and styles, is one of the most important musics in American history. Rap and hiphop are currently two of the world's most popular genres, with local varieties in virtually every country on the planet, while jazz has arguably been America's most significant homegrown music and musical export. *Theorizing African American Music* focuses on the theory and analysis of African American music writ large. TAAM foregrounds work done by BIPOC scholars with this music, as well as work generally done on African American musicians and composers. TAAM includes explorations that might typically fall under the purview of music theory, but also ethnomusicology, musicology, jazz, performance, composition, or other relevant fields that could reasonably include theory or analysis.

As has been discussed widely in recent years, American music theory has historically been, from a racial perspective, unremittingly white. What this means for the many rich genres of music that can rightly be said to have roots in or ties to African Americanism—genres such as blues, boogie-woogie, disco, doo-wop, funk, gospel, hiphop, jazz, Motown, R&B, ragtime, rap, rock, soul, and techno, or other genres not normally associated with black music, such as bluegrass, classical, concert, country, and metal—is that virtually all attempts to analyze and theorize these genres in American music theory were undertaken by white persons, usually men, and strained through a filter of the field's white racial framing. This has resulted, to a large extent, in the appropriation of African American musical genres by mainstream music theory with the intent of legitimizing the music in question to the field so that it can be further mined for its musical resources.

TAAM pulls the discussion of these African American musical genres away from whiteness and (re)engages black and BIPOC voices, thus moving beyond the narrow confines of what has, historically, constituted music theory in the United States. It's difficult to say what "theorizing African American music" is exactly, but the series hopes to create theories of this music on its own terms, with new ideas and concepts, theories that will enhance our understanding not only of African American music but of other musics as well. Importantly, everyone, of any identity, is welcome to contribute to and participate in this book series, but foregrounding black and BIPOC voices remains paramount. TAAM will broaden and enrich academic music while providing inspiration to a new generation of musicians and scholars, thus rightfully placing African American music alongside all other great musics of our planet, as an example of outstanding musical ideas worthy of our collective attention and an exemplar of American music for the whole world to see.

In Kwami Coleman's *Change: The "New Thing" and Modern Jazz*, he situates his topic within multiple fields, including ethnomusicology, musicology, music theory, critical theory, sound studies, ethnic studies, and improvised music studies. He delves deeply into jazz history and theory and offers a fresh perspective on what has often been called "free jazz." Coleman focuses his energy on two notable practitioners, Ornette Coleman and Cecil Taylor, but it's clear that Coleman has extensive knowledge of the field well beyond those two. He extends his knowledge to a Black racial consciousness and vernacular musical practice, and asks us, when thinking about "free jazz," what was so "unfree" about jazz in the first place.

As a practicing jazz pianist himself, and as the son of another significant jazz performer, Coleman brings a unique voice to bear on the subject. He redefines the term "heterophony" to discuss free jazz, formerly known as the "new thing" and usually as chaotic, undetermined, and noisy. Coleman defines heterophony as "an unusually dense sonic texture of centrifugal musical voices that some musicians experimented with in pursuit of immediate and intuitive ways to improvise collectively." In unpacking this term, he reveals the method behind not just a few composers' works but for jazz in the early 1960s, a period that was tumultuous yet of profound importance in American music history. In short, Kwami Coleman's Change: The *New Thing* and Modern Jazz is a must read for all jazz scholars as well as all musicians involved in mid-to late twentieth-century American music, music institutions, and music education.

Philip Ewell
Series Editor, Theorizing African American Music

Preface

"Free jazz means playing any and everything, right?"

It's a common question, one that improvising musicians and pedagogues of music improvisation have probably heard before. This book offers an answer to that question, one that can be concisely summarized as *yeah, kind of, but not really.*

This is my attempt at historicizing a new sound grammar that emerged in the early 1960s—a more abstract approach to improvisation that both grew from and diverted from the musical past. It was, and in some ways still is, a controversial sound. "Free jazz" can, depending on the musicians we're referring to, be an unwieldly and chaotic sound, produced as though the musicians' intent is to confuse and repel the listener. The sound and image of a loud, squeaking and squawking saxophonist may have been conjured in you right now. Free jazz recordings are one thing, but catching an ensemble of improvisers playing "free"—in the immersive context of live performance— can be an intense, disorienting, and potentially unpleasant if not disturbing experience. Depending on one's tolerance for the unknown, however, it can also be exhilarating and inspiring, like watching a group of performers flout or break the rules, customs, and conventions of acceptable performance. Free jazz can signify daring liberation for both performer and observer, and it certainly did exactly that in the early 1960s as it proliferated. Whereas "cacophony" might, understandably, be the most fitting descriptor of the sound in question, I want to suggest that "heterophony" instead captures the essence of the abstract sonic texture represented by "free jazz"—a style that, in the nascent years of the 1960s, was referred to as jazz's *new thing*.

Though none of the musicians in this narrative used the word "heterophony" to describe their music or its sound, it does help illuminate the technique and aesthetic that improvising musicians living and working in, or being cognizant of, New York City's downtown experimental art scene developed in these years. It is a texture of sound insofar as "texture" in music studies refers to the arrangement of discrete streams of sound (like human or instrumental voices) and their relationship to each other; it's a cognate of the Latin noun *textūra*, which translates to "a weaving." Heterophony, I explain in this book's introduction and elsewhere, is a dense sonic texture—a lattice or matrix—of decentralized simultaneity, where autonomous voices (instrumental voices in this case) are woven together and bound by an intuited kind of synergy. In other words, the musicians in this narrative were pursuing an abstract kind of harmony that did not need to rely on the common pillars of musical orderliness: key (tonality) and meter. So rather than a chaotic and disorderly caricature of music, I hope this book contributes to a more informed discourse on this historical period of improvised music and the artists experimenting with the *new thing*. The abstract, heterogeneous mass of sound that a collective of musicians can, by some kind of sorcery, intonate was in the 1960s a new sonic order that language still can't sufficiently objectify, though I spent several chapters in this book trying.

"Change" in the title refers to what these experiments in heterophony represented within the artistic milieu whence it came: the social and professional networks of improvising musicians revolving around New York City's music industry. The city's cultural geography and economy, shaped historically by an ever-changing web of venues, independent and major record companies, and freelance musicians moving to and passing through the city for work, was one important node in a globalizing jazz market that, by the 1960s, extended across both Atlantic and Pacific oceans. "Change" was also a word charged in the 1960s with the energy of potential social and political revolution, appearing in poignant, provocative, and radical media.[1] "Playing the changes" is a colloquialism that improvising musicians use to mean improvising based on a chord progression (i.e., chord changes), so there's perhaps a bit of poetic irony in the fact that the musicians I'm focusing on here sought an alternative to that common practice.

This book started as a doctoral dissertation aimed at understanding the change in style of Miles Davis's mid-1960s quintet in relation to his earlier recorded work. Davis, who was as important an influence on me as a young musician as he was and still is to countless others across the world, seemed to be this permanent avant-gardist who was almost chameleonic in his ability to absorb and adapt to new musical ideas and styles. He would say, in his later interviews during the 1980s, that he changed music several times over his career. That remark, taken at face value, is unforgivably pompous, but I assumed Davis's humility and interpreted it as his "changing" music in the way he changed his wardrobe each decade, starting in the late 1960s up until his death in 1991, in response to the aesthetic and cultural changes of the times. In a *Washington Post* article dated September 28, 1969, journalist Hollie I. West printed remarks by Davis (with unspecified attribution) that would follow him to the end of his career, shaping his legend along the way: "I have to change. I can't look back. It's like a curse. I can't do the things I used to do. There are too many new things out there."[2] So, during that research, I took Davis's word and tried to understand how his style changed so drastically in the 1960s in response to the "new things" in the scene. I found that it was the musicians around Davis—those he listened to live and on records, and the younger musicians he would hire and closely work with in his quintet—who were catalysts for that change. In short, it was *music* that changed Davis, not the other way around.

This is a book about that change in music.

❋

Some important notes on the text:

I refer to many of the subjects in this narrative as Black American to capture the expansiveness of hemispheric black identity, which also includes the Caribbean migrants and their children who settled in the northeast United States, New York City especially. I use the specific term "African American" to denote black culture and experience, rather than people, in the United States.

Historical commercial and unofficial (i.e., bootleg) recordings are a critical primary source in my research; they are the objects of analysis and exegesis that drive the narrative. Many of these recordings are available on digital streaming platforms (DSPs) like Apple Music and Spotify, are available for digital streaming and download, or may be purchased as physical media. You will see the symbol ▶ followed by a timestamp; this denotes the location of an event being described in the narrative text that you can listen to on the digital master of the recording, which tends to be uniform across DSPs. My analytical methodology reflects my interests as a musicologist attuned to the historiography around and intrinsic structural elements that constitute an extant musical work and a composer and musician interested in the knowable and unknowable alchemical processes of creation.

I hope this book contributes to a new understanding of this rich period of musical experimentation and that it continues to inspire music and sound artists to push past what they know, what they think they know, and what they think they must know. This music has certainly had that effect on me.

Kwami Coleman
Greenwich Village
New York City
August 2024

Frontispiece

Bob Thompson (American, 1937–1966), Garden of Music, 1960
Oil on canvas, 78 7/8 x 143 1/2 in. (202.9 x 364.5 cm), height x width
Collection of the Atheneum Museum of Art
© Michael Rosenfeld Gallery LLC, New York, NY
Courtesy of Michael Rosenfeld Gallery LLC, New York, NY

Opening: "Free" Jazz

It began with controversy.

In November 1961, less than a year after recording the experimental album *Free Jazz* for Atlantic Records in New York City, Ornette Coleman and his manager Mildred Fields arranged for the double quartet—the unique ensemble format that Coleman used for the session—to travel to Cincinnati, Ohio, for a concert at the Taft Auditorium. The event was well publicized, with ads running in the *Cincinnati Enquirer*, the city's largest newspaper, for weeks prior, announcing an unprecedented evening of music in the city by "easily the most controversial figure in jazz today."[1] It was, as far as the historical record shows, the first time that a concert of music performed under such an ambiguous and enticing name—*free jazz*—was presented to the public.

Produced by Encore Productions, a company headed by graduate students at two local institutions, Xavier University and the University of Cincinnati's College-Conservatory of Music, the concert was, according to other press coverage, a highly anticipated event. Descriptions promised something enigmatic and novel by an uncanny band and a creation by a jazz iconoclast in pursuit of the musically unprecedented. The evening's program was to contain "[f]ree-wheeling spontaneous improvisation and five original [j]azz compositions" with "Free Jazz—a type of performance which includes a two-minute rehearsed introduction followed by solos, duets, trios, and ensembles made up on the spur of the moment from ideas presented in the introduction" taking up the entire second half.[2] Given Coleman's recorded output to this point, the concert would represent an important milestone in the general public's exposure to the sound of heterophonic collective improvisation, a technique that Coleman had been utilizing in his band's recorded work of the previous two years, and that jazz insiders in the music press referred to as the music's "new thing." But the concert never happened.

The concert was canceled at the last minute, and the *Enquirer* cited flight delays that left inadequate rehearsal time as the reason. The *Cincinnati Post & Times Star* summarized the cancelation as a "fight over fine print" with two divergent accusations: according to Encore, Coleman and Fields pocketed the $900 advance allocated for the band's flights and instead traveled by car; according to Fields, Encore did not have the band's $1,000 fee in hand by the time they had arrived for their pre-concert rehearsal, presumably relying on door sales which, according to the paper's account, amounted to "barely $500," culminating in refunds being issued to 150 patrons for a venue that seats approximately fifteen times as many.[3] Reprinting much of the local reportage and hearsay, the account by *Down Beat*, the premier U.S. jazz magazine, emphasized some of the incident's absurdity: "Dick Shaefer, a former correspondent for *Down Beat*, reported Encore had posters 'all over town, announcing "Ornette Coleman—Free Jazz Concert." People read it literally and actually went to the box office looking for free tickets.'"[4]

This calamity and the press it received likely abetted the confusion and doubts about the seriousness of Coleman and his music and whether the impending new sound in jazz which he seemed to be pioneering had any genuine artistic merit. Was Coleman a serious musical thinker or a charlatan? Was his music the future of jazz or a passing fad? And did *Free Jazz*—the most ambitious example of the *new thing* to date—mark the arrival of jazz's abstract avant-garde or was it an aesthetic turn backward, toward chaos and noise?

This book grapples with the controversy stoked by jazz's *new thing* in the early 1960s and does so by vacillating between three levels of discourse: the *new thing*'s coverage in the consumer print media of the era; first-person accounts by artists of their own creative process as documented in album liner notes, interviews, ephemera, and other archival sources; and my own transcriptions and analyses of performances captured on sound and video recordings. In examining selected recordings as examples of the *new thing*, I bring my own insights as a composer, musician, and musicologist to the task of explicating the concepts, methods, and design details of the performances on these representative and key recordings. My focus on consumer print media, however, also serves to illustrate the fraught, reactionary, and hostile reception of the experimental improvised music critics called jazz's *new thing* during an extraordinary political moment, in the United States and globally. I maintain that the critical consensus on the *new thing*—that it was a reactionary and antagonistic departure from modern jazz—has had an enduring impact on how this period of musical experimentalism is generally understood and taught in jazz and American music studies. The aberration of free jazz/the *new thing* reached its apotheosis in the neoclassical turn of the 1980s and 1990s, a perspective on the music that I was inundated with as a young musician growing up and being educated in New York City at the turn of a new millennium. The presumed illegitimacy of the *new thing* in modern jazz circles in the 1960s and the decades since have obstructed a deeper and more accurate understanding of the aesthetic goals of the musicians involved. My hope is that this book contributes to that fuller and more capacious understanding of the music, its creators, and of the fertile period of experimentation in improvised music out of which the *new thing* developed by situating the sounds and methods of jazz's 1960s avant-garde within the intersecting creative, cultural, and political forces affecting the lives and work of its practitioners.

The methods developed by so-called avant-gardists seeped into jazz's mainstream as they were interpolated by modern jazz luminaries like Sonny Rollins, John Coltrane, and Miles Davis. A goal of this book is to explain this conceptual and methodological diffusion, which I summarize as musicians' common search for new sonic and expressive resources for collectivized and cooperative improvisatory performances. How that experimentation was (mis)understood by jazz modernists, and the terms by which they debated and dismissed the new music, is, as mentioned earlier, part of the story.

Toward the end of the 1960s, the new thing was emblematic of a new radical black consciousness that had been fomenting in the enclaves of industrialized cities since the end of the Second World War. Following the assassination of Malcolm X and throughout the ascendent Black Power movement conflagrating across the United States thereafter, the intensity of the *new thing*'s abstract and opaque sound was taken by its advocates and detractors as the ensoniment of rebellion and revolution. But it was more than that too.

Serious Creative Work

I came to this understanding of the music through my father, Earl Ronald Coleman, born in 1946. He was a pianist and composer from Brooklyn and the first child of Earl Coleman Sr. and Mildred Randolph, followed shortly by my aunt Dorette and uncle Jimmy. Big Earl, as my grandfather was called, was a baritone saxophonist who for a time led his own big band, and Grandma was a seamstress and hairdresser who played the alto saxophone in her youth. The family first lived in 511 Decatur Street, then 2011 Fulton Street, both in the Bedford-Stuyvesant neighborhood; as my uncles Ricky and Michael and aunt Bunny were welcomed into the world the family relocated to 104 Rodney Street in South Williamsburg. My father's formative years were spent traversing these neighborhoods, which included sizable Black American (African American and Caribbean), Puerto Rican, and Ashkenazi Jewish enclaves, but, as an aspiring musician, he was drawn to the bohemian culture of lower Manhattan. It was there, in one of the many cafés in Greenwich or the East Village, that he was first exposed to jazz's *new thing*. He adopted Islam as a teenager and joined the Nation of Islam at sixteen (lying about his age, as membership was granted only at eighteen), enthralled—as many black youths were—by Minister Malcolm's fearless indictments of white supremacy, racism, and the complacency of "well-meaning" yet complicit white and black people.

Proselytizing by the Nation's most successful recruiter, Malcolm X, on street corners, in pool halls, and prisons, and his willingness to engage with the press drew many curious, searching, and otherwise disaffected black urbanites in New York City and beyond. Congregants at Muhammad's Temple #7 on 116th Street and Lenox Avenue were electrified by the young minister's sermons, which blended Garveyite self-empowerment rhetoric, etiological parables that centered Black Americans—descendants of enslaved people—as the progeny of enlightened and powerful ancient African civilizations, new mythology, analyses and indictments of systemic racism that excoriated its perpetrators, and the promise of grace and earthly salvation through Allah via the anointed messenger, Elijah Muhammad. Minister Malcolm instructed his black congregants and audiences that their self-worth and worldview should be erected apart from and outside of societal norms and the expectations of white people, and that they should be proud of their racial identity. He hooked young black men with his own redemption story, telling lurid tales about his time as a street hustler and petty criminal—the lifestyle that led to his incarceration—and his subsequent salvation, which he found in Islam while still in prison. Malcolm used himself as an example of the kind of self-invention, empowerment and agency that can be seized despite the intrinsic disadvantages of a hateful, hostile, and exploitative society. I imagine the impression that Minister Malcolm had on my father and his peers, who were being told compellingly and charismatically that not only were black people not inherently inferior and thus fit for slavery, as white American Christianity taught, but that we had internalized that hatred, inflicting a kind of existential bondage ("mental slavery," as he called it) unto ourselves that was hindering our full potential.

My father never really spoke to me in detail about the years he spent in the Nation. I've since gathered that it's because he grew disenchanted with the organization after Malcolm's censure and subsequent murder and, like so many of his generation, embarked on a more self-directed and exploratory journey of (self-)discovery and political engagement. He found community in local black Islamic networks like the Ahmadiyya, a sect of Islam propagated by the Punjabi mufti Muhammad Sadiq in urban black communities along the East Coast and the Midwest. He found peers and elders who were on complementary spiritual journeys: those who sought a restorative and more expansive theology than what Euro-American Christianity—revolving around a white male messiah—could promise. This social network cohered around an ethos of cultural excavation, knowledge production, and pride in the face of a white supremacist orthodoxy that assumed the inferiority of the nonwhite Global South, particularly Africa and Asia. This network is how my father met many other black musicians with similar interests, one of which was Rashied Ali, a Philadelphia-born drummer ten years his senior who shepherded him through the after-hours world of professional musicians in New York in these formative years.

My father had a story about how Ali brought him to a rehearsal for John Coltrane's band, of which Ali was a member—a profound experience that made a lasting impression on him. The experience offered him a glimpse into the world of the black musical vanguard; among black improvising musicians of the mid-1960s, Coltrane was seen as a creative and spiritual leader and the sound of his music symbolic of a new musical vernacular and transcendent, if not radical, consciousness. In thinking about the few times that I heard my father talk about this experience—which was always directed at his adult music students and friends, not me—it seems to me now that it was almost a rite of passage into a social and professional world largely absent in narratives about free jazz, especially in the academic fields of jazz and American music studies.

The rehearsal Ali invited my father to (I'm not sure whether it was in lower Manhattan or in Long Island, where the Coltrane family lived at the time) occurred when Coltrane first worked with two drummers, Ali and Elvin Jones, which would place it somewhere in 1965. My father turned nineteen years old that year. I don't know who else was in attendance, but it was likely the musicians who recorded *Meditations*: Ali and Jones on drums, McCoy Tyner on piano, and Jimmy Garrison on bass. My father arrived to find Tyner already warming up on the piano, and soon Jones walked in and made his way through the room to set up the kit. Coltrane was not yet in the room, but, according to my memory of my father's telling, the ambience was already electric. The degree of excitement and anticipation in his account, it is clear to me now, spoke to how meaningful it was for my father to be there. He remembered Jones, a powerful drummer whose fiery personality was well-known anecdotally, even among aspiring improvising musicians in New York City like me, a generation later, in the late 1990s and early 2000s (Jones passed in 2004), as being particularly mischievous that day, culminating in a zesty exchange between Jones and Tyner that extended to the other Muslims in the room. Proclaiming loudly that he had not yet eaten and was hungry, Jones announced that he was going to the corner store to pick up a ham sandwich and asked Tyner, loud enough for everyone to hear, if he'd like one too. Tyner was an observant Ahmadi Muslim, for whom pork products and alcoholic beverages are *haram* (forbidden), so, in my father's telling, Tyner just ignored Jones and kept his attention on the piano. That only made Jones start up again, and he declared—this time louder—that he was also thirsty and intended to pick up a cold beer at the corner store too, asking Tyner again if he cared for one. Here was Jones actively starting shit by vibing a dear and observant colleague with threats or temptations of *haram* contraband. Naturally, everyone in the room found this hilarious.

The repartee carried on, with Jones snapping harder and Tyner becoming more visibly annoyed, which only encouraged Jones further, and it all boiled over into a jovially hostile match of the dozens that every musician in the room became entangled in. If Jones's goal was to rile people up, he succeeded. The result was a loud and wonderfully profane tirade of shouting, curses, and laughter. It is a bittersweet memory for me, because I cannot remember or ask about the specific jokes and insults that my father would gleefully recite, but I do have a vivid memory of the wonderment that remained in his eyes each time he told this story decades after. There he was, in the room with some of his heroes—professional black men and architects of a new sound grammar representative of jazz's avant-garde—who were relatable and accessible to him through community networks. Their intimidating artistic powers clearly did not prevent them from engaging the mundane joys of wicked banter. In the story's inevitable climax, my father, imitating the sudden solemnity of the moment, would intone with a brief dramatic pause, "And then, John walked in . . . and all that shit stopped."

In marking the quick turn upon Coltrane's entrance, which signaled the official beginning of the rehearsal, my father recapitulated the unique reverence that many held for Coltrane and the intense focus he brought to the task at hand. His was a story of bearing witness: to serious artistry and playful camaraderie. It was a life-altering experience of an intimate black creative space in the global capital of the jazz industry. That industry was embedded in a multiethnic, heterogeneous city beset by racial and economic segregation and deprivation. The firsthand perspective illustrated by my father's story has informed my own listening to Coltrane and other musicians the industry called avant-gardists in my own formative years; I was led to understand jazz's "new thing" not as a genre or cohesive aesthetic or political movement but as an emergent moment of experimentation that expanded the content and sound of improvised music, especially among black musicians. One method and effect, heterophony, accounts for the dense, opaque, and at times overwhelming sound of the compositions as described in periodical literature and recorded performances known in the 1960s as the *new thing* in jazz. My father died in 2007 when I was twenty-three, and much of my research work since then has been driven by an impulse to understand why this historical moment was so impactful to him and the generations of improvising musicians that followed, mine included.

Heterophony Is Change

Music like that captured on Coltrane's *Meditations*, recorded in November 1965, was experimental insofar as it was accomplished with newer, unconventional methods of collective improvisation that emphasized intuition, deep listening, and close, sympathetic exchange and collaboration between musicians in the act of performance. The ensemble utilizes heterophony, which is a multivoice (or multi-instrumental) texture where cohesion in the ensemble is achieved by means other than the conventional centripetal sonic forces in Western music: tonal center and meter. In heterophony, voices and instruments can play "together" without being in the same key and/ or without a common meter, but musicians may also choose to improvise (a) within a shared tonal center with a more fluid sense of time or, more commonly, (b) within the context of a steady pulse in a tonally open (or multitudinous), chromatic, sound-oriented way (which the drummer and composer Tony Williams, and fellow members of Miles Davis's quintet, called *time, no changes*). Heterophony is a texture, meaning that it describes the relationship between—and aggregate density and motion of—the instrumental or sung voices of a given piece of music. Similarly, a composition and/or a performance can vacillate between heterophony and other ensemble and musical textures, like polyphony, homophony, and monophony. Heterophony does not mean that there is an absence of form, forethought, or other structural parameters that improvisers may abide by. The use of heterophonic textures by black improvising musicians in the 1960s, in cities like New York, Chicago, Philadelphia, and Los Angeles, coincided with evocations and affirmations of African American folkways and cosmology, as well as those of Africa and Asia.

In heterophony, "harmony" is amoebic and conditional; it is constantly changing and unfixed. Heterophony is decentralized, yet cohesion can be achieved through cooperation; it is the abstract sound of heterogeneous simultaneity— a fluctuating web of sound or a matrix of autonomous but still interconnected voices and subjectivities. Musicians improvising heterophonically can potentially be, collectively, in all the keys and none of them all at once. Heterophony invites a different way of listening too, one that's expansive enough to capture, absorb, and process a dense and unwieldly wall of sound. If heterophonic improvisation represented a profound conceptual change for those musicians experimenting with it in the 1960s, it also represented, according to them, an unwanted and unwelcome change elsewhere in the music industry, among other musicians and particularly among those who exerted influence on the employment and livelihood of musicians: club owners and critics. In this book I index also the change in the coverage of the *new thing* in print media, which slid gradually from a discourse of high (avant-garde) modernism to that of grievance and aesthetic failure. I think that discursive shift in 1960s music criticism says something important and revealing about consensus mainstream music aesthetics and the expectations of people who felt entitled—and had platforms—to defend modern jazz as they understood it. The writers who balked against the change heralded by jazz's *new thing* did so with an ear and eye to the acts of dissent igniting across urban America and to the wars and revolutions abroad.

My goal in this book is not to depoliticize free jazz. When it was better known as jazz's *new thing*, musicians—experimentalists, modernists, traditionalists, and all in between—made public statements about political issues and engaged in activism and acts of dissent. Instead, I show how musicians breaking with convention, experimenting, and discussing or provoking change through art by invoking race and ethnic identity, political action, religion and cosmology, Africa, Asia, and future worlds were, ipso facto, challenging entrenched power. I am also interested in the possibility that curious and determined musicians sought a music that was meaningful to them regardless of modern jazz's orthodoxy, a music that emphasized immediate and intuitive cooperative action, experimentation, and a mutual liberation of oneself and, simultaneously, others. I read the liberatory potential of the *new thing* with a wide lens, one that encompasses musicians' individualized goals of creative transformation as well as their expressed concerns, as human beings, for their own histories of subjugation and the freedom struggles of oppressed people in the United States and across a globe alight with anticolonial struggle.

Limits of Modern Jazz

I strategically misappropriate heterophony in this book to mean an opaque texture of heterogeneous sound (and sonic subjectivities) where the organization of and "harmony" between sound(s) occurs without a common key (i.e., tonal center), a centralized meter, or both simultaneously. Groups led by Ornette Coleman, Cecil Taylor, Sonny Rollins, Archie Shepp, John Coltrane, Miles Davis, Sun Ra, and others experimented with heterophony. The term "heterophony" in modern music studies was coined in 1908 by Viennese musicologist Guido Adler, one of the disciplinary founders of musicology in Western Europe and the United States, to mean the disorderly multivoice song practices of European peasants and the "savage" races of Africa, Asia, and the Americas. Under the racist assumption that these are all simple, primitive peoples, Adler insisted that the "harmony" in their music was haphazard and coincidental, occurring as singers improvised variations to a main or central melody carried by a leading voice.[5] While the term is rarely used in contemporary music studies, I am plucking "heterophony" from its colonialist, imperialist origins and rehabilitating it to mean something closer to its etymological Greek roots: *different* (hetero-) *sounds* or *voices* (-phony). My theorization of heterophony in jazz's *new thing* stands upon Martiniquais poet Édouard Glissant's theory of opacity in human relation, where it functions as a metaphor—an effect and affect—for the dense and hazy "filter" that exists between two or more humans (subjectivities) that inevitably thwarts one's ability to see "through" the other/Other person and to understand them as a fully knowable and transparent object. The opacity of heterophonic improvised music invites an unconventional and invested way of listening if the many "liberated" simultaneous musical voices—the multiple subjectivities—are to be heard. The technique can invite a listener to engage attentively with this otherwise unknown and unfamiliar sonic environment—an experience that may inspire them to question, loosen, or abandon expectations that the music and sounds therein should "make sense" and be understandable and enjoyable in a recognizable or familiar way.

Heterophony is what made the *new thing* "new," but modern jazz was the ideological context that gave the music's "newness" meaning. Writers for jazz-oriented magazines and other publications focused on what the *new thing* appeared to be lacking: order, tonal harmony, accessibility, and beauty. Some writers, like Nat Hentoff, A. B. Spellman, and Amiri Baraka, who spoke directly with these experimentalist musicians, sought to relay in equally bold terms their rationale and expressive goals, while others who were musicians themselves used Western harmonic theory to gain insights into the new music. The term "new thing" was coined by Martin Williams in the pages of *Metronome* magazine in 1961; Williams, a prolific writer on jazz, would be among the first in his critical milieu to advocate for Ornette Coleman to the literary, jazz-interested public, citing him as a leader of what appeared to be jazz's new aesthetic stage.[6] Baraka, Williams's colleague at the magazine, wrote "The Jazz Avant-Garde" for *Metronome* earlier in 1961; there he names musicians he sees as heralding jazz's aesthetic revolution (among them Coleman and the members of his *Free Jazz* double quartet, saxophonist Wayne Shorter, pianist Cecil Taylor, and others).[7] It was Baraka whose theories on the aesthetics and political meaning of the new music contributed to a shift in discourse on the *new thing* from jazz modernism to black cultural production, agency, and affirmation, which, by 1966, was interpreted by white writers and readers of these publications to mean that the music is fundamentally antiwhite and antijazz.

It is not difficult to understand why these white writers felt so targeted and otherwise offended by Baraka's writing. The tone in his writing at the middle of the decade is combative, polemical, urgent, sardonic, and unflinchingly critical. He castigates the aesthetic orthodoxy upheld by jazz's overwhelmingly white industry leaders and writes bluntly about the impact of institutionalized and systemic racism on the lives of black people generally, and black musicians specifically. As a result, racism's impact on black people's lived experience and its entrenched nature in American life kept white critics from fully appreciating and more thoroughly understanding the music.[8] Baraka himself became fodder in the emergent narrative spin that took hold by 1966 that portrayed the *new thing* as an insurgent, radical, and nihilistic aesthetic and political movement. For self-appointed jazz modernists, the *new thing* was a rejection of and assault on modern jazz and its white consumer base, and the means by which they denounced the new music was not too different from the mounting anticommunist rhetoric across the American political spectrum during the Cold War that repudiated nonconformity and dissent as pathological or otherwise malicious functions of an encroaching Soviet threat.[9] As stated earlier, this book indexes the change in discourse that occurs as Baraka writes the essay "The Changing Same (R&B and the New Black Music)" in 1965–1966 and, in doing so, makes a case for how serious engagement with the creative strategies and goals of the musicians at the center of polemics and controversies were lost within this noise.

The *new thing* is probably best thought of as an epithet for the conceptual break that exists between jazz and *something else*, where that "else" was everything that didn't neatly fit into a narrow genre concept. My book's focus on the development of jazz's *new thing* in the 1960s is ultimately a study of how free creative practice outpaces established music epistemes and traditions, answering more to creators' imperatives and their attention to the moment than the quasi-divine authority of an idealized past.

In 1960, modern jazz was synonymous with harmonic erudition and technical mastery. It was a quotient determined by critics based on musicians' proximity to the repertoire and sound of bebop, the small group music invented in after-hour cutting sessions at Minton's Playhouse in Harlem before migrating downtown to the nightclubs and bars along 52nd Street, which was then the northern edge of Manhattan's redlight Tenderloin district and the heart of the city's nightlife culture. My definition of modern jazz in this book references important musicological work of the past two decades that explains jazz modernity as a discursive invention in postwar America that satisfied the needs of both white critics interested in locating a progressive, racially integrated music of high aesthetic value, and black artists who found in the aptitude required to perform this challenging music a signifier of black excellence.[10] But it was critics who, with the authority granted by their platforms, shaped the idea of a post-bebop modern jazz as a sophisticated modern art for their readership. This was accomplished in the surge of journalism and books on jazz and its history published in the 1950s.[11]

Scott DeVeaux's 1997 study *The Birth of Bebop: A Social and Musical History* surveys in detail the economic, cultural, and creative forces behind the stylistic school known as bebop, making the point that intrepid critics like Leonard Feather idealized bebop as the revolutionary arrival of jazz modernity in part because of its presumed anticommercial ethos and abstract sound and the challenge that the virtuosity of its musicians posed to the casual listener.[12] The myth of bebop's antipopular, anticommercialist ethos drove the legitimization of modern jazz as a "serious" art form and, thus, a more sophisticated niche music for informed connoisseurs.[13] Patrick Burke, in the 2008 book *Come in and Hear the Truth: Jazz and Race on 52nd Street*, like DeVeaux, makes the point that bebop's comparatively meager commercial success in the 1940s record business (compared to the big bands of the 1930s) was due to dramatic changes in the music industry and larger economic forces that musicians were forced to adapt to, not their desire to distance themselves from the mainstream.[14] Improvising musicians, as soloists and in small ensembles, capitalized on the sound, prestige, and market hype around modern jazz, as they still do today.

Guthrie Ramsey's " 'We Called Ourselves Modern': Race Music and the Politics and Practice of Afro-Modernism at Midcentury," in the 2003 book *Race Music: Black Cultures from Bebop to Hip-Hop*, focuses on black musicians' perspective on jazz modernity. It begins with a quote from the influential drummer Kenny Clarke: "The music wasn't called bop at Minton's. In fact, we had no name for the music. We called ourselves modern. . . . That [bop] label did a lot of harm."[15] Clarke's statement draws attention to the (self-)recognition among the musicians at the center of the so-called bebop revolution of a new and emergent musical aesthetic that was being misrepresented in the press of the moment. Ramsey theorizes the consciousness expressed by Clarke and his professional peers as an instance of "Afro-modernism," a term that encompasses musicians' awareness and navigation of an industry and society where black artistry is being celebrated while, paradoxically, black life is systematically devalued. Ramsey expands the Afro-modernism concept in the chapter "Afro-Modernism and Music: On Science, Community, and Magic in the Black Avant-Garde" to include modes of creative experimentalism that become increasingly visible in black musical output up to the 1960s.[16] And saxophonist and musicologist Ekkehard Jost's *Free Jazz* of 1975 is the first monograph on the new music to address its innovative structural design principles in lieu of its literary misrepresentation and subsequent marginalization while noting the interconnectedness of its social context and musical elements. Jost's prescience and general, intervening arguments—that the musicians in question put a lot of forethought and intentionality into their "free" performances, that motivic exchange between musicians during improvisation is a salient way to decode the "logic" of these performances, and the primacy of sound creation over notation—form the bedrock of my own analytical insights.[17]

The *new thing* marks a moment in American music history when black artists—composers and musicians—exerted an unprecedented degree of creative agency. They were experimentalists who conceptualized performance as a catalyst for the production and exchange of musical sound in a more intuited and decentralized way. Compositions, then, are the blueprints for living sonic environments where new and multiple subjectivities can be expressed and heard simultaneously in the course of performance. Coleman's *Free Jazz* did indeed liberate musicians—even established "modernists" like Rollins, Davis, and Coltrane—to explore more abstract and unknown creative terrain. Their engagement with the *new thing* in the middle of a decade of activism, political violence, social upheaval, and revolution amid civil rights and anticolonial struggle reinforced the notion that it was the sound of radical change.

Method and Scope

This book is the product of extensive archival research at the Institute for Jazz Studies at Rutgers University, the New York Public Library's Schomburg Center and Schwarzman Research Division, New York University's Fales Library and Special Collection, Répertoire International de la Presse Musicale (RIPM) Jazz Periodicals database, and Tom Lord's Jazz Discography, among other archives; formal and informal interviews with Reggie Workman, Denardo Coleman, A. B. Spellman, Archie Shepp, and Wayne Shorter; and musical analyses of several key demonstrative recordings between 1960 and 1966. I foreground primary source material in the narrative to situate the reader in the middle of a dynamic and indeed heterophonous literary discourse on the *new thing* that occurred between musicians, record producers and venue operators, writers, and the literary public concerned with modern jazz and the new music. Music magazines like *Metronome* and *Down Beat* that aimed at a "middlebrow," presumably majority-white readership are key in providing a mainstream consensus on the *new thing*. Despite their being promotional tools, I rely heavily on LP liner notes as primary sources—outlets where musicians directly addressed their audience in, often, their own words, even when speaking through a professional writer. Secondary sources in the jazz scholarship of the past three decades help to add critical perspective on primary sources. My goal in synthesizing these sources is to reposition the ontology of free jazz toward one that foregrounds musicians' creative methods, their thoughts on their own work, and their worldviews. As such, *Change* is a study that tries to avoid any grand narratives about a heterogeneous artistic scene populated by various musicians with their own idiosyncratic sonic identities. Instead, this book offers a genealogy of free collective improvisation in a specific moment and industry and how that concept proliferated and evolved in a few short years. Memories of my father's stories of this moment, when he was a young musician still establishing himself in New York City, are my point of departure.

I use my knowledge and experience as a composer and improvising musician to supplement the archival research; my own creative practice orients my ear and analytical insights into this music. My goal is to explain—clearly and concisely—how the music on key recordings "works": what the musicians accomplished and what it took for them to get there. In doing so, I take the difficulty and opacity of this music as marking a limit in an established epistemology and aesthetic regime that lacks the proper tools to decipher new creative sensibilities and methodologies. I take seriously Sylvia Wynter's example in her 1992 essay "Rethinking Aesthetics" of developing a "practice of decipherment" attuned to the ways in which art by the subaltern—black artists working in a white supremacist society—contains disruptive or contesting sets of signifying practices, new aesthetic frameworks and cultural forms, and new ways of creating and conveying that evade consistent terminology and stable definition.[18] Secondary sources in the fields of critical music, cultural, and media studies help frame my close reading of primary sources—especially recordings—with the goal of providing an ontology of the *new thing*/free jazz as a manifestation of an experimentalist practice by improvising musicians working in a modern jazz industry centered in New York City.

✳

In the first chapter, "Shapes of Jazz to Come," I sort through several tropes in the jazz literature of the late 1950s to explain the change that occurs in the new decade. I discuss how the idea of modern jazz interpolated visions of jazz's aesthetic culmination and progress toward a model of erudition and refinement that mirrored classical music. I also discuss modern jazz's symbol as a progressive music hinged on interracial collaboration that entailed black assimilation into European and European American cultural forms, using the

Modern Jazz Quartet and Dave Brubeck's ensembles as examples. This "classical" signifier overshadowed a new consciousness emergent among black musicians seeking out Africa and Asia, appropriating more Eastern sounds as a way "out" of Western forms, and I take Yusef Lateef's work in the late 1950s and early 1960s as an example.

I focus on Ornette Coleman in Chapter 2, "Free to Not Make Sense," after he had become a paragon of the *new thing* after his 1959 New York City premiere at the Five Spot, on the Bowery in Manhattan's East Village. The chapter explores Coleman's critical misrepresentation, where his music was taken as an assault on modern jazz aesthetics, and how that was fueled by his musical autodidacticism and impulse toward nonconformity. As a Texas-born, black male musician tenaciously experimenting with some of music's foundational structural elements (tonal harmony and meter) in the competitive market of New York City, he and his music were described in pathological terms. After outlining his music's skeptical if not overtly negative reception, I explain how, for Coleman, music was a matter of the breath: the sound a musician produces should be as natural, free, and unique as the way they breathe. This conceptual revelation is what led to Coleman's use of heterophonic ensemble textures (though Coleman would go on to use the term "harmolodics" to describe his approach)—a more decentralized kind of group improvisation where distinctions between soloist and accompanist are minimized or blurred, and a method that is fully formed by his double quartet recording *Free Jazz* of December 1960. That kind of improvisational freedom meant, for Coleman, that the musician could play in ways that were more emotionally honest because they and their colleagues, on stage or in the studio, no longer had to be so focused on harmonic "rules."

Chapter 3, "Interlude: Points of Departure," is a detour from the forward-moving chronological arc of the book and a close look at the improvisational methodologies of several musicians the jazz press identified as avant-gardists. The title comes from pianist and composer Andrew Hill, who, in March 1964, recorded an album titled *Point of Departure* for Blue Note Records that utilizes heterophony and other avant-garde affects. I provide an overview of musicians' creative premises and concepts in the first part of this chapter through select recordings by several improvising musicians in the first half of the 1960s. In the chapter's latter section, I examine how calls for censure of the *new thing* swelled in music literature due to Baraka's provocative writing, and how his work and the controversy it provoked shaped how the *new thing* was discussed in music literature up to 1966.

Chapter 4, "Sound and Fury," is about the pianist and poet Cecil Taylor. His abstract, bombastically "busy" playing marked him as an avant-gardist in a modern jazz landscape, but his unique abstractions were explained to the public as stemming more from contemporary modern classical music than black vernacular musical traditions—a characterization that Taylor grew to resent. I explain how jazz writers' focus on Taylor's conservatory training and interest in modern classical music alienated him from jazz and created a problem in categorization—a break—that Taylor filled with provocative sonic and prosaic statements. Understanding Taylor precisely as existing "within the break," as Fred Moten would call it, of received aesthetic categories and traditions means taking the vexation around his categorization as pointing to nonnormative practice where Taylor, as a music conceptualist and improviser, subverted improvisatory and compositional conventions in striving for kinetic and immersive collaborative musical environments.

In Chapter 5, "Anti Jazz, Anti Music," I locate techniques of free improvisation diffused in the works of more established black improvising musicians. Their desire to experiment with new sounds and more abstract and immediate collectivized approaches to improvisation provoked them to change and forge through new improvisatory terrain. I discuss the recorded work of Rollins, Davis (through the younger experimentalist drummer Tony Williams), and Coltrane: each sought unique paths by experimenting with—and hiring musicians involved in—the avant-garde. My goal is to show how free (heterophonic) collective improvisation proliferated beyond the initial core of musicians identified as avant-gardists in the early 1960s, becoming something of a new sonic grammar for improvising musicians in and outside of New York's jazz scene and industry to grapple with. As in previous chapters, I also pay attention to how these sonic experiments were misinterpreted by writers for music and culture magazines in 1965–1966, now stoked by the blunt and provocative statements that musicians like Shepp, Taylor, Abbey Lincoln, and Max Roach made publicly about racism, the black vernacular, and their own visions for music making and society. Here I underscore the point that controversy around the *new thing* became entangled with the perceived threat of insurrection—by unruly black people in cities, students on and off college campuses, colonized peoples in the Global South—which provoked music critics to conflate its abstract sound with racial and political animus. That distortion remains a strain by which the *new thing*/free jazz is understood and interpreted up to the present, and this chapter explains why.

In "Closing: Black Power," I try to disentangle the trope of racial and political animus projected onto the *new thing* in print media from the affectual force of sonic-haptic energy as a medium by which ideals of empowerment and transcendence could be communicated from the performer to other performers and listeners. Sun Ra's cosmic orchestra, the Arkestra, and his early exploration of electric keyboards and theatrical space-age performativity—which began in the 1950s—are central to my reframing of the abstraction and heterophony of the *new thing* as a generative and conceptually expansive force, not simply just grating, cacophonous noise. Ra's visions and sonification of a new, cosmic plane of existence situates the *new thing* within yet another important experimentalist discourse: Afrofuturism.

I seek in *Change* to provide a more accurate and hopefully useful context for listening to abstract, heterophonic improvised music—music that was once considered to be groundbreaking, disruptive, and bewildering. Some listeners may still feel that way about this music. If anything can be taken away from this book's attempt at a genealogy of method and style, the *new thing/ free jazz*—and the heterophony that made it "new"—was anything but unstructured and unintelligible. It marked a moment of sonic experimentation into heterogeneous sound fields (eventually spanning the range between the acoustic and electronic) that has continued in unceasing, myriad ways in the decades since. The change that the *new thing* represented was, ultimately, in the possibilities embedded in the more expansive way of thinking about, creating, and listening to music that comes when acknowledging that the limits of the past are but a pretext for the possibilities of tomorrow, because:

> *Today is the shadow of tomorrow*
> *Today is the present future of yesterday*
> *Yesterday is the shadow of today*
> *The darkness of the past is yesterday*
> *And the light of the past is yesterday*
>
> *. . .*
>
> *The wisdom of the past is the light of the past*
> *The light which is to be is the wisdom of the future*
> *The light of the future casts the shadows of tomorrow.*[19]

1
Shapes of Jazz to Come

The 1950s are the decade when jazz becomes "modern." That is because, Marshall Stearns wrote in 1956, it was the extraordinary result of "a three-hundred-years' blending in the United States of the European and West African musical traditions; and its predominant components are European harmony, Euro-African melody, and African rhythm." A graduate of Harvard and Yale and a professor at Hunter College in New York City, Stearns narrates the "ancient and honorable history" of jazz, from its roots in West African and European musical traditions to the current panoply of styles and scenes in cities across the United States. Like several other music critics, Stearns was confident that he was witnessing the unfolding of jazz's modern stage, where its sensibilities and aesthetic refinement reflected the result of a "great tradition" comparable only to European classical music, even if the two retained some "crucially different characteristics."[1]

One big difference, Stearns says in *The Story of Jazz*, is harmony—chords, their sequences, and their relationship to the melody—and how classical composers and jazz improvisers (who may also be composers in their own right) utilize and navigate harmonic structures. Just as the "great and complicated structure" of the symphony evolved over centuries, so too had the harmonic language of jazz evolved in only a matter of decades, but just not as completely as is evident in the artful music of Europe.[2] "Since we are all immersed in the classical tradition of Europe and, consciously or not, tend to accept its standards as universal, classical music must inevitably serve as a basis for comparison and contrast in defining jazz," Stearns wrote. "It is true that, except for more modern experiments, the harmonies of jazz are relatively simple . . . [but] to say this and no more is to miss the point. The European harmony adopted by jazz simply forms the mold into which the jazz performance [improvisation] is poured."[3]

In focusing on harmonic sophistication as a signifier of musical modernity, Stearns echoed an attitude held by an entire cohort of postwar critics in the United States who founded, edited, and wrote prodigiously for magazines devoted specifically to jazz, as well as newspapers and lifestyle and culture magazines. Like previous monographs on modern jazz by Leonard Feather

Change. Kwami Coleman, Oxford University Press. © Oxford University Press 2025.
DOI: 10.1093/9780197780121.003.0002

(*Inside Be-Bop*, later *Inside Jazz*, of 1949) and Barry Ulanov (*A History of Jazz*, 1952), both of whom were editors at *Metronome* magazine, Stearns's book upholds bebop as the tipping point. The harmonic erudition of musicians like Charlie Parker and the comparative lack of commercial appeal compared to big band swing had all the trappings of an elite modern art. Writers like Stearns chronicled its evolution, assessed players and records of note, and served as stewards and self-appointed crusaders of this rare, racially integrated domestic artform. Modern jazz, Stearns wants the reader to know, is a progressive music that, because of the collaboration of black and white musicians and its global appeal, represents the harmonious potential of the collective "human spirit."[4]

Stearns's vision of a modern jazz as a hip racial utopia came after the passage of landmark civil rights legislation—the Supreme Court's *Brown v. Board of Education* decision of 1954—and the graphic national press coverage of young Emmett Till's 1955 murder. "Modern" jazz, unlike so much else in American society, was both a musical style and a culture that aspired to a color-blind vision of racial harmony seemingly unattainable elsewhere, where black and white musicians are equals in their concern for making sophisticated and beautiful music. He posits black vernacular music and, by extension, black people as occupying a central and essential part of the "American character," and modern jazz as a respectable and aesthetically elevated music, an emblem of American exceptionalism and triumph over white supremacy.[5]

But this vision of modern jazz was inoculated against the structural depth of racialized difference and discrimination, as well as any other kind of troublesome politics responsible for so much unrest in society. It also presupposed that modern jazz would follow a path of aesthetic evolution comparable to classical music. What would it have meant to Stearns if it didn't? How does Stearns's vision compare with how the black musicians at the center of his narrative understood their own identities and creative goals? Could this vision of modern jazz accommodate sounds and ideas from musical traditions outside of jazz and classical music? How, then, would critics and jazz theorists like Stearns talk about and assess sounds and references that were opaque and unfamiliar?

In this chapter, I consider some of the ideals and contradictions in modern jazz circa 1960 and how race and aesthetics interweave at points of ideological tension. I do so by focusing on the modal music of John Lewis's Modern Jazz Quartet, Dave Brubeck's ensembles, and Yusef Lateef's turn toward sounds that signified the Eastern hemisphere, the Middle East and South Asia specifically. My goal here is pull back the veil of modern jazz's promise of sophisticated hipness and universal appeal and to show how a politics of racial color blindness still carried attitudes among jazz modernists about the centrality, if not supremacy, of classical music. Lewis and Brubeck, skilled and industrious as they were, played significant roles in establishing modern jazz as a brand. The ideals instilled into the modern jazz brand stand apart from important currents in "Afromodernity" that drove the creative direction of other "modern" musicians. I focus on and compare the shared preoccupation with modes in the work of Brubeck and Lateef as reflecting their search for stimulating alternatives to chordal harmony and how their unique quests to broaden their musical language with uncommon scales and melodic formulae reveal cultural affinities in two contrasting cultural hemispheres, West and East.

This shift among improvising musicians beyond orthodoxy bore several creative manifestations, one of the most influential being drummer and composer George Russell's Lydian Chromatic Concept of Tonal Organization. Russell, Ingrid Monson writes, sought to recalibrate the conventional tonal harmonic system that improvisers were accustomed to using by positing the Lydian mode as a better and more modern "parent scale" of a vertical major sonority (e.g., an improviser playing a C Lydian melody over a C major chord). This Lydian Chromatic Concept and the system Russell developed for it aimed at freeing the improviser from the already ossifying conventions of modern jazz improvisation based in major and minor chords and keys toward a music-making process that is transcendent—aligned with the deeper cosmological powers addressed in science and spirituality—and that satisfies the seeking musician's quest for creative introspection and deep, esoteric knowledge sourced especially from Eastern metaphysics (Hinduism, Buddhism, and Sufism).[6] By 1960, that "Eastern" esotericism and musicians' exploration of conceptual terrain outside of functional Western harmony represented a step toward something else: a "new thing."

John Lewis's Modern Jazz Society

Modernity as an art concept in Western intellectual history has always required the "primitive" to have meaning and, because it implies a recent or current point of arrival directed by time's forward-pointing arrow, an advanced if not superior era. The "modern" also contains the conditions for what is known as the "avant-garde": an imperative among creatives and intellectuals to march across the frontier of expressive culture, chartering a path toward the unknown. "Both modernity and modernism go back etymologically to the concept of *la mode*," writes Italian literary critic Renato Poggioli in 1962, "but only the second agrees with the spirit and the letter of it."[7] Whether the avant-garde is a complementary part of or an antagonistic reaction to modernity has been a subject of debate in Western art and literary theory since the 1930s.[8] Modern art, Poggioli theorizes considering the past half-century of artistic production, restores or reinvents ancient and classical values, while art that uses the "modern" only as a hollow aesthetic (as a means of being current and fashionable) is best thought of as being only in a modernist style.[9] Writing a few years before Poggioli in 1958, John Tasker Howard and James Lyon set out to introduce the general reader to "modern music," defined as that created by trained specialists that advances beyond convention, shirks trite commercialism, and is usually not readily accepted by the masses. Even so, modern composers still have a common reference in the art of the past and evoke it in their work: "Music is almost always an expression of the age in which it is written. If it isn't we may be sure that the composer himself belongs spiritually to another age, or that he patterns his work after the music of earlier composers, unconsciously or perhaps deliberately."[10]

Modernity in Western intellectual history, philosopher and anthropologist Bruno Latour argues, is a known object that moderns must protect from the regresses of ignorance and savagery. The promise of an enlightened modernity in Western intellectual history was driven by an impulse to fully know and control nature through empiricism, standardizations of measurement, efficient production, and refinement.[11] Modern art is an entity measured in relation to the "primitive" and less sophisticated past; modern music, then, is so because of the specialized knowledge, technical mastery, and technology required to create and play it. Musical modernity in the United States emerged most forcefully in the Jazz Age of the 1920s, musicologist Carol Oja writes, as concert programming, sound recordings, and literature emanating from New York City's music industry shared the qualities of "iconoclastic, irreverent innovation, sometimes irreconcilable with the historic traditions that preceded it."[12] These attitudes and ideals were invested in the notion of modern jazz in the American music literature of the 1950s, and critics like Marshall Stearns who wrote books historicizing jazz for a general literary public helped to propagate these ideas. Modern jazz, Barry Ulanov wrote in 1950, was "a serious form of music . . . [a] new way of thinking [that] shaped musicians, pushed crude entertainment aside for imaginative ideas, and at least suggested the disciplined creative potential of the young music."[13] Leonard Feather, Ulanov's coeditor at *Metronome* magazine, insisted in his 1949 book *Inside Bebop* (later *Inside Jazz*) that "the advances made by bebop [have] made so much that preceded it seem unimaginative and trite by comparison."[14]

European classical music, its periodized, centuries-old evolutionary aesthetic history, and its modern concert culture served as a model for modern jazz aesthetics; the demands of "serious music" on its composers, musicians, and audiences—of erudition and refinement—were a source of prestige that jazz modernists sought to emulate and integrate. European expatriates had served as beacons for American musical modernists since after the First World War. By the 1950s, composers like Arnold Schoenberg, Paul Hindemith, Igor Stravinsky, and Edgard Varèse, with their unmistakenly modern, abstract works for orchestras, small ensembles, soloists, and (in the case of Varèse) electronics, had been concertized and recorded in their new country of residence in conjunction with the rise of college-level music education, and they received university teaching appointments, designed curricula, and were sought after as lecturers across the country.[15] Schoenberg, who emigrated to the United States in 1933 as a Jewish refugee of Nazi Germany, held an appointment at the University of Los Angeles from 1936 to 1944, and his highly chromatic, systematically dissonant music is an exemplar of modern music's new frontier. A prodigious teacher, Schoenberg wrote passionately about new and abstract harmonies within conventional formal structures and on the necessity for an aspiring composer to develop best practices to control that abstraction based on natural musical laws and logical principles. A true artist, he rhapsodized, will experience breakthroughs working within logical systems by virtue of inspiration and their expressive potency. "That which is new and unusual about a new harmony occurs to the true composer only for such reasons," he wrote in his 1911 *Harmonielehre* (*Theory of Harmony*), which was translated into English in 1948. "[H]e must give expression to something that moves him, something new, something previously unheard-of."[16]

Efforts to make jazz more "serious" began in the 1920s as the syncopated, improvisatory music exploded in popularity and demand in the commercial music industry, which composers and bandleaders acquiesced to in ways tinged with the racist paternalism intrinsic to Western musical modernity. In New York City, George Gershwin and Paul Whiteman—who would promote himself as the "king of jazz" in the 1930s—created and presented, respectively, symphonic popular music conceived of as "serious" music for a jazz orchestra in a series of highly publicized "modern music" concerts starting in 1924.[17] Whiteman in particular was explicit about his symphonic jazz as a project involving the elevation of black vernacular music to something closer to classical music with an assured popular appeal, still driven by an impulse to "civilize" the salacious "savagery" of jazz in the context of the presumed aesthetic superiority of European classical music.[18] That centering of European classical music in American musical modernity is a deference that emerges in conspicuous ways in the modern jazz of the 1950s.

Modern jazz's growing prestige and "seriousness" were also promotional tools facilitating its commodification in the American music industry. The industrial boom of the Second World War contributed to a proliferation of recording and playback technology; after 1945, magnetic tape, the vinyl microgroove record, and stereophonic, high-fidelity playback were available commercially, and the appeal of sophisticated modern jazz grew in conjunction with an ascendent "middle" consumer class with the financial means to purchase equipment and sound discs.[19] Professional music critics served this consumer class by evaluating the most enjoyable, important music on record—effectively streamlining consumer choice—thereby helping to establish modern jazz as a connoisseur industry and culture.[20] In the new genre of men's lifestyle magazines of the late 1950s, like Hugh Hefner's modestly pornographic *Playboy* magazine, modern jazz was presented as an integral part of an urbane and hedonistic bachelor lifestyle rounded out by the gratuitous consumption of provocative journalism, fiction, women's bodies, and recorded modern music.[21] While record corporations with wide distribution like RCA-Victor recorded artists in popular and classical music with presumable mass appeal, smaller independent labels focused on niche markets and promising newcomers.[22]

One of these labels was Atlantic Records. Founded in 1947 by Ahmet Ertegun and Herb Abramson in Washington, DC, and later headquartered in midtown Manhattan a block away from Carnegie Hall, Atlantic could boast one of the first Ampex eight-track recorders ever manufactured. Under Ertegun and Jerry Wexler's direction, and with recording sessions engineered by Tom Dowd, Atlantic's studio captured the music of contemporary black artists in an undeniably modern, high-resolution sound. Ray Charles, Aretha Franklin, Wilson Pickett, and Otis Redding, all signed to Atlantic, helped to establish the polished sound of contemporary rhythm and blues, and when Atlantic signed John Lewis's Modern Jazz Quartet in 1956—ending their contract with the indie Prestige label—they invested in a group that seemed to represent, in their name and presentation, the elevated ideals of contemporary jazz. That the MJQ resembled a classical quartet was not lost on music writers: German American composer and musician Gunther Schuller, quoted in a 1955 article for *High Fidelity* magazine written by Nat Hentoff, heard in Lewis's all-black group an "extreme subtlety and sensitivity.... If John [Lewis] goes on to develop more freedom both harmonically and in his command of form, he will then, in my opinion, come closer than anyone else I know now in jazz—except perhaps Dave Brubeck—to the level of the best contemporary classical music."[23]

Lewis's engagement with classical music started in childhood. Born in Illinois in 1920, Lewis was raised and schooled in Albuquerque, New Mexico, studying piano at an early age. He was drafted into the army in 1942 before graduating from the University of New Mexico, returning after the war to complete his studies in music and anthropology. While enlisted and abroad, Lewis served as a musician in the Special Services, where he met the New York–based drummer Kenny Clarke; the two would play together in the clubs of liberated Paris before Clarke's discharge, which brought the drummer back to New York to play in Dizzy Gillespie's big band. Lewis followed Clarke to New York in 1945 and was introduced to Gillespie, lauded as one of bebop's founders, with whom he would go on to perform and record while simultaneously studying piano, composition, orchestration, and music theory at the Manhattan School of Music. Lewis returned to Paris with Gillespie in 1948, extending his stay to live, work, and compose, establishing an enduring connection to the city and cosmopolitan Western Europe more broadly.[24] Upon returning to New York, Lewis recorded with the Charlie Parker All-Stars, Miles Davis's orchestra, and Davis's small groups that regularly performed at the Royal Roost club in Manhattan's midtown Tenderloin district. Schuller eagerly attended those gigs and was in the audience when Davis, with Lewis on piano, performed new music that would soon be recorded and released as singles by Capitol Records, later compiled onto the LP *Birth of the Cool.*

Lewis met Schuller through his brother-in-law Leon Bibb, a cast member in the Broadway show *Annie Get Your Gun* at the same time Schuller, a French hornist, was subbing in the pit orchestra. Schuller deeply admired Lewis's erudition, seeing him as a classically trained musician operating at the vanguard of modern jazz. Schuller jumped at Bibb's offer to meet Lewis: "It was such a chain of unforeseeable coincidences that led to the meeting with John Lewis that crucially influenced both our lives and careers. And beyond that, John was my closest ally in the battles over a whole new genre of music located halfway between classical music and jazz, the so-called Third Stream concept."[25]

In 1951, Lewis became a member of vibraphonist Milt Jackson's quartet, with whom he had worked in the past, joined by Kenny Clarke and the bassist Ray Brown. Lewis formed the Modern Jazz Quartet a year later out of Jackson's group, hiring bassist Percy Heath (another long-standing collaborator) to replace Brown, and they recorded their self-titled first album for Prestige featuring Lewis's originals "La Ronde," "The Queen's Fancy," and "Vendrome." On their 1955 LP *Concorde,* the MJQ's last for Prestige before signing with Atlantic (featuring Connie Kay replacing Clarke), Lewis's classical influences are made more explicit. In the album liner notes Ira Gitler, then a freelance writer for *Metronome* and *Down Beat,* praises Lewis's use of many different contrapuntal techniques. The title track, a fugue, is one of Lewis's "important" originals, according to Gitler, because of its counterpoint, and Lewis's ability to use this Baroque-era compositional technique is the mark of a modern composer. References to European art traditions and evocations of European cosmopolitanism by the MJQ were noticed by the music press, and Lewis took advantage of this renown in his aspiration for new venues and audiences (Figure 1.1).[26]

Figure 1.1 A promotional photograph of the Modern Jazz Quartet, ca. early 1960s. Pictured left to right: bassist Percy Heath, drummer Connie Kay, vibraphonist Milt Jackson, and pianist John Lewis. Photo credit: James J. Kriegsmann/Schomburg Center for Research in Black Culture, Photographs and Prints Division, New York Public Library.

Lewis and Schuller were close collaborators in the late 1950s and shared the belief that a "serious" kind of modern jazz could match and possibly dislodge the aesthetic superiority of classical music, possibly becoming a new genre unto itself. Lewis explained the impetus in his founding of the Modern Jazz Quartet as an attempt to create a more intellectually rigorous improvised music that was grounded in intricate notated arrangements that would appeal to "the mind's ability to appreciate through the ear."[27] Jazz, in Lewis's MJQ, was exact in its design and execution: it was an improvised music for discerning listeners who would appreciate its refinement and references to European culture.

Lewis's writing for the MJQ featured intricately arranged popular songs and original pieces set in canonical European forms, and members of the ensemble engaged in a more contrapuntal approach to improvisation as though the parts of a fugue were distributed across the four instrumental voices of the quartet. These gestures worked to distinguish the Modern Jazz Quartet as a chamber ensemble of improvisers with a command over a broad stylistic repertoire that spanned the popular and classical. According to Schuller, formal clarity was important to Lewis; he derived it from the Romantic ideal of organic unity central to European art music aesthetics, an ideal articulated by influential nineteenth-century literary figures like the Prussian E. T. A. Hoffmann, who extolled the cogency and sublimity of Beethoven's symphonies. That quality is what, for Schuller, made the MJQ so successful, and it put their music, as Hentoff writes in 1955, in a rarefied league along with other "experimental work of other modern jazz units." The MJQ presented a sophisticated, concert-oriented music that in 1950s American music culture was legible as a more highbrow, "modern" music in the way of classical music. Their music was, in the words of critic Ralph Gleason, "at once complex and orderly; whose excitement is controlled; where the soloist uses structure as well as dynamics to create a climax; and where inspiration finds logical channels for expression."[28]

Lewis cofounded the Modern Jazz Society with Schuller in 1955 to promote his new modern music in venues outside New York's more fickle nightclub circuit.[29] The first concert they organized was in Manhattan's Town Hall in March 1955; they scheduled a second concert for 1956, but it was postponed because of the premiere of Schuller's own *Symphony for Brass and Percussion* with the New York Philharmonic. The Town Hall concert represented for Schuller "a time when the long-standing artificial barriers between jazz and classical music still kept the two musical worlds segregated, but were just beginning to break down." The high-fidelity, microgroove record that was produced from the concert's original tape was released as *The Modern Jazz Society*

Presents a Concert of Contemporary Music on concert impresario Norman Granz's Norgran label.[30]

The album features five of Lewis's original compositions, two, "Django" and "The Queen's Fancy" (inspired by the coronation of Queen Elizabeth II), arranged by Schuller, who also played French horn. "The compositions center on and depend on the jazz soloist and they incorporate jazz and classical techniques," Lewis wrote in the record's liner notes. His conspicuous European references in song titles like "Midsömmer" (explained as being derived from the Swedish holiday and festival), "The Queen's Fancy," and "Little David's Fugue" reflected his vision for modern jazz, one more closely aligned with European classical music and its accompanying cultural prestige.

"Midsömmer" is what Lewis describes as "an adagio in a general first Rondo form." The baroque stylings of its fugal opening are identifiably "classical," and the ensemble's instrumentation—tenor saxophone, clarinet, trombone, flute, bassoon, French horn, harp, bass, and drums—is much closer to a small chamber ensemble than a nightclub jazz band. J. J. Johnson, on trombone, introduces the fugal subject in A minor over Connie Kay's ride pattern on cymbal, and Stan Getz reintroduces the subject on tenor saxophone a fourth above, in D minor; as the two musicians complete this statement, Anthony Sciacca on clarinet reintroduces it at a fourth above in G minor (▶ 00:13), and then Manuel Zegler reintroduces it on bassoon in C minor. The exposition of "Midsömmer," where each voice enters a fourth above the previous, concludes with two final statements of the subject by Sciacca and Zegler again, in F and B-flat minor, before the ensemble moves into what Lewis calls a "second theme" area (▶ 00:39) in which Johnson, Getz, and Sciacca improvise over a strophic (looped) chord progression. The musicians' articulation is noticeably "straight"—minimal vibrato, sharp attack and release—during the exposition, like a classical wind ensemble. That changes in the second section, which is more syncopated and swung, rhythmic attributes racially coded as "black." "Midsömmer" reflects the kind of stylistic and cultural hybridity that the Modern Jazz Society's "contemporary music" offered, where the rhythmic sensibility and improvisation of jazz are interpolated into elaborate arrangements fitting for concert music and for an idealized discerning listener.[31]

Modern jazz's interracial collaboration was, however, what distinguished it most from classical music. Aspirations toward this kind of musical and fraternal universalism were ardently pursued by Schuller in the development of his "third stream" concept, which he envisioned as an aesthetic *third space* between jazz and classical music.[32] Born in 1925, Schuller, a child of German émigrés who enjoyed a middle-class upbringing in New York City and Germany (his mother was a visual artist and his father a violinist for the New York Philharmonic), developed a passion for European art music and jazz in his youth, as well as a grievance that the latter was not granted the same "serious" attention and prestige as the former. In his memoir, *A Life in Pursuit of Music and Beauty*, Schuller recounts his epiphanic realization that his favorite jazz was just "as good" as the modern classical music he also obsessed over. The confusion of his parents, "the implication they gathered from my sudden interest in jazz—my seemingly intractable notion that Beethoven's and Ellington's music were qualitatively equal—really puzzled and disturbed them. . . . [In] due course I began to devote my musical energies equally to both musics. . . . [T]hose things that I heard in great classical music, that is, memorable melodies or themes, striking harmonies, interesting captivating rhythms, a fascinating variety of sonorities and timbres, stated in clear forms and structures—not to mention technical mastery—I also heard in the best of jazz."[33] After completing high school, Schuller was hired as the principal hornist for the Cincinnati Symphony Orchestra, where he stayed for two years until his parents beckoned him back to New York; his father arranged for an audition with the Metropolitan Opera orchestra directed, somewhat unofficially, by the famed conductor of the New York Philharmonic George Szell. During his tenure as the principal hornist at the Met, which lasted until 1959, Schuller made his recording debut in 1950 with Miles Davis's Capitol Records "Birth of the Cool" sessions—a series of intricately orchestrated pieces for nonet arranged by Gil Evans and some of the participating musicians, including baritone saxophonist Gerry Mulligan and pianist John Lewis.

These Capitol sessions catalyzed Lewis and Schuller's professional relationship but, more than that, were emblematic of modern jazz's vanguard: sophisticated harmonies, technical precision, intricate arrangements, and white and black musical collaboration.[34] This blend or assimilation is what Schuller had in mind when he coined the term "third stream." He used it in a lecture at Brandeis University in 1957 to describe the convergence—or assimilation—of jazz and classical music's autonomous streams. His first attempt at forging a "third stream" was that summer at Brandeis's Creative Arts Festival, when he was asked by the university's administrative staff to organize a "really special jazz concert," which he did by commissioning six new pieces ("three by jazz composers and three by classical composers"):

I chose Charles Mingus, George Russell, and Jimmy Giuffre, at the time, in my mind, the most progressive, innovative composers on the jazz side, and Milton Babbitt (of Princeton University) and Harold Shapero (on the Brandeis composition faculty) on the classical side. By common consent I was also asked to compose a piece for the occasion. In addition, I programmed two other works: Duke Ellington's *Reminiscing in Tempo*, as the all-important historic forerunner in jazz of multisectional, completely through-composed, extended-form composition, with a duration of fourteen minutes; and Thelonious Monk's *Eronel*, as arranged by [French jazz critic and composer] André Hodeir, who by 1957 had already written (and recorded) a whole series of extended-form pieces that incorporated many ideas and techniques propounded by the European twelve-tone avant-garde.[35]

Schuller's imperative was notated, extended-form music composed with the same attention to motivic development and organic unity as modern (classical) instrumental music: "As diverse as the six compositions were in form, harmonic language, and style . . . they had one thing more or less in common: all six pieces were to some extent based on or developed out of thematic ideas, a long-standing concept intrinsic in classical music, but not really endemic to jazz."[36] He wrote about this in published essays, first in "The Future of Form in Jazz," published in the *Saturday Review of Literature* in 1957, and then in "Sonny Rollins and the Challenge of Thematic Improvisation" for the inaugural 1958 issue of *The Jazz Review* edited by Nat Hentoff and Martin Williams. That same summer, Schuller joined Lewis in founding a summer workshop for jazz at the Music Inn, a club in Lenox, Massachusetts, in the Berkshires, where the summer concert series at Tanglewood—inaugurated by Boston Symphony Orchestra's conductor Serge Koussevitzky in 1936—occurred annually.

"Jazz had never been allowed to enter or even come near those sacred precincts," recalled Schuller, "but then suddenly . . . there were jazz concerts, and symposia, and panel discussions on jazz." Schuller participated in a panel discussion on the future of jazz sponsored by the Inn's owners Stephanie and Phillip Barber in 1955, co-moderated by Stearns, the same year the Barbers invited the MJQ to perform at their adjacent venue, the Berkshire Music Barn. Ornette Coleman was twenty-nine years old and living in Los Angeles when Ahmet Ertegun and his older brother Nesuhi, Atlantic's head of artists and repertoire and jazz division, arranged for him to attend the Lenox School summer jazz workshop on a scholarship in 1959.[37] (Coleman's relationship with Schuller, Lewis, and jazz modernity more broadly are discussed in greater detail in Chapter 2 of this book.) The MJQ recorded their sixth album for Atlantic, *Third Stream Music*, joined by the Beaux Arts String Quartet and playing original music by Lewis, Jimmy Giuffre, and Schuller, in 1959.

Brubeck's *À la Mode*

Modern jazz was increasingly marketed to white, college-age and -educated men at the end of the 1950s. Visually, on album covers, artists (and thus, by extension, the music therein) were represented as refined, erudite, and cool, as such helping to sell the sound object and their musical creator as an appealing cultural commodity for the modern (white) consumer.[38] The classical-sounding jazz of Dave Brubeck made use of conspicuous sonic signifiers of European art music and, like Lewis's MJQ, took advantage of its aesthetic prestige. Their "classical" modernism helped propel the Brubeck quartet to success, but some suspected that Brubeck's position as a white male musician heading an inter-racial band was part of why, going into the 1960s, his modern music and fame eclipsed that of black musicians—a discursive frame through which Amiri Baraka theorized the arrival of a black jazz avant-garde in an essay published in *Metronome* magazine in 1961. The industry's whitewashing of modern jazz was a factor in what Baraka decried as a stonewalling of experimental black artists, a trope that A. B. Spellman, writer and friend of Baraka—*Metronome*'s only regular black contributor—articulated in his 1966 book *Four Lives in the Bebop Business*, later republished as *Four Jazz Lives*: "If managers of record companies and club owners appear as villains in these pages, it is because they are: blameless villains, perhaps, but villains nonetheless. They are, of course, businessmen, and the commercial value of a group or musician is their foremost consideration. That a Dave Brubeck can be approaching millionaire status while Cecil Taylor, Jackie McLean, and Ornette Coleman are relative paupers is, from my perspective, outrageous; but why be naive? Has it ever been different?"[39]

Born in Concord, California, to a musical family, Brubeck spent his youth studying piano, working on his family's cattle ranch in Stockton, and playing in local dance bands on the weekend. He enrolled at the College of the Pacific in Stockton, majoring in music and, after graduating in 1942 and serving in the army, enrolled at Mills College in Oakland to study with the French composer Darius Milhaud. He formed an octet in 1947, a trio in 1949, and, in 1951, a quartet with whom he recorded and performed in clubs on the East and West coasts, but also, notably, on college campuses.[40] Fantasy Records, the San Francisco–based indie label owned by Jack Sheedy, became a vehicle by which Brubeck—who was also an investor in the label—marketed his music to a youthful, college-attending audience. Already thirty in 1950, Brubeck sought to dislodge his brand of "respectable" jazz from the indecency of the night-club scene, stating in a 1954 television interview that such a separation was good because "the thing that's held jazz back has been the environment. And every time a club is run decently, there's an audience, a wonderful audience, that usually won't go into a nightclub." As musicologist Kelsey Klotz notes, the "environment" of the urban nightclub was widely understood to be contaminated with drugs, alcohol, prostitution, and crime and was often coded as an illicit and black or nonwhite space.[41]

Shirley Hoskins's liner notes to the group's third LP, *The Dave Brubeck Quartet* of 1952, regales the group for appealing to a sophisticated class of music lovers, the "selective group of lovers of classical music who have found in Brubeck's music something of the depth of the classics . . . its intellectual and emotional nature." Hoskins calls the album's music "elusively subtle and complex; always exciting." She informs the reader that the group lives up to its name—a *quartet*, like the prestigious string quartet ensembles that play at Carnegie Hall—because it is "four creative artists evolving an intellectually and emotionally stimulating experience for the highly trained ear capable of appreciating the subtleties of progressive jazz."[42] That sentiment is illustrated in caricature on the cover of *Jazz at the College of the Pacific*, recorded live on the Stockton campus that same year. Brubeck's all-white quartet are drawn leaning against a miniature Ionic-style pillar, dressed in Ivy League ties and Oxford shirts underneath their graduation gowns. Only Brubeck wears a graduate's cap.

Brubeck's concerts on college campuses in the United States increased exponentially when he signed with a major label, Columbia Records, in 1954, and the caricatures on the Fantasy LPs he kept recording even with his new contract vividly convey his branding strategy. For instance, on *Brubeck Plays and Plays and Plays*, recorded for Fantasy in 1957, Brubeck is drawn seated at the piano, smiling and unbothered by the scowls and glares of a roster of long-dead canonical figures in classical music. Perhaps his most impactful modernist statement of the 1950s is the album *Time Out*, recorded in the last summer of the decade. Now famous for its use of odd time signatures, like the 5/4 meter in the ubiquitous "Take Five," the LP secured the Brubeck Quartet's renown as jazz modernists; in 1960, the quartet achieved the unprecedented in joining Leonard Bernstein and the New York Philharmonic in recording *Bernstein Plays Brubeck Plays Bernstein* for Columbia in 1960.

The conspicuous use of medieval European modes in Brubeck's music from this period is another important genre-defining gesture in line with the group's stakes in musical modernity. In this they were not alone; Miles Davis—Brubeck's labelmate at Columbia—recorded the minimalist "Milestones" in 1958 with his sextet as compositions and improvisations built on modes (and not just the major and minor tonalities of popular music) became fashionable signifiers of musical (and specifically classical) erudition. Paul Horn, a wind player and sought-after session musician in California who also recorded for Fantasy, commented to *Down Beat* in 1961 that "modal forms" afforded modern jazz the variety and conceptual freedom of classical music by drawing from the latter's ancient precedents. Modes "give the player more freedom to improvise," Horn remarked, "because he doesn't have to get involved in the [chord] changes. The conception is more melodic than harmonic.... [I]nstead of the melodies arising from the harmonies, the reverse is the case." Jazz is a sophisticated art, Horn emphasizes: "[I]t demands a much higher technical knowledge as a musician. And the people getting into it today don't have any choice—they've *got* to have the knowledge."[43]

Brubeck's album *À la Mode* was recorded in May and June of 1960 for Fantasy Records; it features William (Bill) Smith on clarinet—the composer of each of the album's ten tracks—Eugene Wright on bass, and Joe Morello on drums. On the LP cover the musicians are huddled around a small table in an ice-cream parlor. Wright sits left of center, beside Brubeck, leaning forward and smiling broadly over his ice-cream soda. Colorful mounds of ice cream sit in a single decorative glass in the lower center of the frame, a key part of the picture of the musicians' festive conviviality. Wright is a black man sitting among three white men, presumably having just received service at a privately owned business in an unspecified town or city in the United States at a time when racial segregation is commonplace. In 1960, de facto and de jure segregation was being directly challenged in acts of nonviolent protest by college students and youth throughout the segregated southern states. What appears to be an anodyne, inviting, and maybe unintentionally saccharine album cover was, as Todd Decker points out, unmistakably a profoundly mollified reference to the lunch counter sit-ins boldly challenging Jim Crow segregation during this time, which were routinely met with violence.[44] This album cover is representative of what Kelsey Klotz calls Brubeck's "southern strategy," whereby he "leveraged his whiteness to support integration efforts, even as he continued to benefit from a racial capitalist system that privileged his voice over those for whom he advocated." *À la Mode* displays his new promotional strategy that "married commercial interest with political ideology."[45]

News of black Americans sitting at food counters in the southern United States, in willful defiance of Jim Crow segregation and white supremacy, circulated in the press for years without much photographic evidence. When the African American Methodist minister Douglas E. Moore led a demonstration on June 23, 1957, at the Royal Ice Cream Parlor in Durham, North Carolina, with eight other black people, reportage didn't go beyond the local papers. Seven of the eight demonstrators, including Moore, were arrested for trespassing; they appealed the case twice unsuccessfully in county and state courts and were ultimately denied a hearing at the Supreme Court, leaving the protestors with more than $400 in fines.[46]

By contrast, pictures of a sit-in three years later in Greensboro, North Carolina, caused a national stir. Four black students from North Carolina Agriculture and Technical State University—Ezell Blair, Franklin McCain, Joseph McNeil, and David Richmond—sat at the whites-only lunch counter at the Woolworth department store in the middle of the city's commercial district on February 1, 1960. Woolworth's reserved counter seating for white patrons; black patrons were allowed to eat only at a narrow standing counter. Unlike Durham, the student protestors in Greensboro attracted the national press; Woolworth's was one of the most profitable stores in the region, and the students' direct action posed an overt challenge to the status quo. The store manager closed the lunch counter and left them unattended until closing time, opting not to have them arrested, and the four students—now with Billy Smith and Clarence Henderson sitting in for Blair and Richmond—were photographed at the counter for the *Greensboro Record* at the end of the second day, joined by twenty-three other students.[47] Demonstrators shut down the business on the third day after sixty-three other students joined.[48] By April, sit-in demonstrations had been held in fifty-four cities in nine states, and the Student Nonviolent Coordinating Committee was formed in Raleigh, North Carolina, to help organize and sustain these efforts. Student-led activism combating racial segregation and voter disenfranchisement continued to flare up across the country, and, by Brubeck's recording sessions in May and June 1960, the national press made it clear that a national civil rights movement had been ignited.

The incongruity of moods of the Greensboro Four photo and Brubeck's album cover (both pictured above in Figures 1.2a and 1.2b, respectively) is striking. The black college students at the counter are cautious, wary; the gravity of their action is registered on their faces, captured clearly by the photographer Jack Moebes, who had to shoot from above the hands of the manager, Clarence "Curly" Harris, trying to block his view.[49] The members of Brubeck's interracial quartet, by contrast, are relaxed and cheerful, beckoning the record buyer to join their fun. In their uniform black suits and long ties, the musicians project a sense that the music contained therein is *à la mode*: fashionable, sophisticated, and agreeable in affect. Theirs is a modern jazz created by black and white musical collaboration, a kind of soft advocacy that avoids any mention of white culpability or indemnity.

Figure 1.2a (above) Photo of the second Greensboro Four sitting at the Woolworth's lunch counter, taken on February 2, 1960. Pictured (L to R): Joseph McNeil, Franklin McCain, Billy Smith, and Clarence Henderson. Photo credit: Jack Moebes, courtesy of the Jack Moebes Photo Archive, http://jackmoebes.com.

Figure 1.2b (below) Album cover of Dave Brubeck's *À La Mode*, Fantasy 3301, 1960.

"Dorian Dance," the first track, sets the general mood of the album. This tune, like the others, was written by clarinetist Bill Smith. It is a thirty-two-bar song form in D Dorian with one eight-bar refrain ("A") in duple meter, 4/4, and two contrasting strains ("B" and "C") of eight bars, half of which are in triple meter, 3/4: an ABAC form. A short motivic cell in the A-section (bars 1–2) is played by Smith and Brubeck's right hand in the piano's upper register that repeats (bars 3–4); each statement of the motif receives an echo-like answer by Brubeck's left hand and Wright on bass. This call-and-response happens four times in the "A"-section, twice at ^1 (D) and then twice at ^5 (A), all in the context of D Dorian. The "B" and "C" sections consist of minor chords built upon the pitches of two diminished seventh chords, E-flat (▶ 00:07) and E-natural (▶ 00:21) that descend across the four bars of triple meter before the half and final cadence of the form. The shifts from triple to duple meter dissolve in the improvisers' solo section, which comes after the band states the melody, bringing into relief the audible structural complexity of the exposition. Over Morello's snapping hi-hat, Smith and then Brubeck solo mostly in the Dorian mode, but also make use of the blues scale and, at cadential parts of the form, the C-sharp leading tone that pushes the sonority to D minor.

Elements like metric modulation (from 3/4 to 4/4) and modal mixture (Dorian and diatonic) in "Dorian Dance" present the musicians with novel parameters by which to improvise while also being sonic signifiers of musical erudition. Though certainly not classical music in an aesthetically strict sense, Brubeck's quartet provided their college audiences with a school-friendly modern jazz that, by design, might appeal to—and be marketed to—the intellectual and discerning listener.

Smith, who wrote all the pieces recorded on *À la Mode*, did so during the height of the 1960s early music revival in the United States and Western Europe, a period when composers and music scholars like Paul Hindemith at Yale designed curricula and ensembles (collegia) devoted to excavating, understanding, and performing European medieval and Renaissance music repertory. College-level music students received an education that included new and deeper insights into early modal theory, counterpoint and polyphony, and period instruments. Musicological scholarship on early music informed students' understanding not just of historical performance practice but of the components of style and the theoretical principles that undergirded the works of long-dead composers. Putnam Aldrich, a harpsichordist whose Harvard dissertation was on ornamentation in French Baroque keyboard music, was hired at Stanford University—thirty-four miles south of Mills College—in 1953. Aldrich's hire was the beginning of an influx of early music specialists arriving in the Bay Area, like the Yale graduate Richard L. Crocker at Berkeley.

Smith, an Oakland native, spent less than a year at Julliard in 1946, returning home to study composition at Mills with Milhaud and in 1952 pursuing a master's degree in composition at the University of California, Berkeley under the tutelage of composer Roger Sessions, an alumnus of both Harvard and Yale.[50]

Smith certainly seems to have made use of his education in writing and naming the ten tunes on the album.[51] Track 3 is "Invention," which, in its title and construction, evokes Johann Sebastian Bach's contrapuntal keyboard pieces that would be familiar to any pianist receiving formal training in the repertoire. Similarly, "Catch-Me-If-You-Can" features fast and close imitative polyphony between Smith and Brubeck, with Morello keeping time and adding accents and flourishes; Brubeck, playing only with his right hand on this track, sounds like he is directly quoting Bach's keyboard music. The mood is softer and more subdued in the "Lydian Line," track 4, where the mode's unique sound—its "raised" fourth scale degree, *à la* George Russell—is the pretext for an odd-length thirty-one-bar composition that, like "Dorian Dance," blends unfamiliar abstractions, like the modulation from duple to triple meter (▶ 00:40), within familiar formal and idiomatic conventions.

These homages to canonical European music were part of what bolstered Brubeck's image as a modern jazz musician, one that was already fundamentally aided by his whiteness. Perhaps more than Lewis's MJQ, Brubeck's interpolations of elements that signified classical music represented a modern jazz elevated beyond the sordid nightclub. Brubeck's aesthetic of "respectability" was, by 1960, integral to his fame; it was, Klotz writes, an implicit racial coding that promoted Brubeck as an acceptable choice for college campuses and concert halls and a draw for college-educated white audiences to jazz. The popularity of the quartet's college tours made Brubeck the "face" of modern jazz on the covers of *Time, Vogue, Good Housekeeping,* and *Life* magazines, and his features in these literary venues highlighted, among other things, the music's relative virtue.[52] The Brubeck Quartet and the MJQ contributed to the branding of modern jazz as music for the discerning listener—a music with a sophistication and prestige comparable to European classical music.

Yusef Lateef's Eastern Sounds

A black Detroiter born in 1920 in Chattanooga, Tennessee, William Emanuel Huddleston changed his name to Yusef Lateef in 1948 when he embraced Ahmadiyya Islam after being drawn to its doctrines of universal peace and goodwill for humankind.[53] Lateef's religious adoption paralleled that of many other urban-dwelling black Americans in the 1940s. This was a time where the few Islamic sects established in industrialized U.S. cities during the 1920s or earlier, like Chicago's Ancient Egyptian Arabic Order of Nobles of the Mystic Shrine (the "black Shriners," founded in the 1890s), flourished into a constellation of distinct and overlapping organizations: the Ahmadiyya, Noble Drew Ali's Moorish Science Temple, and the Nation of Islam, which was founded by one of Drew Ali's disciples, W. D. Fard Muhammad.[54] Lateef recalled how being an only child in a working family meant a lot of solitude—time spent, as a particularly sensitive child, becoming "more aware of nature."[55] He took up the tenor saxophone in high school and began working with local bands thereafter in the 1940s. As a young novice he toured with several prominent black musicians, such as Oran Thaddeus "Hot Lips" Page and Roy Eldridge, travel opportunities that surely exposed him to the latest currents in urban black cultures in and outside of Detroit. His first known recording date is in late 1948 in Chicago, with Eugene Wright's Dukes of Swing and the Dozier Boys vocal group. In early 1949, he joined Dizzy Gillespie's orchestra and toured in New York City, Chicago, and Los Angeles. He was introduced to the basic tenets of Ahmadiyya Islam—"unity of mankind, and brotherhood"—during his time in Chicago by a fellow musician, trumpeter Talib Daawud, which inspired Lateef to visit the New York mission house when he was in town. He embraced Islam in late 1949 because he "thought it was the right thing to do and it seemed right." Through Islam, Ingrid Monson writes, Lateef found "a path of intensive study, as well as ethical and spiritual development that guided his life," drawing musical inspiration from a spiritual system connected to Africa and Asia.[56]

For the droves of black migrants from the American South and Caribbean who made their way north in the first half of the twentieth century, Islamic metaphysics offered an alternative cosmology and cultural identity distinct from white Christianity. It was rooted neither in Europe nor in chattel slavery and was a global religion with a strong presence on the African continent and in the Near and Far East. For many skeptical black urbanites of the 1920s, the Christianity practiced by white Americans represented a religion that perpetuated the racial subjugation purported by white slave masters to be justified by holy scripture. This, with the steady news of lynchings in the South (heroically reported by the investigative journalist Ida B. Wells, who fled Memphis for Chicago under threat of violence) and de facto racial segregation of industrialized northern cities, made daily life even more intolerable for black urban dwellers, especially for the veterans and laborers who helped secure victory in Europe. Their sacrifice in Europe under the flag not being enough for white Americans to respect their inalienable rights as citizens made clear to a postwar generation of black Americans the intransigence of white supremacy.

The acceptance of this social and political fact inspired many to search for an alternative "nationhood."[57] Black Americans' embrace of Islamic theology, in any of the several iterations being practiced in urban America, was a means to catalyze an autonomous cultural identity and community that was diasporic in its reach and outlook. Black Islam in the United States was, Sohail Daulatzai writes, a "counter-citizenship" that reached toward a "Muslim International" that spanned Africa and Asia.[58] Embracing Islam allowed Black American urbanites to reconstruct ties to a history and heritable religious identity that had been severed by slavery, forging links through religious instruction and mythology to civilizations outside of whiteness and Europe.[59] The "outsider" identity adopted by practitioners of Islam helped cultivate ideological autonomy and a critical perspective on the false promises of white American modernity. Its appeal to black adoptees was also due to its ability to channel internalized feelings of alienation into agency through religious expression, community building, and civic engagement within the ummah. Accepting Islam as the "original" religion of West Africans before the Atlantic slave trade forged an affinity with "Eastern" cultures of Africa and Asia, one that Lateef channeled as a musician in the context of modern jazz. I will attempt in the section that follows to trace out the Eastern elements in Lateef's music.

The mufti Muhammad Sadiq was born in Bhera in 1872 and arrived in Philadelphia in February 1920, charged with the mission of spreading the Ahmadiyya movement abroad. As a young man, he made the pilgrimage westward from his hometown in Punjab to pledge devotion to Mīrzā Ghulām Ahmad, the prophet and founder of the Ahmadiyya movement in the city of Qadian. Ahmad, the son of a middle-class Muslim landowner, assumed prophethood in 1879 and in public debates and a prodigious amount of writing over the next decade made claims that upset the Sunni orthodoxy, Hindus, and Christians alike. Among them was his revelation that the messiah Jesus had not died on the cross after his persecution but had instead gone to India, where he died and ascended into heaven. Ahmad also advocated for a continuous prophecy—an ongoing process of interrogation and revelation—that contradicted the orthodox tenet of *khātam an-nabīyīn* (seal of the prophets), which held the sixth-century Muhammad ibn Abdullāh as the final prophet and the Qur'an as the authoritative textual source of his divine insight and teachings. Perhaps most upsetting to his detractors was that his followers believed Ahmad to be the second coming of Jesus and a *mujadid* (divine renewer, or Mahdi)—the earthly incarnation of each of the Muslim, Christian, and Hindu messiahs.[60]

Ahmad's social impact was in his success at promoting a new vision of Islam that responded to the political pressures of colonial Indian society, where British imperialists took advantage of religious and ethnic conflict. He advocated against violent jihad toward nonbelievers and, instead, encouraged followers to engage in a "war" of words and ideas in the pursuit of piety and interethnic and interfaith harmony.[61] In 1901, the Ahmadiyya became a formally recognized religious entity in colonial India, and after Ahmad died in 1908, Khalifa-Masih Il Mīrzā Bashir-ud-din Mahmud Ahmad assumed leadership and sought to expand the faith beyond India.

Muhammad Sadiq, serving as Mīrzā Bashir-ud-din Mahmud Ahmad's trusted emissary, established an Ahmadiyya mission in Harlem in April 1920. He had been held previously for months in a New Jersey detention center, accused by U.S. immigration authorities of seeking to spread polygamy, which he successfully appealed. His unfavorable entry to the United States paralleled that of other Indian migrants, especially Punjabis and Bengalis, who were subject to the Oriental Exclusion Act of 1917, the Johnson Act of 1921 (which established strict quotas for Asian immigration), and the Johnson-Reed Act of 1924, which privileged immigrants from Europe. Part of this xenophobic campaign included prohibiting Indians, understood as Caucasian based on their geographic origin, from being classified as "white," which the state reserved exclusively for migrants of European origin.[62] The racial categorization of South Asian migrants may have helped them establish a sense of solidarity with other nonwhite people in the United States.

Sadiq supported himself and his mosque financially by lecturing in the city and writing, for various periodicals, essays intended to disseminate Ahmadi teachings. His first converts were both white and black, but he found his most ardent supporters among black New Yorkers attracted to the depth of his spiritual conviction and the Ahmadi ethos of pacifism and self-reinvention.[63] Converts were required to establish a new identity through Islam (which included adopting an Arabic name) to signify their shift in religious conviction and worldview. After amassing a small following in Harlem, Sadiq moved the Ahmadiyya headquarters to Chicago in October because of its centralized location and his desire to build ties with the region's Syrian, Lebanese, Jordanian, and Palestinian Muslim communities, which led to the Ahmadis expanding to Detroit by the end of the year. Ceding leadership to Maulvi Muhammad Din in 1923, Sadiq returned to India, leaving the Ahmadis in the United States to continue their outreach and expansion; by 1940, the Ahmadis had a national presence, having amassed somewhere between five thousand and ten thousand members.[64] The shared experience of racial discrimination and exclusion established a spiritual, ideological, and material connection between Black American and South Asian Muslims, and, with the latter's presence in urban black communities, Black Americans were also exposed to South Asian customs and cultural expressions.

Lateef, while still based in Detroit, recorded in New York City several times in 1957. These were his first as an ensemble leader, and the music captured on the very first session on April 5 was released by Savoy Records as *Jazz for the Thinker*, a title clearly meant to convey its modern sound. That same band recorded again for Lateef's session a few days later, on April 9, which Savoy later released as *Jazz Mood*; in contrast to the more conventional pieces recorded in the first session, Lateef, trombonist Curtis Fuller, and bassist Ernie Farrow play Eastern instruments in alternation with Western. A scraping gourd and the Arab *arghul*, a tambourine and finger cymbals, and a Bedouin *rabab* (played by Lateef, Fuller, and Farrow, respectively) are prominently featured on the album's cover art (Figure 1.3).[65]

Figure 1.3 Album cover of Lateef's *Jazz Mood*, Savoy MG 12103, 1957.

The Eastern instrumentation spoke to a dimension of Lateef's spirituality, and, as he recounted years later, the music from this period was an attempt at a transcendent kind of music that promoted spiritual uplift in the listener. Serving in this context as signifiers of Asia and global Islam, Eastern instruments are the medium for that transcendence.[66]

The *arghul* is a key element in Lateef's "Eastern" sound. Typically found in the Nile River region that spans Egypt and Palestine, it consists of two bound, multipart bamboo reed pipes that are played simultaneously as two mouthpieces, with a shorter pipe used for playing melody while the larger, lower-register pipe keeps a sustained drone.[67] The *arghul* is an ancient instrument, a prototypical hornpipe played by musicians in the Fertile Crescent between the sixteenth and tenth centuries BCE. Lateef's use of it has signifying and symbolic power—it's an heirloom of his spiritual home region and produces a sound that invokes "the East" in the ear of a Western listener. The *arghul* in Lateef's music, and its distinct modal temperament and Arabic character, is a statement of his identity and a new sonic resource to be experimented with.

Lateef opens the album's first track, "Metaphor," with a forceful introduction on the *arghul* before moving on to the Western flute for the main melody. However, "Morning," on the LP's second side, is where more distinctly "Eastern" elements are featured. It opens with Farrow strumming on the *rabab*, a lute that is ubiquitous across West, Central, and South Asia in several regional variations and may even be related to the Moroccan *sintir* played by the Gnawa people, whose mystical and syncretic practice of Islam is related to Sufism. Farrow's repeated, syncopated, single-note pattern on the *rabab* becomes a mantra—a plucked, oscillating loop upon which other sonic events are overlaid. Lateef scrapes a gourd, Fuller jangles a tambourine, and Hugh Lawson plays a mixed minor-modal chord progression on the piano while Louis Hayes marks the duple meter on the hi-hat. The horns play the blues-inflected melody (▶ 01:04), which Lateef follows with his tenor solo (▶ 02:03) and then Fuller, followed by Lateef's second solo on tenor. The *rabab* is spotlighted during Farrow's solo, which happens toward the end of the performance, with the pattern he's maintained since the beginning. Afterward Lateef and Fuller return to their Eastern percussion instruments before restating the melody on their Western instruments for a final time.

The year 1957 was a busy one for Lateef. He recorded for Norman Grantz's newly formed Verve label just a week after finishing *Jazz Mood*, completed two more sessions for Savoy, and recorded for the indie label New Jazz in October. One of the Savoy sessions produced *Prayer to the East*, where Lateef continued his Eastern sounds with a rendition of "A Night in Tunisia," a piece written and made famous by Dizzy Gillespie in the early 1940s that the band begins with the burst of a gong and low drone on the double bass. Lateef plays an *arghul*-like double reed instrument (unspecified in the liner notes), with small bells and cymbals jangling underneath him.

The song title alone, chosen by Gillespie, conjures images of an enchanted night in Islamic North Africa; like other American song writers of the twentieth century, he was keen on the public's appetite for romantic and caricatured depictions of the mystical Orient—an exotic, faraway Eastern land filled with fantasy, magic, and esoteric, mystical knowledge. Al Jolson, the celebrated Lithuanian-born vaudevillian who became a worldwide phenomenon with the 1927 film *The Jazz Singer*, starred in the 1918 Broadway musical *Sinbad* as a porter in old Baghdad who's transported to exotic, faraway locales by various fabled characters. (*The Jazz Singer* was a technical advancement in the age of silent film because of its synchronous soundtrack; Jolson portrays a singer who becomes a star singing "jazzy" derogatory "coon songs" in blackface.) Improvising musicians like Thomas "Fats" Waller, a Harlem star born in Manhattan's Greenwich Village, capitalized on songs with outlandish Orientalist stereotypes. In his 1938 hit rendition of "The Sheik of Araby" (a comedic song written after the unexpected popularity of *The Sheik*, a 1921 film starring Rudolph Valentino) Waller sings lyrics written by Harry B. Smith and Francis Wheeler of a "bold Sheik" who, after riding over the "desert wild and free" and followed by an "Arab band," lays claim to his female object with an enchanting song, promising to creep into her tent at night when she's asleep to whisk her away.[68] In the lyrics that Waller leaves out, the sheik "proudly" scorns his submissive captive in spite of her cries as they ride away over the desert because he will "soon conquer [her] love by fear"—the "joke" of the song being that this sheik's absurd romantic courtship is actually an abduction.[69]

Orientalist tropes pervaded mainstream American popular culture in a potent way through film. Hollywood features loosely based on Antoine Galland's 1704 translated volume *One Thousand and One Nights*—itself a French-language translation and corruption of *Alf Layla wa Layla* (*A Thousand Nights and a Night*), a collection of stories preserved in Arabic on a fourteenth- or fifteenth-century Syrian manuscript—trafficked in stereotypes of an imaginary Arab world fabricated by the fantasies of European colonists of the nineteenth century.[70] Films like *The Sheik*, *The Thief of Baghdad* (1924, remade in 1940), and *Arabian Nights* (1940) romanticized the "dark forces" that lurked in a dangerous and beguiling foreign society that, Samuel Scurry argues, was counterpoised with Western civilization and necessitated domination to bring to order.[71] Disruptions to colonial fantasies of the Far East spread across the globe in the mid-1950s, starting with the Bandung Conference of April 1955, when representatives of twenty-nine Asian and African governments convened in Indonesia under the aegis of political self-determination and the abolishment of imperial rule. Anticolonial struggles intensified with the Afro-Asian People's Solidarity Organization conference in Cairo in 1957. The visual and sonic signifiers that Lateef used to point to the East blend Orientalist schtick with imaginings of a postcolonial world ushered in by Afro-Asian solidarity.

The cover art for Lateef's *Prayer to the East* depicts an Orientalist fantasy; it's an alluring close-up of a cobra perched in a defensive posture, its forked tongue extended outward as though it's being hypnotized by the snake charmer's flute just outside of the photo's frame. That special flute, called the *sapera been* (snake charmer's flute) in Punjabi, is a double reed instrument, like the *arghul*, with a single mouthpiece that produces a similarly nasal and piercing sound. It is possible that Lateef is playing either the *been* or the *arghul* in the introduction to "A Night in Tunisia," and the instrument's sound echoes the album cover in evoking an exotic and exoticized Middle East. The band presents this complicated blend of the genuine and the inauthentic in the track "Prayer to the East," which begins with another gong crash before pianist Hugh Lawson's bluesy introduction.

Lateef's *Prayer to the East* is representative of his effort to forge a new sound in modern jazz derived from his spiritual identity and interest in cultures beyond the United States. His "prayer" is a figurative reach outward to the Eastern lands where his faith originated and toward a particular cultural geography made audible through South Asian instruments. In signifying Asia thematically and sonically, Lateef sounds a new cultural awareness and identity—a diasporic Afro-Asiatic identity, separate from ideological white supremacy—emerging in urban black communities across the United States. Here, "Eastern" sounds operate as what Monica Miller calls a "social semiotic," legible in a particular cultural context.[72]

On September 5, 1961, Lateef's ensemble began recording *Eastern Sounds* for Prestige's Moodsville imprint, and they use similar strategies to signify "the East" throughout the album. The first track, Lateef's composition "The Plum Blossom," is similar to "Metaphor"; Farrow plucks on a single muted string of the *rabab* a one-bar pattern that simultaneously provides tonal grounding for Lateef, playing a *xun*, and pianist Barry Harris. The Chinese *xun* (埙, or 塤 in traditional Chinese) is a clay ocarina with origins in China's Neolithic period (ca. 4000 BCE or earlier); it is the size of a fist, shaped like an egg, and sound is produced by blowing into a hole carved through its top and covering holes for the thumbs and fingers elsewhere on the instrument's surface. Lateef, Joe

Goldberg writes in the liner notes, searched for the instrument in Manhattan's Chinatown after reading about it in a book about Chinese music, and he uses it (along with the *rabab*'s ground note and the piano's A-major to B-diminished vamp) as part of a broader musical gesture toward the "East."

That no specific Asian music tradition can be identified in "The Plum Blossom" runs the risk of the imprecise cultural gloss endemic to Orientalism in Western music, where "Eastern sounds" signify the "exotic." Goldberg implies this much when commenting, patronizingly, that Lateef's skill *and* naïveté are driven by his sincere interest in "the close relationship between American and Near-Eastern improvisational music."[73] The most evocative track on *Eastern Sounds* is "The Three Faces of Balal [*sic*]," which, Goldberg writes, Lateef wrote for a friend whose "three faces" were that of his wife and twin daughters. The historical Bilal ibn Rabah is an important figure in the hadith, the collected sayings of the Prophet Muhammad, where he is presented as a dark-skinned Ethiopian slave who, upon hearing the Prophet Muhammad's message, converted to Islam and was tortured for it. Bilal was saved from persecution by the Prophet, whom he then served, and was entrusted by him to be the first reciter (*mu'azzin*) of *adhan*, the call to prayer that reaches the ears of all within proximity to the Ka'ba ("sacred home," or mosque). Edward E. Curtis IV underscores Bilal's symbolic importance to twentieth-century Black American Muslims as a black former slave who prevails not just because of religious conviction but also because of his uncanny, divinely inspired musical ability.[74] Lateef's portrait of Bilal features Farrow playing a two-note figure (grounding a pitch close to "E") on the *rabab* while drummer Lex Humphries plays woodblocks, chimes, and cymbal over Lateef's melody and subsequent solo. Lateef evokes *maqamat*—the different melodic "modes" that populate Arabic music across North Africa and the Middle East which each have their own intervallic profile and melodic character—the pentatonic blues scale, and the E octatonic series.[75]

Compositional and performance details, including *maqam*-like pitch collections, ground-note pedal tones, and regional instruments—inspired by Asian musical practices—helped Lateef carve an interstitial space between Western and Eastern musical sources. It is a modern stylistic hybrid, but one that was responsive to a unique set of cultural concerns in postwar Black American urban life. In this way, Lateef's music of this period reflected community-specific efforts to develop an alternative to the implicit Eurocentrism and presumptions of European cultural supremacy in modern American culture. He did this by drawing from his impressions and sense of connection to an "Eastern" Afro-Asiatic world that he shared with other black musicians in this period. This radical worldview symbolized by his adopted

Arabic name and faith was ultimately a deeply personal form of creative expression. Lateef's determination to forge a new aesthetic path outside of normative modernity also reflected the ethos of creative autonomy that writers in the early 1960s would associate with jazz's "new thing."

It was during a 1949 rehearsal at the Click Club in Philadelphia when Lateef first met Coltrane, almost six years his junior, while he was on tour with Gillespie's big band.[76] Lateef remembered Coltrane as being very kind and humble, someone who was either "eclectic by nature, or he developed that attitude. And if he was on the road, there would always be several books in his room. He'd be studying something, whether it would be mathematics or esoteric astrology. I remember that once he and Naima [Coltrane's first spouse] recommended a book called *Esoteric Astrology*, which dealt with the hidden planets and things of that nature, and Naima would see that the various books and things were in his study. She was very essential to his growth."[77] When asked by Leonard Brown about Coltrane's spirituality, Lateef pointed to Coltrane's 1964 album *A Love Supreme*, saying, "I could hear, semantically, the songs of Islam, if you will, and he was married to a Muslim lady . . . Naima Coltrane." Monson provides context to their friendship and Coltrane's spirituality, noting that Ayesha Lateef, Yusef's widow whom Monson interviewed in 2019, observed that though Naima was Muslim she was not an Ahmadi, and Coltrane's proximity to Islam did not purport to include his full conversion to the faith despite the comparative similarities between his poem printed on the album jacket and the opening surah of the Qur'an, the Al-Fatiha.[78] Regardless, Lateef's friendship with Coltrane included a shared interest in spiritual growth and exploration, one that involved rigorous study and an awareness of important cultural currents within the community.

2

Free to Not Make Sense

Student musicians in 1960 could finally learn the art of modern jazz at a school. "The teaching of jazz music is a very difficult task to perform because jazz is mainly a state of mind," says the Dominican-born saxophonist and composer Manny Albam in an alluring advertisement for the newly founded Berklee School of Music in Boston printed in *Down Beat* magazine. "However, in order to achieve this state of freedom in musical thought, the language of music, and the mastery of the instruments by which it is voiced, must be taught by musicians who have themselves experienced the exhilaration of jazz performance."[1]

Applying newly acquired musicianship skills—specifically in harmonic theory and arranging—toward expressive freedom under the tutelage of experienced professionals is what schooling in modern jazz promised the novice musician at Berklee. Like the Lenox School in western Massachusetts that John Lewis and Gunther Schuller were programming, Berklee was aimed at institutionalizing jazz education.[2] That an improvised music with Black American roots was treated as a "serious" subject of study went in tandem with the more widespread legitimization of jazz in literary discourse, particularly by music and culture critics concerned with digesting and assessing the latest in live and recorded jazz and speculating on its current and future aesthetic direction. "Art form? There are still some who may pull up short at that," writes John Clellon Holmes for *Esquire* in an issue devoted to jazz. "They will add that never in the history of man's need to express himself in song has half a century sufficed to transform a folk music into an art music. But one of the wonders of our time is that precisely this has happened in jazz."[3]

But Ornette Coleman, an alto saxophonist who played what looked like a white plastic version of the instrument (it was the Grafton Company's acrylic and brass model, a less expensive option than fully brass saxophones) and whose 1959 LP *The Shape of Jazz to Come* on Atlantic Records attracted critical attention, was, by 1960, an increasingly divisive figure.[4] He'd received a ringing endorsement from Martin Williams, who wrote the LP's liner notes; Williams quoted the Modern Jazz Quartet's John Lewis saying, "Ornette Coleman is doing the only really new thing in jazz since the innovations in

Change. Kwami Coleman, Oxford University Press. © Oxford University Press 2025.
DOI: 10.1093/9780197780121.003.0003

the mid-forties of Dizzy Gillespie, Charlie Parker, and those of Thelonious Monk."[5] "Mr. Coleman is a newly hailed jazz radical from California," writes John S. Wilson for the *New York Times*. "He plays a plastic alto saxophone, producing short, disjointed phrases in a series of smears and runs that appear to have little definite form or orientation. However, when he joins with his trumpeter Don Cherry (who plays an oddly truncated instrument), they create some extremely affecting and unusual melodic lines. One gets the impression that Mr. Coleman is still searching for the proper form and setting for the type of playing that he has undertaken."[6] In an open letter printed in *Down Beat*, critic and pianist John Mehegan takes up the "question" of Coleman:

> I feel I must state my position in this Ornette Coleman controversy, since he raises so many pertinent questions for jazz and all jazzmen. I assume Ornette is sincere, but what he is doing certainly has nothing to do with jazz and, I'm afraid, very little to do with music in any form.
>
> First of all, he does not swing; neither does his rhythm section for that matter. Any talk about "pan-chromatic" or "serial" jazz is ridiculous. Most of Ornette's playing seems to consist of endless noodling around the I [tonic] chord with an occasional flurry of non-diatonic tones. I would say that Coleman is riddled with the very thing that he is supposed to be free of—namely a scaler-key center. Compared to a Rollins, a Coltrane, a Getz, not to even mention Parker, Coleman is a fumbling neophyte.
>
> But perhaps Coleman's playing is not the real issue here. His reputation is completely the result of artificial promotion by a small group of kingmakers. . . . Musicians arise! Rescue jazz from the cabalists, the metaphysicians, the hucksters, the ward healers.[7]

Rare was it that one musician warranted such a definitive takedown in the music press, but for Mehegan and other skeptics, Coleman's lack of harmonic sophistication disqualified him from the ranks of "serious" jazz modernists.

Down Beat, the leading jazz magazine in the United States, made efforts to acclimate their readership to Coleman's music and stoked the hype. "The Controversial Mr. Coleman," a paragraph-long piece printed in late November 1959, a month before Mehegan's open letter, acknowledged that critics were indeed put off by "one of the most talked-about young musicians in jazz today," which some critics heralded as "the start of a new direction in jazz."[8] This odd, unauthored notice appeared in print a week after Coleman's quartet began their nightly engagement opposite the Art Farmer–Benny Golson Jazztet at the Five Spot Café, a bar and restaurant popular among beat poets in Cooper Square—the northern end of the Bowery—in Manhattan's East Village. Their first date was November 17, and the turnout was large enough in the following week for Joe Termini, the venue's proprietor, to extend Coleman's quartet until December 1. The buzz around Coleman's group was steady, and the quartet was booked at the Five Spot "indefinitely" by late January 1960.[9] Jazz magazines quickly picked up on this rare phenomenon and its greater significance. Reflecting on the quartet's opening nights as a "preview for the press," George Hoefer luridly recounts the crowd's mixed reaction to their performance: " 'He's a fake.' 'He's a genius.' 'I can't say; I'll have to hear him a lot more times.' 'He has no form.' 'He swings like HELL.' 'He's out, real far out.' 'I like him, but I don't have any idea what he's doing.' Jazz can well use a new thrill, idea, or sound, something similar to what happened when a jaded swing era spawned Charlie Parker, Thelonious Monk, and Dizzy Gillespie in the early 1940s. But many critics feel that Coleman is back where Parker was in that groping period."[10] The several weeks they spent playing at the Five Spot, at the precipice of a new decade, symbolized to those reporting on the quartet the arrival of jazz's bewildering *new thing*. One anonymous writer observed in *Harper's Bazaar*, "The intense, cacophonic jazz of alto saxophonist Ornette Coleman has the veteran way-out world all agog. Coleman on his first trip to New York Pied Pipered the beatniks into the bulging Five Spot until dawn."[11]

In this chapter I focus on Coleman in the first three years of the 1960s, his commercial recordings and his coverage in the press, to show how he came to represent, from that point onward, the most prominent and controversial figure in what writers understood to be jazz's burgeoning avant-garde. My goal is to demonstrate how Coleman, through his own words on musical meaning and design, was fundamentally within the modern jazz paradigm in these years. I focus specifically on how his recorded music was taken as an assault on modern jazz's aesthetics, and how this notion was fueled by his musical autodidacticism, unique nomenclature, and general impulse toward nonconformity, idiosyncrasies that, for a black man, connoted deviance in normative society. The ways in which he—a southern, black male musician tenaciously developing a personalized sound and trying to build a career in a competitive market—and his music were described in pathological terms conforms, I argue, to the orthodox paternalist attitudes that white liberal elites held over what they saw as a poor, black underclass disinterested in, or perhaps incapable of, formalized education and social assimilation.

How seriously could a musician interested in experimenting with some of music's foundational pillars—harmony and meter—expect to be taken in the early 1960s, when modern jazz, its experts claimed, reached an apotheosis? According to the literary archive, not very, but this outcome was not just due to malice. The reaction to Coleman and his ensembles in these years conveys the difficulty that (self-)appointed experts on modern jazz had when confronted with an experimental practice for which there was no apparent precedent. This chapter is also about what happens when a creative practice surpasses formalized knowledge and ceases to make sense to the experts. Coleman, in his quartet, was experimenting with what he saw as a more organic approach to collective improvisation, where musicians could play in an autonomous yet coordinated way, guided by intuiting musical action instinctually and sympathetically, not just by thinking about it. The environment and sonic texture that these musicians developed is best described, I argue, as heterophonic.

For Coleman, music was a matter of the breath, in that the sound a musician produces should be as natural and unique as the way they breathe. What would it sound like if we all could hear ourselves breathing, at our own natural rate, along with the other human beings we share a space with at the same time? The result of this conceptual approach to music performance is a heterophonic ensemble texture where distinctions between "soloist" and "accompanist" are blurred, creating a more decentralized kind of group action and improvisation.[12] That kind of improvisational freedom meant, for Coleman, that the musician could play in ways that were immediate and more emotionally or affectively honest because they no longer had to be so focused on abiding by strict harmonic "rules." I touch on Coleman's musical output up until his self-produced December 1962 concert at Manhattan's Town Hall, which he organized under financial and personal duress and of which only a portion was ever commercially released. Coleman's "far-out" conceptualism and his obstinate determination to be heard, despite unsupportive peers, skepticism and denunciations in the press, and the general condescending attitudes that white liberal society held toward the black "underclass," fed the notion that he was pathological—an assumption that shaped the controversy around his music. In fact, Coleman was interested in expressing a more natural and human "feeling" in his music. In the context of modern jazz, some heard in his quartet's "formless" improvisations only cacophonous noise, but there were also musicians, writers, and consumers who heard in Coleman's sound *something else*.

Ornette's Something Else

Booked for almost two months at the Five Spot Café, between November 1959 and January 1960, and brought back again for April, May, and July, Coleman's quartet went from being unknown to the most controversial group in New York City's jazz industry at the start of the new decade (Figure 2.1).[13]

Figure 2.1 The exterior of the Five Spot's original location in Cooper Square, on Third Avenue and 5th Street in the East Village. A sign advertising the Ornette Coleman Quartet appears underneath the neon letters in the window on the right. Photographer unknown. Courtesy of *PopSpotsNYC* (blog).

Critics emphasized his outlier status. Leonard Feather wrote of Coleman's newfound notoriety in *Down Beat*'s first issue of 1960, after the quartet's engagement had been extended; he focused on Coleman's unique background and his difference from "rank-climbing musicians." "The initiative in molding new stars has been seized by other experts, including some who were among the slowest to accord reluctant recognition to Dizzy Gillespie and Charlie Parker," Feather chided. "Coleman has been the subject of the kind of extravagant praise normally reserved for a musician backed by years of big-time experience. Though it is much too soon to determine how important his contribution will really be, the indications are that he has indeed found a style of both writing and playing that is valid, fresh, and exciting."[14]

Critical hype fed the controversy surrounding Coleman's music. Those writing in support focused on the same qualities as the detractors: Coleman's melodies were striking and emotive but unconventional and unstable because of the music's formlessness, and the musicians improvised with abandon and without chord progressions tethering their playing. Coleman's music sounded simple and complicated all at once, and his few abstruse public comments on his compositions and the ensemble's methods gave professional critics little insight for further commentary.[15]

Michael Frayn, a reporter for the *Manchester Guardian* writing on the jazz clubs of New York, described Coleman's quartet, which he encountered at the Five Spot in December 1959, as "making the most extraordinary noises, far out on some limb of its own. A famous English dramatic critic sitting about two feet in front of Mr. Coleman's deeply disturbed saxophone shouted to me, 'I think they have gone too far.' I think perhaps they had."[16]

Coleman's reputation among peers as an experimentalist musician began when he was living and working in Los Angeles, though his impulse toward nonconformity started years before. Born in Fort Worth, Texas, in 1930, Coleman settled in California in 1953 after years as a saxophonist touring the American South and playing with a wide array of ensembles: a vaudeville troupe, a rhythm-and-blues band, a white "western swing" band, and blues "shouter" Pee Wee Crayton, who first brought Coleman to Los Angeles in 1951. Crayton effectively abandoned Coleman in Los Angeles while they were on the road, leaving the young saxophonist with the challenge of finding work in a new and unfamiliar scene. He struggled to do so, like so many black southern migrants of his generation living under Jim Crow segregation.[17]

Coleman was an obstinately self-taught musician; as a young man he eschewed formal training for on-the-job learning and the unforgiving hustle of a freelancer. He started on the alto as a young teen but switched to the tenor in high school, determining that he would find more and better work playing in the busy bars and nightclubs of the city's vice district throughout the school week and on weekends.[18] According to writer Howard Mandel, Coleman was offered a scholarship to a local college in Texas but, shortly after enrolling, dropped out. He told an interviewer years later that the pretenses adopted by his fellow black students, who "acted like they're Einstein," led him to seek an education outside of what he saw as elitist institutions.[19] In his earliest comprehensive interview for the press, conducted by Nat Hentoff for *Esquire* magazine in 1961, Coleman recounted harrowing early experiences on the road after high school. He was fired from a touring band in Natchez, Mississippi, for trying to make a fellow musician a "bebopper" and was forced to leave town under threat by the police for his unconventional long-haired, bearded appearance. After relocating to New Orleans, he was beaten and his saxophone was destroyed on a trip to Baton Rouge, presumably also for his unconventional style, appearance, and mannerisms. He told Hentoff that he was determined throughout these terrible experiences to persevere and remain as "uncommercial as possible."[20]

The travails wrought by his eccentricity was one trope that permeated Coleman's early reception in New York; another was his "miseducation." John Litweiler, one of Coleman's biographers, asserts that Coleman's autodidacticism, fed by his long-standing skepticism of rote learning and formal education, led to his fundamental misunderstanding of some aspects of basic musicianship, including the relationship between transposing instruments—like his alto saxophone—and concert pitch.[21] His "deficiency" in this regard was for Gunther Schuller, one of Coleman's earliest supporters (whom Litweiler quotes) a "handicap" that fed his innate genius:

> He'd write things down and they never made any sense. He'd write B flat when he really was hearing D flat, and it was all screwed up. So he said "Let me study with you." He came to my apartment religiously every week for something like eight months—he never was late. . . . I was making good progress, and he was beginning to understand—I felt there was like a light going on in his brain.
>
> Suddenly he stared at me and said, "I think I'm feeling sick," and he started to groan. He quickly got up and rushed into the bathroom and vomited for about ten minutes—it was unbelievable. Then, afterwards he came back and said, "Gee, I'm sorry, Gunther, I don't know what happened, but I realized something that I never realized before, and it really hurt me." His eyes were fill of terror—if a black man can turn white, he turned white. That's not just some casual little experience, that was a mind-blowing, earth-shaking experience for him. He never came back for another lesson. . . . I have always said that because he did not learn these things in the traditional way, he became the extraordinarily original improviser that he is, it's his genius.[22]

It is difficult to assess the veracity of Schuller's claim in archival sources, but his anecdote, which portrays Coleman as a kind of clueless savant (or, even more pejoratively, an archetypical "noble savage") lacking fundamental musical knowledge, does reinforce a trope that distances Coleman from musical modernity. Hentoff explained Coleman's notoriety as being a product of his idiosyncrasies and imperfect (or absent) formal musical education, qualities that also made him an anomaly among the educated and sophisticated musicians active in New York. Features like Hentoff's 1961 *Esquire* profile helped establish Coleman's image as a soft-spoken yet resolute nonconformist, an undeterred outlier and potential "natural" genius pursuing an ideal despite facing persistent doubt and rejection by musical gatekeepers and professional peers.[23] The lack of formal education and presumed dysfunction of poor and working-class Black Americans—which precluded their ability to assimilate into modern American society—was, as I explain later, taken as a matter of social fact by other influential writers in American cultural criticism.

Coleman's unique way of thinking and playing is why, Hentoff reported, Crayton abandoned him in Los Angeles and why he was regularly snubbed at jam sessions by more established musicians from whom he sought mentorship. Coleman worked odd jobs in Los Angeles while continuing his self-directed musical study, meeting trumpeter Don Cherry and bassist Don Payne in this period. Payne convinced veteran bassist Red Mitchell to facilitate a recording opportunity for Coleman at Lester Koenig's indie label Contemporary Records in February 1958. The ensemble Coleman organized for this session, released as *Something Else!!!! The Music of Ornette Coleman*, was standard, small-group modern jazz instrumentation: Walter Norris on piano, Payne on bass, Billy Higgins on drum set, Cherry on trumpet, and Coleman on saxophone.

The nine tracks on *Something Else!!!!* are Coleman's original compositions, each in a conventional song form: either a twelve-bar blues or a thirty-two-bar (AABA) song form. "Chippie" and "Angel Voice," two of the thirty-two-bar songs, interpolate the familiar chord progression from the Gershwin brothers' 1930 showtune "I've Got Rhythm." The use of common song forms and chord-based improvisation in a style emulative of the 1940s bebop generation puts *Something Else!!!!* squarely in modern jazz practice. But Coleman's distinct conceptual approach is heard in how the ensemble approaches melody in relation to the meter and form, where it is "exhaled" with the kind of free outward flow of speech and breath—an effect that the ensemble utilizes in moments of improvisation vis-à-vis the underlying chord progression of the form. Coleman, who explained the approach to Hentoff for the album liner notes, wanted a creatively liberated and more collectivized, dialogic kind of music-making experience that emphasized the individual musician's approach to "pitch," a term that Coleman and Cherry use unconventionally in their conversation with Hentoff to mean a musician's timbre, or unique sonic signature. Blending the individuals' highly personalized sound (which they produced on their instrument as a product of their technique and sensibility) with spontaneous and instinctual exchange with other musicians—whose "pitch" and sensibility they'd become familiar with—during dialogic improvisatory flow imparted an intuited, almost speech-like quality to melody and rhythm.[24]

Using "pitch" outside of its standard (academic) meaning, which might be the deliberate or inadvertent result of his self-directed education, Coleman articulated an interest in musical expression achieved by going beyond standardized parameters like temperament, diatonicism, and centripetal meter, noting that writing out music to be "technical and right" was "not hard to do, [and had] no meaning by itself," where the ultimate goal should be achieving the "human sound of a voice" on one's instrument. Coleman emphasized his preference for melodies and rhythms that were "natural," closer to speaking and breathing, predicting that one day "music will be a lot freer. Then the [chord progression] for a tune, for instance, will be forgotten and the tune itself [i.e., the compositional melody, including how the musicians are improvising spontaneously and collectively in relation to it] will be the pattern, and won't be forced into conventional patterns. The creation of music is just as natural as the air we breathe. I believe music is really a free thing, and any way you can enjoy it you should."[25] Hentoff quoted Coleman several years later in an article for the *New York Times* saying that his music "doesn't have any real time, no metric time. It has time, but not in the sense that you can time [i.e., count] it. It's more like breathing—a natural freer time. 'People have forgotten how beautiful it is to be natural. I like spread rhythm, rhythm that has a lot of freedom in it. . . . [With] spread rhythm, you might tap your feet a while, then stop, then later start tapping again. That's what I like.' "[26]

Despite this album's modernist leanings, Coleman's preoccupation with musicians' idiosyncratic "pitch" and improvisational freedom resulted in a harmony that is a conditional "effect" produced by the simultaneous streams of melody and sound created by musicians playing freely together. Instead of a musician developing their improvisation "logically," emphasizing pitches that are harmonically soluble and aligned with the syncopation of the underlying swing rhythm or rigid meter, Coleman's vision of "free" music is where harmony is a circumstantial phenomenon, contingent on the musicians' coordination and cooperation, and in constant flux. The ensemble does not fully realize this ideal on *Something Else!!!!*; the unusual thirteen-bar melody of "The Disguise," for instance, where, according to Coleman, "the first and last bar change places," still leads to a conventional twelve-bar blues in D major that the soloists navigate in the typical "modern" way. Coleman asserted his conceptual vision on later recordings, pursuing an ideal where melody (precomposed and improvised) and its character (shape, rhythm, and articulation) informed the improvisatory action of musicians, not the form's chord progression: "the tune itself will be the pattern [i.e., *form*], and won't have to be forced into conventional patterns [i.e., *forms*]."[27]

In *Tomorrow Is the Question! The New Music of Ornette Coleman*, his next record for Contemporary recorded in Los Angeles in January 1959, Coleman dropped piano from his group and thus reduced the possibility that any one instrument could produce anything resembling a chord.[28] Now, with an ensemble of mostly monophonic instruments—saxophone, trumpet, bass, and drums—and no explicit, identifiable chords, Coleman could better realize his vision of unique "tunes" that optimized the expressive freedom of musicians. He would work with this sparser ensemble texture almost exclusively for the next decade.[29] In the *Esquire* interview, Hentoff underscored the unrelenting hardships and rejection that Coleman faced in this period despite his deal with Contemporary, and he relayed Coleman's story of a pivotal encounter during the band's trip to San Francisco in 1959, when Payne convinced veteran bassist Percy Heath of the Modern Jazz Quartet to sit in with the ensemble. Heath recorded six of Coleman's nine compositions on the LP, one of which is "Compassion." The A-section of its "tune" is first played by the bassist (Heath or Mitchell) and the drummer (Shelly Manne); a long, sinuous melody that rises and falls is followed by a repeated declamatory motif that ends with a strong cadence. "Compassion" starts and stops in a manner that mimics speech, outside of the regular pulse of metric musical time. All four musicians play the repeat of the A-section, which is broken up into a call-and-response exchange between the bassist and the rest of the ensemble (▶ 00:14); then the band moves onto a very short four-bar B-section (▶ 00:30) before repeating the A-section. Coleman and Cherry improvise freely while the bassist and drummer maintain the pulse without abiding to a precomposed form, thereby keeping metric "time" without chord changes.

Excited and confused by Coleman's music and his experience playing it, Heath introduced the quartet to John Lewis with his ringing endorsement, and Lewis arranged for Coleman's group to record for Atlantic Records, with whom he already had a contract, and to attend the Lenox School that summer. Lewis made his enthusiasm for Coleman's music public, commenting in an interview for the *Jazz Review*, "I've never heard anything like them before. . . . [It's] not like any ensemble that I have ever heard, and I can't figure out what it's all about yet. Ornette is, in a sense, an extension of Charlie Parker. . . . [T]hey are not playing an imitation but actually something new."[30] In May 1959, the new Coleman quartet, with bassist Charlie Haden in Payne's place, recorded the portentously named *The Shape of Jazz to Come* in Atlantic's studio in Hollywood.

In the opening track of this LP, "Lonely Woman," another Coleman original, the "tune" (i.e., compositional melody) is carried by Coleman and Cherry, and it floats above Haden's low open-string "D" pedal tone (above which he overlays an improvised melody) and Higgins's propulsive wash of percussive color. The form of the "tune" is a loose thirty-two-bar AABA, "loose" because the ensemble vacillates in and out of phase with the pulse (meter), and the three streams of sound—the two unison horns, bass, and drums—align in a fluid and fluctuating way, like a group of people simultaneously wailing. The sound mass produced by these three streams expands and contracts: the group sonifies an emotional state like anguish, keeping with the title of the tune. During Coleman's solo, Haden maintains the pedal tone and provides rhythmically active "free" counterpoint, while Higgins leans into the ride cymbal, driving the ensemble with fluid, metallic sound. This coordinated and cooperative "formlessness" has a heterophonic texture, and it demands that musicians carefully listen and empathetically respond to each other's direction and subtle inflections.

The heterophony of the Ornette Coleman Quartet (pictured on the album cover of *This Is Our* Music of 1960 in Figure 2.2) is most dramatic on "Change of the Century," the title track of their last recording session in California, which occurred on October 8 and 9, 1959. This abstract AABA "tune," played by the horns in unison, is embedded within a maelstrom of activity by Haden's untethered bass melody and Higgins's bright, propulsive cymbal (though he ghost-notes the rhythm of the "tune" on the snare). Coleman and Cherry alternate as soloists, skimming above and weaving in between the other two independent musicians in a decentralized environment of musical activity. Coleman proclaims in the liner notes, "[Perhaps] the most important new element in our music is our conception of *free* group improvisation":

> The musicians have complete freedom, and so, of course, our final results depend entirely on the musicianship, emotional make-up and taste of the individual member. . . . Many people apparently don't trust their reactions to art or to music unless there is a verbal *explanation* for it. In music, the only thing that matters is whether you *feel* it or not. You can't intellectualize music; to reduce it analytically often is to reduce it to nothing very important. It is only in terms of emotional response that I can judge whether what we are doing is successful or not.

He tells Hentoff in the *Esquire* interview that while his eccentric ideas were received better by New York audiences, his audaciousness and general presence still provoked hostility by critics and more established improvising musicians on the scene: "They *had* to listen because what we do automatically catches your ear, but I could feel their anger. I guess it's shocking to hear someone like me come on the scene when they're already comfortable in Charlie Parker's language. They figure that now they may have to learn something else."[31]

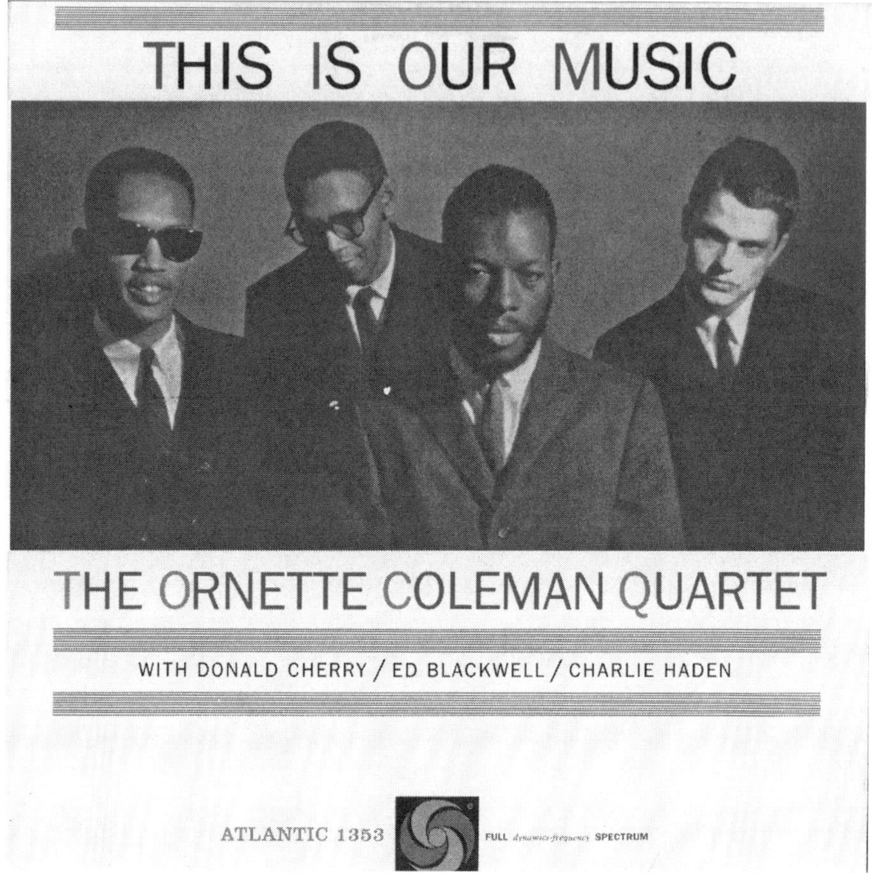

Figure 2.2 Album cover of the Ornette Coleman Quartet's 1960 LP *This Is Our Music*. Photo credit: Lee Friedlander.

Presumed Dysfunctional

When Democratic Party candidate John F. Kennedy was elected president over the Republican contender Richard Nixon in November 1960, it marked a new era of American liberalism. Born into an affluent and politically connected Massachusetts Irish-Catholic family, the Harvard-educated Kennedy made keen use of television to promote his image as a younger, progressive candidate for the new decade. During his campaign, he cultivated strategic alliances with organized labor, made appeals to urban-dwelling ethnic minorities, and joined former president Harry Truman's renunciation of the red-baiting House Un-American Activities Committee despite his brother's relationship with disgraced senator Joseph McCarthy and his father's more conservative political leanings.[32] The incoming Kennedy administration also struck a hardline stance against the Soviet Union, with Soviet communism poised as the antithesis of American democracy and the existential threat of nuclear warfare a foil for American industry and military imperialism.

The Kennedy administration's vision of American progress was powered by an economy oriented toward a burgeoning multinational free market, trade between "friendly" nations, and a prosperous middle class. As the youngest elected president, whose sartorial flare and charmed marriage to the equally media-primed Jackie Kennedy only added to his celebrity, Kennedy's "manufactured" image marked, for historian Gary Donaldson, the first "modern" U.S. presidential campaign.[33] The ideal of American liberalism that Kennedy embodied at the turn of the 1960s was youthful, educated, elite, white, but receptive to the grievances of racial minorities, advocating for racial integration but still staunchly anticommunist and intolerant of deviance from and subversion of the status quo. Kennedy's reluctance to enact legislation to protect the civil rights of racial minorities was a calculated political strategy to avoid further alienating white southern voters invested in racial segregation and the prevailing social order and whose vote he only narrowly secured to win the election.

The industrialized American city was a site onto which both the promise and the problems of a modern society were projected in 1960. Cities became centers of trade, industry, and migration, and urban populations were intrinsically heterogeneous; civil unrest in northern and southern metropoles, initiated especially by Black Americans challenging their incomplete citizenship, discrimination, and police violence, threatened to interrupt the flow of capital and social order. The only viable solution—racial integration—was, for Daniel Patrick Moynihan, Kennedy's assistant labor secretary, a long shot because of the seeming unbridgeable gap between the demands of a modern society and the plight of poor and marginalized black people who could not seem to assimilate.

By the time Moynihan completed *The Negro Family: The Case for National Action* in 1965, he had already established himself as an expert on urban reform. The "Moynihan Report," as it became known, warned of an "approaching new crisis in race relations" emerging from poor and neglected black urban dwellers.[34] Along with "the racist virus in the American blood stream," the depraved conditions of the black poor were due to a "tangle of pathology," a concept Moynihan cribbed from anthropologist Oscar Lewis's "culture of poverty" theory to describe an inherited, irrational, and dysfunctional outlook and lifestyle that perpetuated the poor's self-destructive behavior and propagated social failure throughout generations.[35] In Moynihan's report, the culture of black urbanites—the unwitting, intergenerational victims of slavery, brutality, and discrimination—was suffused with trauma. Impoverishment and its deprivations impeded Black Americans' chances for gainful employment and a better, more integrated place in modern American society. Such errancy, fomented by broken families and welfare dependency, was positioned as the antithesis of the social fitness of men of pedigree, presumably men like Moynihan himself, whose whiteness, elite education, and proximity to political and economic power were convincing signs of cultural superiority.[36]

Moynihan served as Lyndon B. Johnson's assistant secretary of labor at the time of his report and held faculty positions at Wesleyan University, then Harvard, but his ties to government and academia began in the late 1950s. He served as staff to New York governor Averell Harriman and completed a doctoral program in international relations at Tufts University while holding a faculty position at Syracuse University. It was around this time that he began writing for *The Reporter*, a magazine directed at career politicians and diplomats that was founded by Max Ascoli, a refugee of fascist Italy who was devoted to the defense of liberalism, a political ideology that promotes free-market capitalism as a guarantor of a free democratic society.[37] *The Reporter* pledged informed political analyses grounded in objective fact and enlisted writers like Moynihan to comment on civic politics and public policy from the perspective of their specialization.

Moynihan wrote pieces on urban planning, transportation, and organized crime—all matters of concern for administrators in a functioning metropolis. His editor Irving Kristol introduced him to Nathan Glazer, a Columbia-trained sociologist who also worked for the Kennedy administration. At the time, Glazer was working on a study aimed at profiling and comparing the largest ethnic groups of New York City and invited Moynihan to contribute to his project; in 1963, *Beyond the Melting Pot: The Negroes, Puerto Ricans, Jews, Italians, and Irish of New York City* was published by MIT Press. Moynihan was not a trained social scientist, but the ideas that he and Glazer presented about ethnocultural differences were fundamentally assessments of each racialized group's relative success and social fitness in the modern metropolis.[38] Both Moynihan, an Irish American, and Glazer, a Jewish American, with their combined academic pedigrees and governmental affiliations, enjoyed a rare and elevated platform that lent their views an uncanny authority. They based their enumeration of New York's largest ethnic groups on the previous decade's census data and their own anecdotal observations; glaring exclusions were Asians (who were mentioned only in reprinted census data and categorized as "white") and "old stock" Anglo-Saxon Protestants and other long-since-assimilated Europeans, whom the authors imputed to be the only "non-ethnic" Americans.[39]

Beyond the Melting Pot was an attempt at an objective study of the social and labor relations in a modern, multiethnic city; these were social and labor relations that affected freelance musicians as well. Glazer and Moynihan sought to diagnose the inherent problems of a "merchant metropolis with an extraordinarily heterogeneous population. . . . [Their] languages have been mutually unintelligible, their religion radically different, their family structures, values, ideals, cultural patterns have been as distinct as those of the Irish and the Southern Negro, of urban Jews and peasant Italians."[40] The success of these ethnic groups in a modern economy, Glazer and Moynihan concluded, was tied to how well they assimilated into American culture and its norms; acclimating to ideological and cultural commonalities ensured good social relations and labor prospects, which, the authors suggested, are the ligaments that hold together an orderly society. Their ultimate claim, however, was that the melting pot analogy for the American populace did not live up to reality and that certain harsh objective truths about New York's ethnic mélange could offer policymakers a better path forward, especially with regard to the economy.

"To speak of the Negroes and Puerto Ricans," they wrote, "one also means unorganized and unskilled workers, who hold poorly paying jobs in the laundries, hotels, restaurants, small factories or who are on relief."[41] And though they acknowledged that discrimination and poverty contributed to the low status of African Americans and Puerto Ricans within the social hierarchy, they surmised that their relative unfitness, compared to the other ethnic groups, prevented them from competing in the labor market—the consequence of their inability to properly assimilate into the "homogeneous American mass."[42] Moynihan posited a "nonethnic" city of industry where talent, in the arts and cultural fields, was competitive and essentially "colorblind." Their assumption here was that merits, like talent, ensured one's ability to compete in and successfully integrate into a "modern" American society and economy.

Glazer and Moynihan's book offers a window into the chauvinistic attitudes of an elite, cosmopolitan, and white liberal class in the first half of the 1960s that understood culture in the terms of a social hierarchy. The authors posited a lack of education and useful, employable skills as contributing to the unemployment and social failure of urban blacks. City-dwelling Black Americans—southern migrants and their descendants—suffered from the lasting ancestral trauma of slavery, which inculcated an environment plagued by vice and broken families and produced a culture of pathology incompatible with mainstream society. The best chance that Black Americans had for social fitness, Moynihan and Glazer argued, came from the "middle-class and well-to-do and educated Negroes" who could successfully navigate or assimilate into modern—white—American society. The integrationist project was a goal to be met by Black Americans, an argument they made throughout their book: that ethnic groups' ability to integrate into mainstream white society was a marker of success. Moynihan and Glazer insisted that the social failure of the black underclass was a point of contention for middle-class Black Americans who, through education, employment, and normative behavior, were more successful at integrating into mainstream society.

That lack of education and skill training compounded what Glazer and Moynihan called the "somewhat frayed relationship of the Negroes to political liberalism in general," since slavery and the decades of disenfranchisement that followed kept African American political power and social mobility behind that of other groups.[43] The black underclass's social failure was ultimately, for Glazer and Moynihan, what contributed to the city's mounting social and political unrest. The authors utilized this uncritical perpetuation of racist stereotypes to explain what they saw as the "developing tension between Negroes and liberals," which had led to a "new rise of Negro exclusivism and nationalism: the feeling that Negroes have to go it alone and should trust no one but themselves, and the idea that any disinterested common action with democratic-minded whites for public policies to improve the condition of Negroes is an illusion."[44] They cited the black Muslims of the Nation of Islam and other groups as leading a new "exclusivist feeling" among the black underclass, which contributed to interethnic tensions, but determined that the "psychological satisfactions" radical blacks gained by attacking their liberal allies, and their greater goal of separating from white America, would ultimately fail. The authors insisted that protests spearheaded in New York's black communities would necessarily end because, in addition to its limited political returns, "protest leadership shows a tendency to become irrational, shrill, and ineffective."[45]

Considered a landmark text in its time, *Beyond the Melting Pot* promised a new, "objective" study of ethnicity (which the authors racialized) in a modern American society, and it won the Cleveland Foundation's Anisfield-Wolf Award, which recognized important literary works on American race relations, in 1964.[46] Their paternalism and belief in social and cultural hierarchies was shared by writers focused on the constantly fluctuating music cultures of a multiracial metropolis. Music critics who focused on modern jazz began to utilize tropes of deviance and degeneracy the more musicians like Coleman performed in seemingly irrational ways that flouted norms. Here, the "outer," public world as defined by elite, successfully-assimilated white men found a parallel in the "inner" conceptual world of musical expression as understood by elite, successfully-assimilated white men; in both worlds, the "noise" of a disaffected black underclass was the result of pathology and an inability or refusal to assimilate into modernity.

"JAZZ IS SICK," wrote Jean Le Blanc (a nom de plume) for *Esquire* in 1962. "What was once, only a few choruses ago, the unspoiled child of the American arts is now a pain-ridden adult. Neurotic musicians are serving up nerve-wracking music for nervous critics. With the help of the self-appointed experts, jazz has been manufacturing its own mausoleum."

> To qualify among the cognoscenti as a jazzman of consequence you need (a) an active rejection of the public's interest, or preferably no public interest at all, (b) a police record, preferably for violation of the narcotics laws, (c) an utter lack of concern for beauty of sound, (d) a death certificate and/or (e) a capacity for solemnity and the conviction that jazz is a deadly serious business. This narrows the field neatly. In (a) you have Miles Davis, who turns his back on audiences, and Thelonious Monk, who seems unaware that they exist. We won't go into the unhealthy details of (b); the constant newspaper headlines, though slanted, are basically factual. Chief contenders for (c) are Ornette Coleman, John Coltrane and Sonny Rollins; in (d) Charlie Parker and Lester Young, in (e) John Lewis, Gunther Schuller and a handful of other Third Stream jazzniks. . . .
>
> Where once we hear the exquisite purity of Johnny Hodges' alto, we face the cacophony of an Ornette Coleman, who rejects tone, chords, harmony and melody, whose champions equate anarchy with progress.[47]

In this, the veiled writer portended the aesthetic decline of the only native U.S. art music which, up until then, achieved its ideal state in the "pure" sound of Johnny Hodges (Edward "Duke" Ellington's star altoist) and Dave Brubeck's highly popular small group, whose album *Time Out* he considered "ingenious." Apostate critics were to blame even more than the musicians themselves for this aesthetic degeneracy because, in their determination to stay on top of the latest and noisiest fads, they abandoned rationality and good taste. The author's surprising inclusion of Rollins as a transgressor of beauty occurred months before his collaborations with Don Cherry, the trumpeter in Coleman's quartet, which began in July 1962. And Le Blanc's condescension toward the Third Stream's "seriousness" implicated the classical music strivings of "jazzniks" as misinformed, if not seditious, communist-like behavior. Musicians like Abbey Lincoln and Max Roach, whose *We Insist! Freedom Now Suite* was the source of this purported "Crow Jim" controversy, had choice words for Le Blanc; in a refutation published as an op-ed in the *Amsterdam News* they called out Le Blanc's thinly veiled racism, the "God complex" from which he dismissed open-minded critics, and general ignorance about creativity in jazz, questioning how this so clearly sick "self-appointed critic of the critic" could possibly know what emotional health was.[48]

There is a parallel in how Moynihan saw the black underclass as being on the periphery of modern America's progressive monoculture and the divergence that black avant-gardists represented for Le Blanc in relation to modern jazz. In both cases, not assimilating was construed as pathological, and the chaos fomented by a dysfunctional class of people as a threat to modernity. Both Moynihan and Le Blanc understood an inability or refusal to assimilate as pathological and the unsettling "noise" of musicians abandoning modernity as like that of the chaos and unrest in cities across the country.

The ideological haze created by this manufactured culture war emanated from policy and cultural criticism. For writers like Le Blanc, the new jazz was pathological, and musicians like Coleman were deviant and intent on rejecting "beauty." The aesthetic change represented by Coleman's quartet had a greater context in Black Americans' claims of agency that, as I discussed in Chapter 1, involved questioning, subverting, and diverging from the status quo and establishing an identity that aligned with one's convictions and subjecthood. Originality was an imperative for abstract modernists like Monk that distinguished musicians in their milieu and could serve as an effective marketing tool, as Robin D. G. Kelley has shown in his prodigious biography of the musician; it was also a strategic tool of resistance against structural oppression and the pressure to assimilate.[49] Black radical creativity, La Marr Jurelle Bruce argues, is the outgrowth of an expressive culture that developed within and in opposition to Western modernity in that it "imagines, manifests, and practices otherwise ways of doing and being—all while confounding dominant logics, subverting normative aesthetics, and eroding oppressive structures of power and feeling."[50] In this way, the heterophonic textures developed by Coleman's ensemble in the act of performance were an abstract kind of "harmony"—a sound mass of opaque and coordinated musical simultaneity—and not just irrational, pathological "noise."

Autodidacticism and idiosyncratic creative practices cultivated by Black American improvising musicians in the 1960s, George E. Lewis explains, opened new conceptual and expressive terrain while asserting their right to self-expression.[51] Understanding Coleman's early 1960s recorded work, then, as an experimentalist practice developed outside of musical orthodoxy is to hear in it the noise of a new creative syntax being tested and developed. Because there was no available theoretical rubric for this new music—no publicly available lead sheets or scores—and only parabolic language from its creators printed in magazines and album liner notes, Coleman's presence in the music discourse of the early 1960s was one of regular debate and controversy. The "free" and "formless" heterophonic "harmony" in Coleman's quartet music pushed past the accepted sonic frontier of modern jazz and into abstract affective terrain.

Creative abstraction served a dual aesthetic and political goal for postwar black artists in that it resisted assimilationist expectations of universal intelligibility and understanding. For marginalized subjects, rejecting the expectation that one's work should be intelligible and palatable to a general audience can function as a bulwark against superficial engagement and the exploitative traps of capitalist industry. A black writer's commitment to opaque abstraction in prose writing, argues Phillip Brian Harper, upends any "promise of easy and transparent communication in light of which none of their cognitively disjunctive features can fail to make an impression, since these evidently violate that very promise."[52] Harper finds a similar abstractionist practice in pianist Cecil Taylor's rendition of the Rogers and Hammerstein showtune "This Nearly Was Mine," recorded on *The World of Cecil Taylor* LP of 1960. Drawing from Amiri Baraka's 1962 album review in the avant-garde magazine *Kulchur*, Taylor's abstraction of the tune's melody and metric time, for Harper, distorts the original in a way that disorients the listener and disappoints their expectations, thus potentially beckoning them to listen to Taylor's take as though it is an unfamiliar, original tune.[53] It is helpful to understand the "new thing" represented by Coleman's music in this way: as initially frustrating a listener's normalized expectations and, potentially, inciting a different kind of listening experience.

In a heterophonic ensemble texture, the absence of a tonal center and/or meter creates an amorphous and potentially disorienting sound mass that demands a dedicated and proactive kind of listening. Processing the totality of sound in one hearing is beside the point because it is humanly impossible to hear every voice in a clear and isolated way, since they overlap with and intrude upon one another. In heterophony, "hearing," "understanding," and "knowing" are exercises in approximation and repetition, leading the listener, in the words of Édouard Glissant, to "focus on the texture of the weave and not on the nature of its components."[54] It was Glissant who, in *Poetics of Relation*, first proposed "opacity" as a theoretical concept—and a mode of being and engagement—that describes and promotes a human being's right to difference in relation to others.

For Glissant, opacity is an embrace of the irreducible totality of human existence, a "filter" through which genuine human interaction and mutual understanding ("relation") occurs. Opacity is not the absence of clarity but the recognition of the many artificial limits that the privileging of objectivity and orthodox knowledge sets against our attempt to understand humanity in its multitudes. "Agree not merely to the right to difference," Glissant demands, "but, carrying this further, agree also to the right to opacity that is not an enclosure within an impenetrable autarchy but subsistence within an irreducible singularity. Opacities can coexist and converge, weaving fabrics."[55] Getting comfortable with the lack of clarity that comes with embracing opaque multiplicity, according to Glissant, is a poetic alternative to the rigid Enlightenment model of universalism—a totality that all human beings are expected or forced to acquiesce to.[56]

"Some musicians say, if what I'm doing is right, they should never have gone to school," Coleman told Gary Kramer for the liner notes of the 1959 Atlantic LP *Change of the Century*. "I'll say, there is no single *right* way to play jazz. Some of the comments about my music make me realize though that modern jazz, once so daring and revolutionary, has become, in many respects, a rather settled and conventional thing. The members of my group and I are now attempting a breakthrough to a new, freer conception of jazz, one that departs from all that is 'standard' and cliché in 'modern' jazz."[57]

Naming Jazz's Avant-Garde

On the evening of May 16, 1960, Gunther Schuller premiered his latest work before a live audience at Circle in the Square, a theater on Bleecker Street in Greenwich Village. This was the first time that a general New York audience was presented with the kind of hybrid music that Schuller had been experimenting with alongside John Lewis at their summer music school in Lenox. The concert ensemble consisted of the New York Contemporary String Quartet and a variety of notable jazz soloists on the New York scene, like Bill Evans and Eric Dolphy. In style and appearance, Schuller's music faithfully reflected the symbolic welding of modern jazz and classical music, and white and black musicians. John S. Wilson, reviewing the concert for the *New York Times*, dubbed it a "third stream of sound," lifting the "third stream" nomenclature from Schuller's lectures at Brandeis University, and summarized the music as one wherein "jazz and classical techniques were fused."[58] This would be the first time that a more abstract subgenre would be identified in the press, and this term stuck to Schuller's music and any adjacent efforts to blend jazz and classical styles, prompting Schuller to clarify, a year later, that the "third stream" was an adjective and not a noun, an ideal and not a genre.[59]

Schuller would perform some of these pieces again in the fall of 1960 at the Monterey Jazz Festival in California and then record them in December for the Atlantic Records release *John Lewis Presents Contemporary Music: Jazz Abstractions—Compositions by Gunther Schuller & Jim Hall.* The title track of that LP, "Abstraction," a twelve-tone piece Schuller had written specifically for Coleman as a soloist, was first played at the May concert in Greenwich Village with six other pieces.

Whereas Coleman's public association with Lewis and Schuller helped to position his ensemble within the modern jazz vanguard, their abstract, heterophonic "harmony" was, in Baraka's view, what set them apart. He had caught Coleman's quartet during their Five Spot run with fellow *Metronome* contributor Martin Williams, who he recalled as being the first person to refer to Coleman's music as jazz's "new thing," an epithet that would accompany Coleman's music—and that of any other experimental improvising musician who appeared to play in a "formless" and spontaneous way—for the next decade.[60] Williams, in turn, became one of Coleman's earliest advocates in the press, and as the co-editor of the *Jazz Review* (alongside Hentoff) and a *Metronome* contributor (also along with Hentoff), his endorsement carried a legitimizing weight. For Williams, advocating for Coleman involved making his musical thinking more transparent to jazz criticism's readership.

An example of this is "Ornette Coleman and Tonality," a printed conversation in the *Jazz Review* between Williams and composer/theorist George Russell for the June 1960 issue, where both men pontificate on Coleman's improvisatory methods and how they should be best understood, diatonically or otherwise. Russell and Williams agree that Coleman's style is idiosyncratic. Ultimately, they surmise, he is one of many musicians in recent years leading an "assault on the chord," which includes Gil Evans's arrangements, Charles Mingus and his "extended form" music, and Miles Davis's "modal period" with Bill Evans.[61]

After reviewing two fundamental strategies of improvisation—horizontal (where a musician focuses on scales and "sequences of intervals" in their different permutations) and vertical (where they weave a chromatic melody through a sequence of chords)—Russell describes Coleman as a musician who managed to fused tonality and pantonality together into an organic style, and Williams agrees.[62] "Then if a soloist chooses to be completely free, it really makes no difference to which of these centers [tonality and pantonality] he attaches his thinking," Russell explains. "In other words, everything in music is related in terms of close to distant relationships and there is no 'right' and 'wrong.'" Coleman has a unique sense of form, Russell concludes, even if the formal structure of his music is not obvious, but he still has to prove his formal abilities as a composer by producing a "large-form work," something that third stream composers like John Lewis and Jimmy Giuffre have done.[63] In seeking to explain how he improvises, Williams and Russell make a case for Coleman as a mostly "rational" musical thinker who knows the musical rules, even if he chooses not to abide by them.

A few months after Williams and Russell's conversation was published, on December 21, 1960, Coleman recorded *Free Jazz: A Collective Improvisation by the Ornette Coleman Double Quartet* for Atlantic Records. It is a thirty-seven-minute performance and an ambitious example of Coleman's daring conceptualism which contributed to the notion that his music was "formless." I write about *Free Jazz*—its design and reception—at length in my previously mentioned article for the *Journal of Musicology*, so what follows is a condensation of the relevant parts.[64]

Down Beat magazine ran a special double-author record review of *Free Jazz*, published in the January 18, 1962, issue, where the critics expressed two diametrically opposed opinions on the recording.[65] The editors noted that assigning two separate reviewers to assess the recording was a decision made in response to readers' calls for better-rounded reviews, but it was likely also in response to the controversy surrounding Coleman and his music. The two reviewers, assistant editor (and record producer) Pete Welding and associate editor John A. Tynan, took divergent views on Coleman's record. Welding rated *Free Jazz* a full five stars, celebrating the "iconoclast alto saxist [*sic*]" for carrying "to their logical (though some listeners will dispute this term) conclusion the esthetic principles present to a lesser degree—quantitatively, at least—in his previous recordings. . . . It does not break with jazz tradition; rather, it restores to currency an element that has been absent in most jazz since the onset of the swing orchestra—spontaneous group improvisation."[66] In sharp contrast, Tynan rated the album no stars, citing specifically the lack of tonal and structural coherence. Tynan concluded his short commentary by observing, "If nothing else, this witch's brew is the logical end product of a bankrupt philosophy of ultraindividualism in music. 'Collective improvisation?' Nonsense. The only semblance of collectivity lies in the fact that these eight nihilists were collected together in one studio at one time and with one common cause: to destroy the music that gave them birth."[67]

Heard by critics like Tynan as noise yet presented by its defenders as modern jazz's new aesthetic frontier, the "new thing," and *Free Jazz* especially, most upset those who held tonal harmony as the bedrock of musical order. In the aesthetic worldview of the white, male, college-educated writers who made up jazz's critical field, modern jazz's aesthetic sophistication rivaled that of classical music, and its connection to black vernacular culture made it authentically American. In this way, for its critics and gatekeepers, modern jazz represented the ideal integration of Western tonal logic and African rhythmic intuition—and black and white people. Hanging above this discourse is a hegemonic model of formal coherence and "orderly" improvisation central to modern jazz aesthetics, one that could not easily account for nor assimilate the kind of experimentalism that produced *Free Jazz*. The lack of coherence that Tynan found in *Free Jazz* is instead a musical texture imbued with what composer Olly Wilson called a heterogeneous sound ideal which, historically, held great currency in Black American musical practices. The heterogeneous sound ideal is where multiple sounds (or sonified subjectivities) are present in a musical environment—a live or recorded performance— and coexist without the expectation that they fully blend or assimilate into each other.[68] One aspect of musical design—texture—offers a way of understanding *Free Jazz* in terms not of negation (i.e., as inharmonic and disorderly) but of multiplicity.

Understanding *Free Jazz* in the terms of its heterogeneous sound ideal—its heterophonic textures—reclaims it from a discourse of pathology and deviance (where it lacks harmony and formal order and is an attempt at negating or destroying jazz), which is ultimately where the critical discourse goes, and instead embraces multiplicity and opacity. *Free Jazz* is a performance where musicians play prepared material and collectively improvise without a centralized key or meter. Sound creation in *Free Jazz* is fluid and interactive, and distinctions between soloist and accompanist are blurry and muddled. Instrumental sound in *Free Jazz* is heterogeneous, "harmony" is achieved abstractly through coordinated simultaneity (governed by the musicians' deep listening and interactive playing), and tonality is polyvalent and fluid.

As such, a listener engaging with the recording must be willing to expand their field of attention to absorb the dense and amoebic mass of sound. By actively readjusting to various points of interest, the heterophonic textures of *Free Jazz* invite the listener to "perform"—to act—alongside the musicians through active listening. Furthermore, the overall absence of a centralized metric pulse and conventional soloist-accompanist dynamic shatters expectations that intelligible and transparent formal structure or other guideline will help streamline one's attention and concentration during the listening experience. *Free Jazz* does not lend itself easily to conventional formal analysis, and it's not easy to parse. This denial of easy accessibility fed the doubts of Coleman's critics, including other musicians, like Miles Davis, who questioned publicly his musical aptitude and sanity.[69]

Free Jazz does have a formal structure that becomes apparent when listening to the initial thirty-seven-minute commercial release and the shorter, seventeen-minute "First Take" released by Atlantic Records on a compilation LP of Coleman's music, *Twins*, in 1971. Williams, who wrote the liner notes for *Free Jazz*, explained the form this way: "[It] is not a theme-and-variations piece in the usual sense. . . . I don't suppose any jazz performance ever took bigger chances. Not only is the improvisation almost total, it is frequently collective, involving all eight men inventing at once. And there were no preconceptions as to themes, chord patterns or chorus lengths. The guide for each soloist was a brief ensemble part which introduces him and which gave him an area of musical pitch. Otherwise he had only feelings and imagination—his own and those of his accompanists—to guide him."[70] The lengthy thirty-seven-minute double-quartet performance that is *Free Jazz* and the shorter "First Take" share a clear structure. An A-section, where musicians play precomposed melodic motifs (what Williams calls "ensemble parts" labeled "a" and "b" in the event map included in the appendix), is played in sync by the eight musicians, and this alternates with a B-section eight times, with each return foregrounding one of the eight soloists of the double quartet. While one musician steps into the foreground in each iteration of the B-section, they are always subsumed in dialog with the collective. This polyvalent, heterophonic texture is why writers described *Free Jazz* as atonal; any tonal center is fleeting and compounded by others, and melodic and sound creation for the musicians is both self-directed and interactive.

The event map in the appendix is a transcription of both *Free Jazz* and "First Take." There's no known extant score or written instructions that lay out its plan, and the event map serves as an itinerary of what takes place at each stage of intuited musical activity.[71] It also describes the different textural registers on which the musicians' collective improvisation occurs: heterophony, homophony, and monophony. Moments of monophony are where the ensemble play a precomposed motif in a loose, messy unison, and homophony is where the ensemble plays the same rhythm in lockstep but choose (improvise) different pitches/sounds. The ensemble is in a free-heterophonic texture during the "solos" (B-section). Atlantic recorded *Free Jazz* in stereo, and each unit of the double quartet is panned into either the left or right channels, each instrument mirrored on the other side of the field. Dolphy is on bass clarinet (right channel), Coleman on alto saxophone (left channel), Freddie Hubbard on trumpet (RC), Cherry cornet (LC), Haden (RC) and Scott LaFaro (LC) on bass, and Ed Blackwell (RC) and Billy Higgins (LC) on drums.

When one musician is foregrounded (B-Sections) others drop out, thereby thinning the texture, gradually rejoining the soloist with their own improvisations. Bassist Haden (panned to the right) and drummer Higgins (panned to the left) both imply a steady pulse, but any semblance of regularity dissolves as they fall in and out of sync with each other. The rotating solos culminate with a fragment of a lyrical "unison" melody, and the texture's density dissipates so that the final four soloists—the two bassists (with the drummers), then, finally, the two drummers (alone)—improvise. A final co-ordinated "unison" melody closes the performance.

Improvisation in *Free Jazz* unfolds as a heterophonic dialog. Even when a wind instrument is featured as a soloist there is always one bassist (LaFaro, LC) and drummer (Blackwell, RC) improvising simultaneously. The remaining horns rejoin the soloists with background riffs and sonic interventions, aggregating into a collective improvisation that ripples with a fluidity difficult to measure, without a steady, ticking pulse, and existing outside of the context of a singular key or tonal area.

Ethnomusicologist Eric Charry notes how assumptions that Coleman's music in this period was completely free—lacking predetermined design and parameters—led Schuller and others to fundamentally misunderstand or ignore the important clues within his album liner notes into how his music is organized.[72] Charry clarifies that "freedom" for Coleman meant, primarily, an aesthetic or "spirit" of freedom where musicians are invited to co-create in spontaneous and emotionally immediate ways, abandon cliché and fealty to any one particular style, and loosen expectations.[73] In turn, listeners (including critics of the early 1960s) expecting "coherence" in an orthodox and accessible way, and subsequently critiquing Coleman's group for upsetting those expectations, are likely deferring to established and subjective conclusions about legitimate music-making that is anything but "universal."[74] As I've been hinting at in this chapter, while this critique is definitely applicable to 1960s music criticism, understanding the biases of the past can help us rethink and relisten to what by all accounts is still challenging, experimental music. By considering harmony in *Free Jazz* as existing in a new or different epistemological context, contemporary listeners can appreciate it as a fluid and cooperative performance of decentralized sonic simultaneity.

Charry sees in Coleman a creative thinker and committed artist who, through ingenuity and grit, expanded the possibilities of improvised music in ways that did not exclude forethought and organization. I agree with that assessment. In 1961, Coleman's conceptual breakthrough represented also, for Baraka, a provocation and aesthetic break from modern jazz. He compares the paradigm shift represented by Coleman's music to the bebop revolution of the 1940s and imagines the emergence of a new jazz avant-garde more closely tied to the complexity and emotional depth of bebop through the black musical vernacular, not the classical-leaning "third stream":

There is definitely an "avant garde" in jazz today. A burgeoning group of young men who are beginning to utilize not only the most important ideas in "formal" contemporary music, but more important, young musicians who have started to utilize the most important ideas contained in that startling music called BeBop....

I say *particular* avant garde since I realize that there is also another so-called "new music," called by some of my more serious colleagues, *Third Stream*, which seeks to invest jazz with as much "classical" music as blatantly as possible [*sic*]. But for jazzmen now to have come to the beautiful and logical conclusion that BeBop was perhaps the most legitimately complex, emotionally rich music to come out of this country, is, for me, a brilliant beginning for a "new music."

BeBop is roots, now, just as much as blues is. "Classical" music is not. But "classical" music, and I mean now contemporary Euro-American "art" music, definitely can and should be "milked" for as many *definitions* as possible, i.e., *solutions* to engineering problems the contemporary jazz musician's life is sure to raise [*sic*]. I mean, more simply, Ornette Coleman has had to live with the attitudes responsible for Anton Webern's music whether he knows that music or not. They were handed to him along with the whole history of formal Western music, and the musics that have come to characterize the Negro in the United States came to exist as they do today only through the acculturation of this entire history. And actually knowing that history, or those formal Euro-American musics, only adds to the indoctrination. But jazz and blues are Western musics; products of a Euro-American culture.

We are, all of us, *moderns*, whether we like it or not.[75]

In this article, titled simply "The Jazz Avant Garde," published in *Metronome* in September 1961, Baraka threads the needle between jazz as the product of an elite Euro-American music tradition—classical music—and that of Black American vernacular culture. His attempt to theorize what appeared to be a distinct and aesthetically revolutionary movement led by Coleman does so by acknowledging the hegemony of classical music, positioning avant-gardists as resistance against its indoctrination, which he sees as a problem in modern jazz more generally. After distinguishing between new musicians with an original style and those imitating Charlie Parker and other bebop musicians from the 1940s, Baraka praises Coleman for developing new concepts and ideas of his own. He calls these handful of stylistic originals the avant-garde and lists them by name, some in boldface to mark the "quality and quantity of these players' innovations; they are: **REEDS: Ornette Coleman, Eric Dolphy,** Wayne Shorter, Oliver Nelson, Archie Shepp. **BRASS: Don Cherry, Freddie Hubbard. PERCUSSION: Billy Higgins, Ed Blackwell,** Denis Charles (drums); Earl Griffith (vibraharp). **BASS: Wilbur Ware, Charlie Haden,** Scott

LaFaro, Buell Neidlinger, Chuck Israels, George Tucker, others. **PIANO: Cecil Taylor. COMPOSITION: Ornette Coleman, Eric Dolphy, Wayne Shorter,** Cecil Taylor."[76] Eight of these musicians participated in Coleman's *Free Jazz* recording session in December 1960.

Baraka identifies free melody as a distinguishing feature of this emergent avant-garde. Soloists, he observes, improvise with a heightened, irregular rhythmic sensibility, and bassists and drummers are more "melodic," their roles less restricted to time-keeping accompanists: "So if the heavily accented melody springs the rhythm section, it also gives the other soloists more room to swing. The strict 4/4 is missing, and the horn men can improvise on the melodic efforts of the rhythm section. This is one reason why in a group like Coleman's it seems as if they have gone back to the concept of collective improvisations. No one's role in the group is as *fixed*. . . . Everyone has a chance to play melody or rhythm."[77] The abstract expressivity of avant-gardists like Coleman invokes, for Baraka, the vocal tradition of primordial African music—a cultural continuum flowing through the blues and bebop as well. That the avant-gardists he named have not sterilized their music of this influence also distinguishes them from the "third stream." His position on Coleman's music and that of other artists in that orbit is wary of jazz's slide toward a more classical kind of concert music, which shifts the source of its aesthetic legitimacy across the proverbial racial color line. In critiquing the classical leanings of the "third stream" and "so-called West Coast jazz," Baraka frames the jazz avant-garde as a revolutionary music rooted in the black musical vernacular, and its musicians as the leaders of a black cultural vanguard. Baraka's revolutionary framework will also shift the literary discourse around the *new thing*, as I explain in the Interlude.

Ornette Coleman at Town Hall, 1962

Coleman's musical experimentation after *Free Jazz* furthered his reputation as an eccentric among critics and other musicians, and many were divided on whether he and his music should be taken seriously. In *Ornette!*, recorded less than a month after *Free Jazz*, in January 1961, Coleman returned to his more typical quartet format, with LaFaro substituting for Haden on bass. Each of the four tracks, all titled with cryptic acronyms that are purportedly abbreviations of books by Sigmund Freud, are organized in the typical tripartite melody (played by the ensemble in their "unison" style)—free collective improvisation—the reprised melody format common in Coleman's previous quartet sessions.[78] Heterophonic collective improvisation on this album occurs largely between each of the horns (Coleman and Cherry), against a more supportive rhythm section (LaFaro and Blackwell, who, in turn, improvise as a heterophonic duet). Despite having no centralized key area in moments of improvisation, the band members align metrically over a steady, regular pulse. This technique, a kind of semi-heterophony, would be appropriated by Davis's quintet years later under the conceptual direction of drummer Tony Williams, who called it "time, no changes" (i.e., metric time, no chordal harmony).

Coleman returned to his instrument from adolescence, the tenor saxophone, for recording sessions for Atlantic on March 22 and 27, 1961. *Ornette on Tenor* features Jimmy Garrison on bass, who would join Coltrane's new quartet in November, and it continues Coleman's preoccupation with speech-like, gestural improvisation. "Cross Breeding," the album's opening track, features a jagged melody that Coleman and Cherry play in "unison" while Garrison and Blackwell improvise their own complementary melody and sound. As in *Ornette!*, Blackwell and Garrison establish a common pulse but also periodically phase outward into heterophonic autonomy. Unfortunately, Coleman's experimentation upset not only his critics but one of the musicians on this session, Garrison, who left the band after expressing his despondent frustration with the music.[79] Coleman's resolve to present his music despite the rejection did take a significant emotional and psychological toll, specifically around the financial strain of living and working in New York City. He remained steadfast, telling Spellman years later, "I would advise anybody that was sitting on their ass waiting for some wealthy middleman to come along and exploit them because they have talent . . . to go out and do for themselves. . . . If you've got to do something and you feel . . . tired of waiting for someone to come along and give you the chance to do it, don't wait for that. Go out and do it for yourself. Then you'll know."[80]

After several months without recording, Coleman took his own advice and began organizing a concert of his original music at Town Hall, an austere venue just north of Manhattan's old Tenderloin District, in Times Square. The venue's legacy of progressivism began at its founding in 1921 by the suffragist League for Political Education, and it held several landmark concerts over the decades featuring prominent international composers like Richard Strauss, star soloists like Pablo Casals and Marian Anderson, and young prodigies like pianist Ruth Slenczynska and violinist Isaac Stern. Barrier-pushing black artists like Paul Robeson, Langston Hughes, and Billie Holiday performed at Town Hall for the general public, and a concert of small-group jazz on June 22, 1945, starring Dizzy Gillespie, Charlie Parker, and Max Roach marked the concert-stage arrival of what journalists began to call bebop.

Coleman's concert, then, was to be in a lineage of great concert music and, possibly, an effort to make himself part of that exalted legacy. A self-produced venture, this act of self-advocacy and career advancement was, he told Spellman, meant to be a break from the smaller venues downtown. Coleman was wary of the alcohol and drug use downtown and the low wages paid by club owners there, so this was a step toward giving his music a better platform.[81] Funding the concert himself, he advertised it with help from the musicians on the program, and as it was to feature his latest original compositions, a successful evening at such a prestigious venue would be a career milestone.[82] He used a new trio, made up of David Izenzon on upright bass and Charles Moffett on drums, but also organized two other groups: a rhythm-and-blues band, with a pianist (Chris Towns), guitarist (Nappy Allen), and electric bassist (Barney Richardson), and a string quartet (with violinists Selwart Clark and Nathan Goldstein, violist Julien Barber, and cellist Kermit Moore). By having all these ensembles on the same program, Coleman was effectively merging three stylistic streams: small-group modern jazz, rhythm-and-blues, and "classical" European chamber music. The concert, which took place on December 21, 1962, was recorded in its entirety by Blue Note Records, but less than half of the evening's music was released commercially, by ESP Disk, because of legal disputes.[83] The program of contained ten pieces: one original by bassist Izenson, Coleman's piece for string quartet, one piece for the R&B band and trio together, and the remaining for the trio alone.[84]

Spellman, who was in attendance, characterized "A Blues Misused," which featured Coleman's trio combined with an R&B quartet, as being comparable to *Free Jazz* and as "one of the two most important works that he has ever performed. . . . It was as if Ornette had excavated his entire musical past to get to the core of his work.[85] Bill Coss, reviewing the concert for *Down Beat* in January 1963, described "A Blues Misused" as "a sometimes historical, sometimes satirical, sometimes plain funny piece that exhibited the worst of rhythm and blues."[86] In contrast, Coss regarded the string quartet piece "Dedication to Poets and Writers" positively, as providing "insight into things to come" in Coleman's style; he said it was "more delicate, airy" than he expected, and considered it a highlight in a concert seemingly devoted to showing "Ornette Past, Present, and Future." Though there are no extant score or parts to confirm, "Dedication," which was commercially released by ESP, is an almost ten-minute atonal piece that, in its execution by a string quartet, might have symbolized the arrival of Coleman as a composer of "serious" music. The unreleased "Blues Misused," comparatively, was, based on Spellman's testimony, an abstractionist ode to Black vernacular music, and the remaining trio pieces more typical of Coleman's small-group work.

Coleman encountered difficulties getting the four classically trained musicians of the string quartet to express the music in the way he intended, finding that they relied heavily on the written score and could not accurately emulate the phrasing and articulation he demonstrated on his alto saxophone. Straddling both sides of the aesthetic rift in literary modern jazz discourse of the time, Coleman's "classical" and "R&B" pieces answered to two factions: Schuller's "third stream" and Baraka's vernacular-rooted avant-garde. But the hardships of a freelancer in a fraught and exploitative music industry overtook the joys of creative exploration. "If I was rich," Coleman told Spellman, "I wouldn't have to think that I'm fighting the system or that I was being exploited, because I could go out and do my best and be happy. . . . But since I'm not loved and I'm not rich, I just feel fucked up, that's all. But being rich wouldn't make me play the saxophone any better, and I'm not loved because nobody is interested in what I'm doing; they're only interested in writing and talking about it, not the music itself."[87]

Like Coleman's earlier recorded quartet work, the first track on the concert LP, "Doughnut," is in the tripartite structure (melody–soloists' improvisation–reprise of melody) typical of his small-group music. Coleman repeats the singsong tune—consisting of short melodic motifs stated at different pitch levels—twice at the opening, with Izenzon and Moffett gesturing toward the basic contour of the melody simultaneously. The trio then launches into an extended period of heterophonic collective improvisation in unmetered time (which lasts until ▶ 2:00, when they collectively shift into metric time). But "Sadness," the second track on the LP, is perhaps the most unique on the recoding: it begins with Izenzon bowing across the upper two strings of the bass (the G- and D-strings), producing a mournful wail that he achieves by gliding up and down the highest string in an almost infinite portamento. Above Izenzon's wail is Coleman's equally mournful cry that, in its intensity and emotiveness, conveys the essence of the tune's title.

Coleman first plays the head melody in G (▶ 00:22) and, before resolving to the tonic, suddenly plays the entire melody again up a semitone in A-flat (▶ 01:05), mimicking possibly the bump in energy and anticipation that comes with a sudden modulation upward common in a gospel refrain. "Sadness" is about catharsis—from an experience of tragedy and hardship—and Moffett, on drums, accents on the drumheads with brushes, adding bursts of metallic and percussive color in this three-way bereavement.

"Sadness," with its strong and poignant head melody played by Coleman, is a heterophonic lament. In their coordinate autonomy, the trio sonifies three distinct "sad" voices or subjectivities, like mourners eulogizing a recently departed loved one. This is only one possible interpretation; my point is that the heterophonic texture of "Sadness," despite its abstractness, allows for an emotionally direct affect that mimics how human beings cry and grieve: in long howls and shorter bursts of irregular, impulsive sound. Closing the LP is "The Ark," a twenty-four-minute heterophonic collective improvisation bookended by an abrupt, fragmented melodic motif—another typical tripartite head-solos-head structure.

In his *Down Beat* review, Coss concludes that the Town Hall concert was "a musical success; a provocative journey through a particularly personal, strongly individualistic jazz world." But Coleman felt differently. He was disappointed, and frustrated that the concert only broke even, which he felt was symptomatic of an unfair and exploitative business. The Town Hall concert would be Coleman's last public performance for two years. Speaking candidly to Spellman, he lamented:

> The problem is in this business that you don't own your own product. If you record, it's the record company that owns it; if you play at a club, it's the nightclub owners who charge people to listen to you, and then they tell you your music is not catching on. . . . This is the worst kind of suffering. This psychological suffering of knowing that you're being exploited, whether it's whites doing it to whites or whites doing it to blacks or blacks doing it to blacks, it's still the same thing. . . . The insanity of living in America is that ownership is really strength. It's who owns who's strongest in America. It's strategic living. That's why it's so hard to lend your music to that kind of existence.[88]

Coleman entered his hiatus disillusioned at the music industry in general, but he also struggled with the unrelenting public debate about his mental health. He was aware of being perceived as an illiterate musician "who just plays" without planning or writing down his thoughts and designs, an image that not even his work for a string quartet could quash.[89] Coleman remained a symbol of eccentricity and pathology in jazz until the later years of the decade, and his music would remain at the center of a debate on the *new thing*'s aesthetic legitimacy and its suspected political undertones. However, other improvising musicians in and outside of the New York scene would find an affinity with Coleman's musical nonconformity, drawing inspiration from his indelible spirit of freedom.

3

Interlude: Points of Departure

The sounds that were introduced to the general, literary public as the *new thing* were not, by 1960 and the years after, limited to artists living and working in New York City. Ornette Coleman's experiments in "free" heterophonic improvisation began in Los Angeles with other modern musicians, such as Canadian pianist Paul Bley. Before working with Coleman, Bley lived in New York City to study at Juilliard and work on the scene while organizing concerts in his native Montreal, Quebec—where he shared the stage with Charlie Parker—and, in 1957, moved out west with composer and pianist Karen Borg, whom he later married. (She then took the name Carla Bley.)[1] Paul Bley quickly secured a weekly gig leading a group at the Hillcrest Club in Beverly Hills and, in October 1958, organized and recorded a night's set along with the Coleman quartet.

That recording, released over a decade later, features the group playing Parker's "Klactoveedsedstene," Roy Eldridge's "I'll Remember Harlem," and two of Coleman's originals, "The Blessing" and "Free."[2] Generally, the musicians improvise on each tune with a great deal of melodic freedom, playing phrases that do not conform (in a conventional manner of harmonic consonance) to the underlying chord progression. That juxtaposition or textural contrast brings the melody out in relief, and "freedom" from the chord changes also allows bassist Charlie Haden to vacillate between articulating and departing from the form along with the soloists. What they all do abide by is a shared, centripetal pulse (a technique later called "time, no changes"). The descriptive title "Free," in particular, functions as a directive for musical action: it begins with a sixteen-bar singsong melody (that spans an AABA formal structure) executed in Coleman and Cherry's synergetic, breath-like "unison" that was what Michael Bruce Cogswell calls Coleman's dramatically vocal approach to saxophone performance.[3] After the melody, the horns and Bley each take turns improvising over Haden and Billy Higgins's propulsive bass and drums, dispatching themselves over, against, and through the rhythm section's steady pulse in an uncannily complementary way. This dynamic is dialogic; Higgins "answers back" to the soloists' accented rhythms on the snare drum and completely drops out during Cherry's solo, dramatically thinning the sonic texture. In their loosening of melody's close bind to metric musical time and harmonic form, the musicians achieve a "freer" and more collectivized, dialogic kind of improvisational environment. Bley's recording of Coleman's "Free" documents an early instance of improvisers' conceptual turn toward more open, fluid, and unpredictable collaborative musical creation a year before Coleman makes his controversial debut in downtown Manhattan. Coleman recorded "Free" again a year later with his quartet on the Atlantic LP *Change of the Century*.[4]

The Jamaican-born Londoner and saxophonist Joe Harriott recorded the album *Free Form* in late November 1960 for the American label Jazzland, just weeks before Coleman's double quartet recorded *Free Jazz* for Atlantic Records. It, like Coleman's record, was a definitive aesthetic statement portending jazz's—and specifically black musicians'—voyages into abstract sonic realms. The title *Free Form*, like Coleman's "Free" and the later *Free Jazz*, describes both affect and technique, clueing the listener and record buyer into the musicians' creative approach: a conceptualism preoccupied with abstraction. Harriott's tunes "Formation," "Parallel," "Straight Lines," and even the more musically specific "Tempo" are almost programmatic in how they evoke the abstraction of planar geometry, a nod perhaps to the draftsmanship style interpolated by contemporary painters like the British Alan Reynolds, Peter Joseph, and Marc Vaux, and those associated with the German Bauhaus, Dutch De Stijl, and Eastern European Constructivist schools of design. The fourth track, "Impression," is overt in its association with modern abstract art (the tune and most of the soloists' improvisations are modal, in E-flat and B-flat Dorian), while the third track, "Abstract," most literally projects the music's general affect and aesthetic.

The melody of "Abstract" is a quick-paced, long and springy descent in E-flat. After twelve bars, the next part of the tune leaps upward and downward by fourths and fifths—intervals that can destabilize the previously established tonal center (E-flat)—which the pianist, Pat Smythe, supports with tonally ambiguous quartal chords. After repeating the roughly twenty-one-bar tune again, Harriott's group launches into their solos. Flugelhornist and trumpeter "Shake" Keane plays first (▶ 00:30), blurting through scatters and smears of tone color as bassist Coleridge Goode and drummer Phil Seaman steam onward with the pulse. Keane dodges through and floats above the instrumental texture, while Goode and Seaman, initially in metric sync with each other, slide out of phase with each other. Afterward, Harriott, on alto saxophone, sustains a gentle long note behind Keane's playing, but then quickly steps into the foreground (▶ 00:58), interjecting and pushing the quartet into a brief episode of heterophonic collective improvisation. Though the bassist and drummer give the impression of a steady shared pulse, the band falls into metric asynchrony without losing their general cohesion. Like the Ornette Coleman Quartet's "Lonely Woman" from 1959, where the horns play out of phase with the bassist and drummer, Harriott's group pursued an abstract, heterophonic "harmony" outside of conventional tonality and musical time.

Harriott's *Free Form* LP, like the recordings by improvising musicians discussed previously, documents the transatlantic proliferation of a freer, more collectivized approach to improvisation and group performance. However, as with Coleman's music, the musicians' experimentation was generally met with less enthusiasm, if not outright consternation, in print media. "The album title is a fairly accurate description of their musical approach," Pete Welding writes in his two-and-a-half-star review of Harriot's album for *Down Beat*. "Freed of the 'restrictions' of bar lines, conventional harmonic sequences, et al., [they] are thus enabled to follow, individually and collectively, their own musical stars." Though the musicians play together well for most of the recording and seem to utilize collective improvisation more than other avant-gardists, they are ultimately unsuccessful, Welding concludes, because "each of the selections is rather inconclusive and discursive [like] . . . a very clever musical exercise . . . [a] type of musical experimentation, where the development takes place more in terms of an emerging emotional climate than it does on a set formal organization or harmonic structure. . . . It may be challenging to play this music but not to listen to it."[5]

Situated halfway between the California and New York scenes was Chicago, a bustling and competitive market for live and recorded music in the United States. A fiercely racially segregated industrial powerhouse, the city nonetheless was an incubator for musicians asserting a unique and unconventional practice that confronted or ignored the expectations of the jazz industry. Composer, musician, and musicologist George E. Lewis, in his 2008 study *A Power Stronger Than Itself*, chronicles the development of the Association for the Advancement of Creative Musicians (AACM), founded in Chicago's South Side by pianist and composer Muhal Richard Abrams, composer Phil Cohran, pianist Jodie Christian, and drummer Steve McCall in 1965. The AACM grew out of Abrams's Experimental Band, which he established in 1961 with musicians attending the regular jam sessions and rehearsals that occurred at the C&C Lounge, as a workshop to test music with more abstract and extended forms.

Abrams's Experimental Band and the later AACM—whose members, including Anthony Braxton, Amina Claudine Myers, Wadada Leo Smith, Henry Threadgill, and the members of the Art Ensemble of Chicago, went on to create experimental improvised music of their own—emerged to meet a necessity among Chicago's emergent black and creative musicians for a workshop environment to develop musical skills and explore new methods of composition and self-expression.

"As the 1960s emerged," Lewis writes, "the relative informality and flexibility that marked the development of jazz performance practice during the 1940s and 50s was slowly, almost imperceptibly beginning to harden, conditioned by the stark economic pressures that accompanied the endemic undercapitalization of the field."[6] Abrams recalled his convictions at the time in an interview with Lewis: "[W]e were headed outside. We were deliberately breaking some rules. To us, Bird and them were like people who broke ground. We copied them religiously, but that was not the end; we didn't sacrifice our individualism to do it. There were some on the scene who did, but we didn't. We started to draw and paint, because we felt like that—doing things differently."[7]

Pianist Andrew Hill, born in 1937, also grew up in Chicago's South Side. Like so many other professionals in the 1960s, Hill had an eclectic and self-directed musical upbringing. He began on accordion as a child and taught himself piano throughout his teens; a gifted student, Hill complemented his musical studies with real-world work, playing the accordion on the street for money and inserting himself in black Chicago's night life.[8] His embeddedness in the professional field led to a gig as part of a Charlie Parker pickup band in 1954 in Detroit, where, Hill told writer Ben Ratliff in a 2006 interview, the elder saxophonist said something that changed his musical thinking for the rest of his career: "I look at melody as rhythm." Hill reflected on Parker's comment: "It opened my mind up to many possibilities. . . . [If] everything is rhythm, then you just have these rhythms on top of each other. But they're not polyrhythms or pyramids of rhythm: they're crossing rhythms."[9]

The loose, fluid, and interactive relationship between streams of rhythmic activity that Hill cites as an epiphany is a defining characteristic of his recorded work made after his arrival in New York in 1961. He made his first of many albums of original music for Blue Note Records, *Black Fire*, in November 1963, and recorded four more LPs by June 1964 which Blue Note released slowly over the next several years.[10] Leonard Feather, writing in *Down Beat* in 1965, highlighted Hill as a rare talent that was "possibly the most gifted pianist of the new wave, both in freshness of ideas and in technical equipment."[11]

On "Smokestack," the title track of Hill's second Blue Note album, recorded in December 1963, heterophony creates the untethered polyrhythmic effect of the head melody, where members of the quartet overlap and collide with each other in a knotty rhythmic matrix. Hill plays the lyrical head melody in metric sync with bassists Eddie Khan and drummer Roy Haynes, while the other bassist, Richard Davis, freely improvises through the texture. As Hill begins to improvise (▶ 01:01) he slips out of sync with the pulsing bassline, and

Haynes on drums, having already established a loose and fluid ride pattern, begins to play more gesturally, accenting (or "commenting" upon) Hill's punctuated playing, anticipating or intuiting the pianist's pauses and breaks. Just before the return of the head melody (▶ 04:02), the entire ensemble slips into a multivoice, metrically ambiguous "free form" dialog. Abstracting musical time in this way, with "free form" heterophony and departures from convention, led to Hill's association with other avant-gardists in the jazz press. "The new jazz, in fact, is considerably more heterogeneous than the music which immediately preceded it," concludes saxophonist and writer Don Heckman in the album's liner notes: "Andrew Hill's playing style is distinctly his own, but it is nevertheless intimately involved in the solution of musical problems which are in the mainstream of contemporary jazz. Some of his unique and fascinating answers to these problems are provided here."[12]

Point of Departure, Hill's fourth album for Blue Note, was recorded in March 1964 with trumpeter Kenny Dorham, reedists Eric Dolphy and Joe Henderson, bassist Richard Davis, and drummer Tony Williams. Its evocative title hints at the general effect of abstraction and freedom that characterized, for musicians, critics, and record buyers, jazz's *new thing*. Hill's "New Monastery" is written in an asymmetrical form (the head melody is eleven bars) which the musicians repeat before their consecutive solos (Figure 3.1).

Figure 3.1 Autograph score showing head melody of Andrew Hill's "New Monastery." Courtesy of the Institute of Jazz Studies, Rutgers University.

The harmonies Hill writes out in the parts are chromatic and tonally ambiguous: he plays a quartal sonority (marked on the score as "G7sus/F") on the piano that lasts the first two bars while the horns play an angular "atonal" melody that continues into the next chromatic harmony ("Gmaj7(b5)/F#") written in the next two bars.

Like the abstract work of other improvising musicians, the precomposed and improvised elements in Hill's music can be difficult to parse based on the audio alone. That ontological blur is, I argue, an effect of the license that composer and musicians took to create abstract work that resists easy listening and comprehension. With improvisation as the vehicle for each member of an ensemble to exercise that license, musicians found points to depart from convention and cliché.

The commercial recordings of Eric Dolphy, who was on Hill's *Point of Departure*, also utilize descriptive and alluring song and album titles to signify abstraction and unconventionality. In the spring and summer of 1960, before participating in Coleman's *Free Jazz* session in December, Dolphy, who'd moved to New York from Los Angeles in 1958, recorded *Outward Bound* and *Out There* for New Jazz, a subsidiary of the indie Prestige label. These were Dolphy's debut as an ensemble leader and composer, signaling his proximity to an avant-garde of which Coleman was the nominal leader. Joe Goldberg acknowledged this association in *Out There*'s original liner notes: "About [Dolphy's] own work, and the work of the men he's been associated with, [Dolphy] has a final comment to make: 'Something new's happening. I don't know what it is, but it's new, and it's good, and it's just about to happen, and it's wonderful to be here in New York right in the middle of it.'"[13]

Clay Downham, in his 2018 master's thesis on Dolphy, argues that the affective freedom Dolphy achieves in his early albums was the product of "systematic approaches to outside playing," where the musician's note choice in improvisation draws from some of the latent tonality in the precomposed material—a methodology and creative outlook informed by George Russell's Lydian Chromatic Concept first published in 1959.[14] Despite the music's eccentric sounds, Dolphy, Downham argues, thought carefully and methodically about new and interesting ways to improvise and design abstract compositional forms that would best support his more experimental approach. Adding to this, I argue that Dolphy's creative practices extended to heterophony—a textural setting where each musician is "free" to determine their creative action within the collective performance, which accounts for the abstract and "out" sound of the LP's music.

Like Coleman's quartet, Dolphy omits chordal instruments in *Out There*, using instead bassist George Duvivier, drummer Roy Haynes, and Ron Carter on cello. The "harmonies" that emerge from these four instrumental voices throughout the eight tracks on *Out There* are a result of the planned and improvised melody and sound carried by the horn, string instruments, and drums. The title track, a thirty-bar AABA song, features a pair of simultaneous chromatic melodies, one carried by Dolphy and Carter playing in unison and the other Duvivier's bassline, with Haynes keeping a propulsive swing on the snare, with brushes, and the hi-hat. Each melodic pair is organized into seven (A-section) and nine (B-section) bars—7 + 7 + 9 + 7 and neither melodic line of the pair has a strong tonal center, nor does the sum of both concurrent parts. Locking in with Haynes, Duvivier generally maintains the walking bassline (and thus the form) while Carter and then Dolphy improvise freely, phasing in and out of the metric pulse. There are no traditional chords or key in "Out There," and the basic structural parameters (the 7 + 7 + 9 + 7 AABA form) and meter help to put Carter and Dolphy's "out" playing in relief.

The conventions in song and album titling that I've discussed so far, while certainly not specific to experimentalists like Dolphy and others developing jazz's *new thing*, did contribute to its branding as an avant-garde outsider art that could work in favor of musicians' record sales. Descriptive epithets like "free," "departure," and "out" point to an aesthetic of abstraction and new conceptual and musical terrain.[15] This kind of oblique branding is especially conspicuous in Blue Note Records' output of the early 1960s. Saxophonist Jackie McLean's *One Step Beyond* and *Destination . . . Out!!* (both of 1963), trombonist Grachan Moncur III's *Evolution* (1963), *Some Other Stuff* (1964), and several other releases distinguished these artists and their collaborators as avant-gardists to the record-buying public. But the abstract and opaque sound of heterophonic textures in this music led listeners and critics to think of the avant-garde as a gimmick. Bobby Hutcherson, a vibraphonist who recorded with Dolphy, McLean, and Moncur before leading his own sessions for Blue Note, emphasized the challenging requirements of the new music in an interview for *Down Beat* in 1966:

"For one thing," he said, "it's definitely so much more demanding on your creativeness and on your knowledge of music. You have to listen. Like you're out there, and you know there's no chord pattern where you can say 'Okay, on this D-minor 7th chord I'm going to play. . . . Yeah, I know this lick, I can run across that, and then I can do that.' It's not like that. You're out there and you just have to listen. You have to have your ears as wide open as you possibly can, listening to everyone else as much as possible, and at the same time concentrating on what you're trying to do. It makes you so much more involved in what's going on. If you even think about having a drink after—or whatever you're thinking about—you're going to miss the whole thing. You're going to miss somebody's idea of what they were trying to give you. You're going to miss so much."[16]

Transgressive Creative Work

In October 1962, Archie Shepp, the twenty-five-year-old Floridian tenor saxophonist who had arrived in New York City from Philadelphia two years earlier as a new college graduate, stepped into the studio to record with trumpeter Bill Dixon, bassist Don Moore, and drummer Phil Cohen. Theirs was a piano-less quartet that, because the absence of a chordal instrument, primed the ensemble to improvise heterophonically. At the center of each of the four pieces they recorded, released by Savoy Records as the album *The Archie Shepp–Bill Dixon Quartet*, both Shepp and Dixon alternate free improvisations along with Moore and Cohen, who keep a steady common pulse (most audible in Moore's bass lines). That heterogeneous mesh of sound for listeners of modern jazz, accustomed to following a soloist's skillful melodic invention over the chord progression of the form, offered very little to go on. This LP and the string of club dates in Manhattan that followed caught the attention of music journalists like George Hoefer who were curious about their "avant-garde approach." Reviewing a recent performance in Judson Hall, Hoefer mentions the group's "dissonant" improvisations, noting that small, poorly publicized concerts like that one may be "where the jazz of the future will be unveiled."[17]

The dissonance that Hoefer heard was probably the heterophonic improvisation featured on the two Dixon originals, "Trio" and "Quartet," where solos by the alternating horns are bookended by head melodies that seem to channel the speech-like, declamatory playing of Coleman and Don Cherry. Shepp and Dixon also play a rendition of Coleman's ballad "Peace" on the LP, and its final track is an up-tempo and bawdy rendition of Leonard Bernstein's "Somewhere" from the musical *West Side Story*—a variety of styles treated to degrees of abstraction.

Prior to working with Dixon, Shepp spent two years in Cecil Taylor's band. Taylor, the New York–born pianist and a graduate of the New England Conservatory, attacked the instrument with an intense, kinetic energy, and the band's overall sound was idiosyncratically abstruse. I explore Taylor's music in more depth in Chapter 4. A defining quality is its energy: a raw, unrestrained kind of sonic power that Taylor seemed to channel through the piano like volts of electricity. Key to this sound was Taylor's tone-cluster approach—where his tightly bound fingers struck the keyboard like the blunt end of a stick—which departed from the orthodox Eurological technique of the formally trained. By forgoing "good" technique in favor of a sharp, hammer-like sound, Taylor shirked the modernist aesthetics of polish and refined tonal clarity, developing an "unpolished," percussive, and potent sound grammar. That reclamation of creative agency and transgression of the unspoken expectations of musical mastery—conspicuous displays of clarity, control, and restraint—represented something insurgent and, potentially, revolutionary in modern jazz.

I understand the creative license taken by black musicians identified as avant-gardists in the jazz industry of the early 1960s in the greater aesthetic context of black radicalism that, as Cedric Robinson instructs, is an epistemology and practice of resistance and reclamation.[18] These musicians do not, however, fall neatly within the bounds of Robinson's conceptual and historical mapping of the Black Radical Tradition because, however critical musicians were of the music industry and its capitalist exploitation of artists, it was a vocation and, to an extent, a livelihood that commanded a degree of social currency and prestige. Improvising musicians in the black community were respected as specialized, skilled laborers, and musicians benefited—however unevenly and unfairly—from the commodification of their creative labor. I'm not saying or even implying that the musicians identified as avant-gardists in this narrative "sold out," but rather that their radical aesthetics and candor about social politics in published essays, interviews, and liner notes divulge something about the complexities of surviving as a creative musician interested in developing new techniques and untested modes of expression. That said, the jazz avant-garde of the 1960s did reflect the "new habits of thought" and a radicalism that was also being generated in the twentieth century by activists, artists, and community leaders that drew from and inspired social and political change.[19] Musicians identified as jazz avant-gardists did challenge and upset the status quo by asserting sonic signifiers of difference: the collective musical action that produced densely woven, heterophonic sound masses departed from normative jazz practice while still being referential to it. The freedom to create abstract sounds exercised by musicians knowing that they may be felt on a visceral, emotional, and even spiritual level more than be cognitively understood did assert a radical creative agency and, as such, did represent change. This kind of radical assertiveness in the face of normative, respectable behavior can't be extracted from the ethos of disruption and direct action for young and black activists across the United States that inspired new visions of society, community, and mutual aid to enact that change.

Resistance against ossified, unjust, or outdated norms faced its own resistance. Reactionary backlash against racial desegregation reached a new plateau after the 1956 Supreme Court's decision in favor of Oliver Brown over the

Board of Education of Topeka, Kansas, a case that deemed racially segregated schooling unconstitutional. "The desegregation battles of the early 1960s," historian Manning Marable writes, "were conceived, planned, and carried out by young people—and all the impatience and idealism which characterize youth were an organic and integral aspect of this campaign for racial justice."[20] In this climate, being black and subverting or ignoring convention and transgressing upon decorum could easily be construed as an insurrectionary act by those invested in white orthodoxy or supremacy who now felt threatened by change. Saying what you want to say, and in the manner and register you want to say it, was, as a black student or freelance musician, politicized and inherently political, even when declaring and defending your humanity. It was this sense of collective experience, agency, and defiance in the face of white supremacy that Amiri Baraka postulates in his book *Blues People* of 1963 as parts of the "essence" of African American culture that artists—musicians especially—were at the vanguard of articulating. "In Greenwich Village," he concludes, "a place generally associated with 'artistic and social freedom,' . . . young Negro musicians now live as integral parts of that anonymous society to which the [nonconformist] artist generally aspires. Their music, along with the products of other young American artists seriously involved with the revelation of contemporary truths, will help define that society, and by contrast, the nature of the American society out of which these [white] Americans have removed themselves."[21]

Black women artists gave voice to black struggle in these years. Singers Abbey Lincoln and Nina Simone, in particular, were at the vanguard of expressing in lyric and performance rage, indignation, steadfastness, passion, and lament. Lincoln, born in Chicago in 1930, established her career in Los Angeles and Honolulu as a singer, stage performer, and actor, and moved to New York City in 1957 to further her career and record. Now embedded in the city's music industry and black life, she began to feel at odds performing the musical fare expected from a "jazz" singer in nightclubs and cabarets, and she found friendship, mentorship, and solidarity from established black artists who helped expand her political consciousness, like Oscar Brown Jr. (who she met in Chicago), Maya Angelou, and Thelonious Monk.

One of those musicians was veteran modern jazz drummer Max Roach, whom she would eventually marry. In 1960, Lincoln recorded for Candid Records *We Insist!—Freedom Now Suite*, a multipart ensemble work written by Brown and Roach that rhapsodizes black emancipation from past to present and from the United States to Africa. Ethnomusicologist Ingrid Monson, in the book *Freedom Sounds*, explores in detail the influence and intent of the album and its subsequent live settings of the piece, noting that jazz critics reacted to the album's overtly political message and, most particularly, Lincoln's vocal performance. Commenting on "Triptych," a duet between Lincoln and Roach divided into three movements—"Prayer," "Protest," and "Peace"—Monson writes that Lincoln's "stylized screaming" in "Protest" represented the work's most expressive "avant-garde moment."[22] The track begins with Lincoln singing open vowel sounds, invoking a mournful lament, and Roach responding to her phrases gently across the drum set. But at the almost four-minute mark, Roach swells in volume with a roll on the snare that bursts across the entire instrument, sending rippling waves of percussive and metallic sound through the room that Lincoln meets with full-throated hollering. "Protest" is a heterophonic duet, Lincoln and Roach improvising together without a common meter or key but with a fluid and intuited sense of complementarity. The track ends with a more reserved and austere dialog between the two, this time with a steady five-count meter. "Triptych," Lincoln remembered, was an important creative milestone for her: "It was a great tribute for a singer and actress. . . . It was abstract and to the point, and I finally learned to scream and not hurt my voice."[23]

Lincoln's screams in "Triptych—Protest" are a display of emotive intensity and corporeal power, of the kind required by the diaphragm and pelvic floor to push a large amount of air through the lungs and sing loudly. The thematic event that causes Lincoln to scream in the unfolding drama remains hidden, yet her hollering encompasses a range of possible emotions: pain, anguish, catharsis, determination, resistance, passion, and rage. Lincoln's performance interpolates sounds from political reality; it's topical and carries great symbolic power in its immediate cultural climate, echoing the sounds of black voices engaged in protest in the streets. Poet and theorist Fred Moten homes in on Lincoln's work here as a poignant statement that symbolizes a radical "break" from the expectation of decorum in "jazz" performance, motioning toward the ineffable, indescribable, and affectively potent. Lincoln's use of raw, vocal sound—screaming across swaths of her vocal range—instead of lyrics is a sonic irruption (a performance) of a cathartic, revolutionary sentiment. A black woman's screams interrupt and thwart any sense of normalcy or decorum and demand the listener's attention.

The immediacy in the act of screaming and the alertness and anticipation it incites in the listener induce a new and unexpected set of possible responses, and therein exists its power to redirect and provoke action. That Lincoln and Roach engage in a charged and attention-demanding improvisatory exchange of vocal and instrumental sound is just as much a display of renegade creative agency and affective power that, as apposite of decorum and aesthetic conformity, represents, for Moten, the break(ing) power of the black radical tradition. This has a historical point of departure, as per Saidiya Hartman, in the pained screams of black women starting with Frederick Douglass's 1845 account of his aunt Hester's beating in *Narrative of the Life of Frederick Douglass*. That was the creative agency—the freedom—at the root of the *new thing*, and it was a sound of rawness, immediacy, and a disregard for decorum: "That echo [of Aunt Hester's scream] haunts, say, saxophonist Albert Ayler's 'Ghosts' or the fractured, fracturing climax of James Brown's 'Cold Sweat.' It's the re-en-gendering haint of an old negation: Albert Ayler always screaming secretly to the very idea of mastery."[24]

Literary and music scholar Daphne Brooks offers an important framework for understanding eccentric and unruly performances by black artists. Brooks considers the "specific strategy" of black performance—what she calls acts of "Afro-alienation"—"counter-normative tactics used by the marginalized to turn [trauma] . . . into a critical form of dissonantly enlightened performance." These rebellious and "odd" approaches to performance, Brooks clarifies, were fugitive ventures aimed at going beyond the normative expectations, limitations, and moments of dehumanization so much a part of life as a racial and gendered "other."[25] Moten too raises this point: "[W]hat occurs in the New Black Music of the sixties—indeed what occurs throughout the short and accelerated history of the music as the music's historicity—is the emergence of an art and thinking in which emotion and structure, preparation and spontaneity, individuality and collectivity can no longer be understood in opposition to each other. Rather the art itself resists any interpretation in which these elements are opposed, [and] resists any designation, even those of the artists themselves, that depends upon such oppositions."[26]

I see the experimentalism of the new thing accomplishing similar goals in its unconventional sound and emphases on creative liberation and collectivity. If the new technique of heterophony represented any kind of dissent, it was in black musicians daring to abandon restraint and musical decorum for the sake of affective intensity, pursuing instead a process and sound that exists beyond mid-twentieth-century trappings of mastery. The *new thing*'s raw and urgent sound was not as simple as the protestation of modern musical "rules"; it was an arresting and confrontational sound—a sonic aesthetic with wiles of immediate and direct expression of affect and emotion that could, possibly, induce new ways of listening and acting as individuals in a collective, and maybe also a new reality to exist in.

That raw new reality is audible in Nina Simone's performance of her original composition "Mississippi Goddam," which premiered at the Village Gate in 1963, the same year she would headline at Carnegie Hall for the first time.

Performed and recorded by Simone and her ensemble at the Hall a year later, "Mississippi Goddam" is a sardonic and satirical show tune that addresses the shameless and disturbing state violence used to defend racial segregation in the Jim Crow South. It was inspired, Simone would explain later, by Kurt Weill's 1927 setting of Bertolt Brecht's "Alabama Song" in the parody opera *The Rise and Fall of the City of Mahagonny* and is what Brooks calls Simone's masterful "strategic dissonance" and a public instance of liberation in black female performance.[27] Brooks provides a brilliant read of Simone's Carnegie Hall performance and its "work" on the audience, so my own, which follows, will offer only a bare outline.

"The name of this tune is 'Mississippi Goddam,'" Simone announces slowly and emphatically to the crowd as the band keeps a cheery vamp in G major, as drummer Bobby Hamilton punctuates Simone's "goddam" with a pressed snare roll and kick drum lick—a callback to an old vaudeville cliché. The "goddam" in the title—a word commonly used in African American Vernacular English as an emphatic remark, conveys an affect of stunned exasperation that Simone theatricalizes throughout the entire performance. "And I mean every word of it," Simone declares before singing:

> Alabama's gotten me so upset
> Tennessee made me lose my rest
> And everybody knows about Mississippi, goddamn!
>
> Can't you see it? Can't you feel it?
> It's all in the air
> I can't stand the pressure much longer
> Somebody say a prayer.

After repeating the opening refrain another time, Simone and the band modulate down to E minor and the mood of the song grows darker. Simone chimes, "This is a show tune but the show hasn't been written for it, yet." She continues:

> Lord, have mercy on this land of mine
> We all gonna get it in due time
> I don't belong here, I don't belong there
> I've even stopped believing in prayer
> Don't tell me, I'll tell you
> Me and my people just about due
> I've been there, so, I know
> They keep on saying, "Go slow."

The next stanza excoriates the inertia, apathy, and hypocrisy of those who insist that Simone and her people "go slow" with a mocking list of examples of black stereotypes that insist that black folk are, indeed, "too slow," which leave the singer confused and disoriented.

Her direct address to her largely white audience during this E minor section is a moment of catharsis where Simone (pictured in Figure 3.2) articulates with candor the horrifying truths that she observes and that she knows the audience is aware of. Contrasting dissonantly with the song's swift tempo and cheery "oompah" rhythm are Simone's poignant and raw lyrics addressing the suspicion that protests are covert communist plots and damning a deceitful nation and its white people ("You're all gonna die and die like flies; I don't trust you anymore"), which she delivers with aplomb.

Simone's "Mississippi Goddam" is an experiment in song in its blend of humor, irony, direct address, and indignant rage as vehicles for candid testimony and catharsis in the context of a tragic political reality. It departs from the typical lightheartedness of musical theater and the more metaphorical language of earlier politically inflected songs like Billie Holiday and Abel

Figure 3.2 Nina Simone at the piano with her trio, ca. 1964. Courtesy the Hulton Archive via Getty Images.

Meeropol's "Strange Fruit" of 1939. Simone's "Mississippi Goddam" is a raw and unflinching confrontation and condemnation, an abstraction and inversion of a show tune performance.

The "Changing Same"

The *new thing*'s abstraction and potency inspired Amiri Baraka to compare the *new thing* to the blues in "The Changing Same (R&B and New Black Music)," a 1966 essay published in the 1968 book *Black Music*. Baraka theorizes an ontology of African American music that locates its essence in a shared ancestral experience that includes surviving chattel slavery, Jim Crow segregation, and mob- and state-sanctioned violence, which produced a unique cultural identity and aesthetic. The essence of the black experience, for Baraka, also included the coerced adoption of European traditions, including Christian religiosity, at the expense of indigenous African languages and customs. That traumatic break is, for Baraka, the catalyst for black music's dialectic (a process of cultural reclamation and reinvention that spans the sacred and secular) that remains a continuum throughout the generations, what Baraka calls the "blues impulse."[28] The difference in the 1960s, he writes, is that too many rhythm-and-blues artists are concerned with "pleasing" a more general and "universal" (i.e., whiter) audience, whereas the avant-garde responsible for what he calls the "New Black Music" is uninterested in any such popularity or acceptance:

> But the significant difference is, again, direction, intent, sense of identification . . . "kind" of consciousness. And that's what it's about; consciousness.
>
> [At] its best and most expressive, the New Black Music is expression, and expression of reflection as well. What is presented is a consciously proposed learning experience. . . . It is no wonder that many of the new Black musicians are or say they want to be "Spiritual Men" ([some] of the boppers embraced Islam), or else they are interested in the Wisdom Religion itself, i.e., the rise to spirit. It is expanding the consciousness of the given that they are interested in, not merely expanding what is already there, or alluded to. They are interested in the *unknown*. The mystical.
>
> [The] content of The New Music, or The New Black Music, is toward change. It is change. It wants to change forms. From physical to physical (social to social) or from physical to mental, or from physical-mental to spiritual. Soon essences. Albert Ayler no longer wants notes. He says he wants sound.[29]

Like his 1961 *Metronome* article, where he identifies specific musicians as avant-gardists, here Baraka names and endorses specific musicians: Shepp,

Albert Ayler, and the keyboardist and bandleader Sun Ra. This essay differs from that earlier one in that Baraka elevates the *new thing* as the new *black* music of significance while disparaging the popularity and accessibility of R&B. He also chastises white hipsters and musicians whose interest in and "imitations" of the black *new thing* lack the same depth as the music of the black musicians he names. Baraka's championing of the *new thing* five years later is as an abstract and perhaps the most important contemporary manifestation of that black American cultural essence—a music of immense (secular) spiritual power that is diluted with the escalation of white participation in modern jazz. The *new thing*, for Baraka, is a revolutionary new stage of black cultural evolution that he extols with gendered language as strong and masculine, while modern jazz, with its diluted black essence, is degenerately effeminate and undesirably queer: "The New Music (any Black Music) is cooled off when it begins to reflect blank, any place 'universal' humbug. It is this fag or that kook, and not the fire and promise and need for evolution into a higher species."[30]

A poet and playwright, Baraka (pictured in Figure 3.3) was born in Newark, New Jersey, in 1934 as Everett LeRoi Jones. He was educated at Rutgers and Howard, graduating with a BA in English in 1954. After serving in the U.S. Air Force, he moved to Manhattan's Lower East Side in 1957 to continue his studies in the city, where he enmeshed himself in the downtown artistic and literary scenes. Writer and poet A. B. Spellman, Baraka's friend from Howard who moved to the Village, explained that the cheap real estate of the district's tenements and vacated manufacturing infrastructure, along with the ample coffee shops and bars scattered throughout its east and west sides, were magnets for artists. The affordability of Lower Manhattan and the potential exposure that its more casual venues offered made it a desirable and alluring destination for creatives and nonconformists. "You're around people who were creating and producing all the time," recalled Spellman; "the Lower East Side was as close as America ever came to something like Montmartre," Paris's famous fin-de-siècle bohemian district.[31] Baraka coedited an avant-garde magazine (*Yugen*), founded a press, and published the work of beat poets Allen Ginsberg and Jack Kerouac, and, in 1961, published his first book of poetry, *Preface to a Twenty-Volume Suicide Note*. A denizen of and an active participant in this literary milieu, Baraka earned a meager income as a freelance writer, contributing essays and reviews to *Metronome, Jazz, Down Beat*, and other jazz magazines while writing and publishing poetry and plays. After a trip to Cuba in 1959 with a delegation of black artists (where he witnessed the unfolding revolution firsthand) and the murderous deposition of Congolese premier Patrice Lumumba in 1961 by Belgian colonial forces (abetted, it

Figure 3.3 Amiri Baraka (*right*) and John Coltrane, date unknown. Photo credit: N.Y. Jazz Museum/Schomburg Center for Research in Black Culture, Photographs and Prints Division, New York Public Library.

was later discovered, by the CIA), Baraka was by his own admission radical-ized: "So it was in the air, it was in the minds of the people, masses of people going up against the apartheid South. It was also coming out of people's horns, laid out in their music. . . . So there was a newness and a defiance, a demand for freedom, politically and creatively, it was all connected."[32] He left the down-town scene in discontent shortly after Malcolm X's assassination in February 1965, relocating to Harlem.

Baraka's "Changing Same" is a distillation of this shift away from down-town bohemia and toward revolutionary black politics, a change reflected also in how other writers understood jazz's *new thing*. As I've written elsewhere, Baraka's essays in jazz magazines in the first half of the 1960s construed the music and its musicians as the outgrowth of a new and radical black conscious-ness. For him, the *new thing* was the sonic manifestation of black radicalism and situated in the Black American experience unlike the more Eurologically oriented modern jazz that was Gunther Schuller's "third stream." Considered in light of the civil rights legislation (the Civil Rights Act of 1964 and Voting

Rights Act of 1965) and assassinations of black leaders (Lumumba in 1961, activist Medgar Evers in 1963, and Malcolm X in 1965), Baraka's investment in the *new thing*'s abstraction and affective force as the sound of black rage, catharsis, and revolutionary action also works to distance it from the apolitical disinterest and cliché of modern art and modern jazz.[33]

In the decades since, scholars have unpacked Baraka's chauvinism while acknowledging his prescient theories of radical black creative practice. His role as a provocateur and advocate of black avant-gardism set the terms by which the literary public came to understand—and reject—the *new thing* and experimentalist black improvising musicians. On the ownership and entitlement that white hipsters claimed over modern jazz and its musicians, Jon Panish discusses the segregation of and divergent value systems between jazz's black and white audiences in Greenwich Village, which also mirrored their relative social and economic power. "Among Euro Americans in the Greenwich Village jazz community, the sense of ownership . . . is an essential part of their relationship to jazz," writes Panish. "It is this sense, in fact, that obliterates any recognition that there is anything specifically African American about the music, the performers, or the tradition of which they are a part." Baraka's "Changing Same" was his response to white audiences' discomfort with black musicians' assertions of creative and cultural authority, even if "being political" was construed as a sign of aesthetic failure (i.e., selling out) because, Panish quotes a white jazz fan as saying, "the musicians lost all touch with the audience. . . . [T]he musicians began to change."[34]

But Baraka's casting of the *new thing* as the sonification of black revolution flattens the diverse means and motivations of the experimentalist musicians in question. The abstraction of the *new thing* served Baraka's goal of resistance against white society's circumscription and capitalist exploitation of black life, and the sound of the music was enough to inspire and sustain revolutionary ideas and action. In this way, black artists—and especially experimentalists—wielded the creative and political powers required to direct and possibly also carve the path towards black liberation. Baraka made efforts to incite this cultural revolution after his move to Harlem, where he subsequently founded the Black Arts Repertory Theater/School in 1965 to produce and perform plays by and for black people, breaking institutional ground for the Black Arts Movement.[35] Synthesizing Marxist theory with his investment in the Kawaida philosophy of Maulana Karenga (the creator of the holiday Kwanzaa), who advocated for the creation of new myths and folklore as effective tools of cultural transmission, retention, and self-empowerment, Baraka invested the black arts with revolutionary power. Potent revolutionary black art was, in this episteme, essential for inculcating among the black masses a robust and culturally autonomous ethnic identity.[36] By the mid-1960s, the *new thing* was for Baraka the sound of a revolutionary black consciousness, and its utility was liberation. As profound and valorous an intent as this was, Baraka's lens for the *new thing* colored it with his own freedom dreams, which, however capacious, could not account for the diversity and multiplicity of musicians' creative practices.

Baraka's "changing same" in black music is its "blues impulse," the continuum of genuine expression and resistance against oppression shaped by the black experience in the United States that flows into black music spanning the avant-garde fringe and the center of the dance floor, the sacred and the secular. This is precisely Baraka's interest in saxophonist Albert Ayler's sound; he hears in its abstractions of traditional African American religiosity the saxophonist's quest for a cosmology that transcends white (Protestant) Christianity. "Albert Ayler uses the other practical religion as key and description of his own quest. . . . [His] music, which he characterizes as 'spiritual,' has much in common with older Black-American religion forms. An openness that characterizes the 'shouts' and 'hollers' [of Pentecostal black churches and worship] . . . the band is 'free' and makes sounds to tear down the walls of anywhere."[37]

Born and raised in Cleveland, Ohio, to a religiously observant and musical family, Ayler started his musical career early, playing the alto saxophone alongside his father (a violinist and tenor saxophonist) in local churches and community centers, and with his brother, Donald, who began on alto and switched to the trumpet at his father's behest. In high school, Ayler gained some of his first secular professional musical experience touring with the rhythm-and-blues bands of harmonica player Little Walter Jacobs and singer Lloyd Price, eventually starting his own group.[38] Attending but unable to continue paying for college, he enlisted in the army in 1956 and played in the military band, where he switched to the tenor saxophone and, in 1959, traveled to Europe for the first time, stationed in Orléans, France. While there, he played with local musicians, and he traveled across Europe and visited Denmark and Sweden for the first time.

His biographers credit his time in Europe as offering Ayler the opportunity to develop his own idiosyncratic creative voice. He was deeply inspired by John Coltrane (who he would later work with) and interpolated elements from gospel and rhythm-and-blues into his sound and repertoire.[39] Valerie Wilmer, a photographer and writer who memorialized Ayler and Coltrane in her seminal book *As Serious as Your Life*, described his creative angle this way: "He took as his source material the spirituals, funeral dirges, bugle calls and marches of the past, and, though he seldom did so, he could *really* play the blues. He used a tough plastic reed, a Fibercane No. 4—the hardest—and had a sound that scared the shit out of everyone who heard him. Rollins, Coleman and Coltrane had explored the use of the saxophone's harmonics or 'overtones,' but Ayler was the first person to actually base his style on them."[40]

Ayler returned to the States briefly after being discharged in 1961 and tried, unsuccessfully, to find work. He returned to Europe in early 1962, just before his twenty-fifth birthday, and made a home in Sweden. Finding Scandinavians to be much more open to his loud, abstract, and "noisy" sound than American audiences, he began working regularly and, in October, was invited by Bengt Nordström to record before a live audience at the Stockholm Academy of Music with local musicians. That LP, released as *Something Different!!!!!!!!* on the Swedish indie label Bird Notes, documents Ayler's unique take on such show tunes as Sigmund Romberg and Oscar Hammerstein's "Softly, as in a Morning Sunrise," and modern jazz tunes like Miles Davis's "Tune Up," Bobby Timmons's "Moanin'," and Ayler's original piece "Free." Only days after the concert and recording, Ayler met pianist Cecil Taylor in Stockholm and traveled with his group to Copenhagen, performing a lengthy heterophonic collective improvisation with them live on Danish television.[41] In January 1963, Ayler recorded his first studio album in Copenhagen, *My Name Is Albert Ayler*, with a repertoire of almost all modern jazz standards with local Danish musicians. Except for the original composition "C.T.," a dialogic heterophonic improvisation presumably dedicated to Taylor, Ayler's "out" playing clashes with the rhythm section's more conventionally "modern" approach.

Ayler met trumpeter Don Cherry that same month in Copenhagen while the trumpeter was on tour with Sonny Rollins. That encounter, along with his earlier performance with Taylor, encouraged Ayler to try his sound again in the United States. He returned in February 1963, first to Cleveland and then, later in the year, to New York, where he joined Taylor for a set of club dates in downtown Manhattan. A year later, on February 24, 1964, Ayler led an all-day recording session at Atlantic Records' recording studio for the Danish label Debut, featuring metrically "free" renditions of seven well-known African American spirituals, including "Swing Low, Sweet Chariot," in a quartet that includes pianist Call Cobbs, bassist Henry Grimes, and drummer Sunny Murray, the latter two members of Taylor's band. Ayler, with his forceful tone and wide, earnest vibrato, keeps the melodies of the spirituals intact while Grimes freely improvises a countermelody and Murray provides splashes of metallic color on the cymbals.

In these raw, mildly abstract interpretations of spirituals—sacred songs and heirlooms of black folk culture—Ayler demonstrates what Benjamin Piekut calls the "vernacular avant-garde," where artists worked within and abstracted the "so-called low forms" more often associated with common people, an imperative that Baraka understood as revolutionary.[42] Ayler's experimental take on these folk songs at such a significant historical moment in Black American political history carries symbolic weight: it is a gesture of cultural veneration, a statement of creative agency, and perhaps a declaration of Ayler's devout spiritual convictions. In effect, Ayler is, in Piekut's words, combining "established and shared norms with improvisations in response to novel situations," almost as if he means to communicate to the listener that he *really* believes in the power and beauty of these songs, which is why they must be treated anew and in his own unique voice, like a "far out" gospel singer bearing witness.[43]

Ayler carried this affect into another set of pieces he recorded the same day with a piano-less quintet and an additional bassist, Earle Henderson, released separately by Debut as *Spirits*. The LP is a thirty-six-minute heterophonic collective improvisation in four parts (each a separate track): "Spirits," "Witches and Devils," "Holy, Holy," and "Saints." The musicians sustain a trance-like sonic environment filled with ecstatic, declamatory sounds that, at their most intense, evoke a state of spiritual possession. What few moments there are of discernible melody in the musicians' playing are fleeting and fragmented, like the hymn-like tune at the beginning of the last track, "Saints," that becomes evident in its incessant repetition at the end of the performance. The sound of *Spirits* is one of transcendence that frustrates any conspicuous clues of orderly structural organization: it's an environment for collectively improvised sonic action. But its sonic signifiers are indeed conspicuously black and vernacular, evoking the worship practices of the Pentecostal/Charismatic sects of Christianity that proliferated in urban Black American communities at the turn of the twentieth century. That kind of deep cultural reference is a detail that Ole Vestergaard Jensen, the record's producer and writer of its liner notes, spells out for the record buyer:

> This is the music of a new generation of jazz artists. They are all born between can and not. In another way this is also a unique session. The music is all-American and not influenced by European traditions as it has been [*sic*] the case with so many other [avant-garde] jazz and/or third-stream composers. Ayler's compositions [come] direct from the roots of jazz. It is a very blues-oriented music being leaped out with a strong present-day force.
>
> This is the music of the sixties and not a far-ahead thing. . . . If you don't dig the music in this album, you should not blame Albert Ayler, but maybe yourself as being behind of time.[44]

4

Sound and Fury

Questioning what seemed to be modern jazz's increasingly dissonant current phase, Gunther Schuller concluded his essay on Thelonious Monk's concert at Manhattan's Town Hall in February 1959 with an open, lingering question: "Who's next, Cecil Taylor?"[1]

Taylor had been gaining notice in the Greenwich and East Village scenes, his jarring, abstract sound puzzling audiences and critics alike. In a favorable review of Taylor's first recording as an ensemble leader, *Jazz Advance* of 1956, Dom Cerulli calls the performances captured on the album "astonishing" because they are all "marked by such freedom in improvisation that careful, studied listening is required. . . . Whether this is the [only] direction or a [single] direction in which jazz will move remains to be seen."[2]

Born in 1929 in Long Island City, Queens, Taylor had imbibed New York City's rich arts and cultural offerings since his childhood. His father, Percy Taylor, was a domestic worker for a wealthy senator residing on Long Island, and his mother, Almeida Ragland Taylor, an actor, pianist, and dancer, fully stewarded her son's education and musical instruction. His interest in big band and modern jazz flourished during his years at Flushing High School, motivating Taylor to pursue music as a serious career path and to enroll in the New England Conservatory's newer popular music program, graduating in 1951 (Figure 4.1).[3]

By his own account, Taylor's time in Boston was difficult; it culminated with his being rejected from the composition program by the faculty head, who Taylor remembered as a "bigot." He later maintained that he "learned more either outside of school or from the nonacademic aspect of school than I did in the classes."[4] His ambitions in the professional field of modern jazz led Taylor to seek gig opportunities in the jazz clubs flourishing in Boston's black enclaves beyond the South End. Clubs in the Roxbury neighborhood were where Taylor encountered touring New York musicians and embarked on his own career as a soloist. He made his first recording in Boston, *Jazz Advance*, on the fledgling indie label Transition in 1956, and returned to New York afterward, where he performed in the many bars and cafés that populated Lower Manhattan's bohemian scenes.

Change. Kwami Coleman, Oxford University Press. © Oxford University Press 2025.
DOI: 10.1093/9780197780121.003.0005

Figure 4.1   Cecil Taylor in New England Conservatory's yearbook, *The Neume*, 1951. Photo courtesy of the New England Conservatory Archives, Boston.

Nat Hentoff, a coeditor of *The Jazz Review* with Martin Williams, took an early interest in Taylor and, in 1958, produced the LP *Hard Driving Jazz*, where the still relatively unknown pianist leads a quintet of high-profile soloists: John Coltrane, trumpeter Kenny Dorham, and drummer Louis Hayes. The record received mixed reviews in music magazines and prompted a critical debate on Taylor's idiosyncratic approach to the piano, which some suggested aligned more with modern classical music than jazz. One reviewer, Zita Carno, acknowledged Taylor's heterogeneous influences but took issue with his accompaniment behind the other soloists, which Carno heard as an unsuccessful clash of musical styles: "He is a fresh and intriguing soloist with a startling new approach to jazz which is really something else. His studies of Bartók and Stravinsky I don't need to go into; everybody knows about that. The influence of Thelonious Monk is also an old story. These and other factors have been assimilated by Taylor and fused into a highly personal, exciting style. But he is not a good comper [i.e., accompanist]. . . . Taylor is an extremely percussive and busy pianist whose harmonic and rhythmic lines present a continuous challenge to the ear of the soloist."[5]

This noisy and "busy" abstract playing is what qualified Taylor, for writers like Amiri Baraka, as an avant-gardist, yet his conservatory education and assumptions about his understanding and interpolation of contemporary classical music led to ambiguity around which avant-garde he aligned with: the "black" or the "white" one. Writers who understood "jazz" and "classical" as intrinsically distinct—racially coded—musical categories and cultural worlds were unclear about whether Taylor's music was jazz, "third stream," or not "music" at all. In some cases, Taylor's busy, dense, and abstract sound led writers to question his musical competence. Ted White, writing for *Metronome* in 1961, found Taylor's music "monotonous" despite his "classical background" and stifled by overactive piano playing, limited melodic statements, and "stylistic devices." He concluded that if "one plumbs deeply enough to sort out the subtleties, one will find that Taylor has much to say; it is merely his self-limited vocabulary which obscures this fact." That is, the lurking "danger" of Taylor's unabashed idiosyncrasy—which White interpreted as a "complacency of style"—would prevent him from becoming "one of the most important jazzmen of our time."[6]

Taylor bristled at the emphasis that critics put on his conservatory education and interests in modern classical music. He told poet and writer A. B. Spellman that these details were only small facets of his artistry and that he certainly didn't consider his music "third stream." Instead, he situated his style well within jazz's historical lineage ("an extension of period music—Ellington and Monk") because, like these two composer-pianists, his signature sound was his own unique and deliberate invention drawn from various sources, foremost being black vernacular culture. For Taylor, the black vernacular was a cultural heirloom inextricable from his identity and lived experience as a Black American. He insisted that the sounds, customs, and social world of the black vernacular informed the contours of his abstraction.[7]

In this chapter I explore Taylor's music of the early 1960s in the context of the vexed interstitial space—between a black jazz avant-garde as delimited by Baraka (see Chapter 2 and Interlude) and a white (Eurological) modernist avant-garde—and how these categorical distinctions contributed to the controversy surrounding his music in the critical literature of the era.[8] I rely on archival interviews with Taylor, especially his exchange with Spellman in *Four Jazz Lives*, as the source of Taylor's refutation of his image as an aspiring, modern classical musician or a jazz musician whose style was derivative of modern classical music. My argument is that his claiming of the black vernacular as an important source of his abstract style served to protect his creative agency from what he viewed as an exploitative industry upheld by misinformed or clueless critics. I also show how Taylor's claims of agency fed his reputation as a black musical insurrectionist, an archetype increasingly pinned on experimentalist black improvising musicians producing abstract music and speaking out against racism and economic exploitation in a moment of social and political upheaval in the United States and the Global South.

Style and Revolution

Taylor's professional breakthrough came after his performance at the Newport Jazz Festival on September 14, 1956, at age twenty-seven, thereafter winning *Down Beat*'s "Piano–New Star" award in August 1957.[9] He was compared to Lennie Tristano, a pianist who led an ensemble engaging in free improvisation on the sides "Intuition" and "Digression," recorded in 1949, and who, in the decades since, has been cited as a precursor to the *new thing*/free jazz even as Tristano became a fierce and vocal critic of the new music of the 1960s.[10] *Down Beat* compared him to Monk because of his abstract and idiosyncratic style.[11] At the turn of the decade, Taylor was recognized as a modernist pushing at the boundaries of jazz practice, but in a few short years his enigmatic style represented a categorical aberration. Confused about the apparent references and allusions to contemporary classical music in his playing, the bombast of his sound on the piano, and his unflinching verbal statements about racism and economic exploitation, by 1965 Taylor the modernist had become, for critics, Taylor the angry transgressor. Elements of that literary character arc can be found in Schuller's statements about Taylor in 1959, where he is presented as an "erstwhile iconoclast" railing against the status quo who, because of his revolutionary ardor, had recently found acceptance among a broader audience—the same type of listeners drawn to Monk's nonconformist style. "This," Schuller wondered aloud, "may explain why one bewildered listener, not to be cheated of his anticipated 'revolutionary' atmosphere, upon noting the heavy representation of beards in the audience, wondered whether he had strayed into a Fidel Castro stronghold."[12]

To fully appreciate the image conjured by the spectator in Schuller's quote requires understanding the fixation on and paranoia around the presumed ever-present threat of international (Soviet) communism permeating American politics and culture. The description of a concert hall filled with bearded rebels there to see Monk—the same demographic after Taylor—plays upon middle-class anxieties about nonconformist youth and rebellious racial

Figure 4.2 Thelonious Monk, ca. 1959. Photo credit Yoram Kahana/Schomburg Center for Research in Black Culture, Photographs and Prints Division, New York Public Library.

minorities that, in 1959, extended into elite and presumably apolitical cultural spaces (Figure 4.2). The world was ablaze with revolution.

Colonized people in Asia, Africa, the Caribbean, and Latin America were fighting against and, in some instances, thwarting imperial rule, overturning colonial regimes, and gaining national sovereignty. Fidel Castro, the charismatic lawyer turned guerrilla and war hero from Cuba's rural Oriente

Figure 4.3 A 1959 photograph showing "Los Comandantes de la Revolución." (L to R) Raúl Castro, Antonio Núñez Jiménez, Ernesto "Che" Guevara, Juan Almeida Bosque, and Ramiro Valdés in Havana during the first year of the Cuban Revolution. Photo credit: AFP PHOTO/ARCHIVO BOHEMIA via Getty Images.

province, galvanized *campesinos* (farmers) and university students, successfully ousting the U.S.-backed authoritarian regime of Fulgencio Batista in a Marxist revolution called the Movimiento 26 de Julio (26th of July Movement). Journalists around the globe transmitted—in print, radio, and television—images of rugged, uniformed insurgents, parading victoriously through the streets of Havana after six years of sporadic guerrilla warfare. The bearded men and rifle-wielding women of Cuba's new vanguard party, led by Castro, Camilo Cienfuegos, Juan Almeida Bosque, Celia Sánchez, Vilma Espín, the Argentinian-born Ernesto "Che" Guevara, and others, were young, fiery, and determined rebels who had successfully overturned the status quo and the hemispheric superpower backing it. The visibility of black revolutionaries like Bosque and other Afro-Cuban guerrillas also symbolized a victory against the tyranny of white supremacy (Figure 4.3).

Castro relied on Soviet support throughout the Revolution and further normalized relations between Havana and Moscow after Batista's ouster, which culminated in the Soviet-Cuba economic agreement policies of February 1960.[13] Almost a year after Monk's concert at Town Hall, President Dwight Eisenhower initiated an embargo on trade with Cuba in response to their

Soviet alliance and began a military training program for antirevolutionary exiles, a paramilitary force that John F. Kennedy would deploy in the failed Bay of Pigs invasion of April 1961. In depicting Monk's audience as a "Castro stronghold," Schuller, however sarcastically or flippantly, positioned the bearded pianist as the enigmatic leader of some kind of aesthetic insurgency.[14]

Taylor's vanguard status in the early 1960s was, Schuller explained, due to his "atonal" improvisations. Years earlier, in a review of Taylor's first two albums—*Jazz Advance* of 1956 and the Newport Jazz Festival set in 1957—Schuller asserted that Taylor's solos were indeed coherent and cohesive despite the improvised atonality, a legitimacy that, for Schuller, stemmed from Taylor's fidelity to the piece's form (i.e., structural design).[15] Deeply invested in empirical analyses as the best method to understanding and appreciate jazz improvisation, Schuller understood Taylor as a modernist taking jazz to its next aesthetic stage: atonal improvisation and extended, complex forms much like the European modernists of the twentieth century: Claude Debussy, Arnold Schoenberg, Igor Stravinsky, Alexander Scriabin, and Darius Milhaud. They, like Taylor, had explored the "outermost extensions of tonally centered chords and melodies."[16]

Schuller found that Taylor's atonal abstractions ran the risk of detracting from the currents of black vernacular expressivity; the speed at which Taylor created and moved beyond his musical "ideas" in a singular performance sounded like he was "objectively performing a function . . . and hid[den] from us what he feels about the blues." For all of Taylor's intelligent abstractions and adherence to form, his style, Schuller argued, was problematic because it was *too* cerebral and, because of this, lacked the emotional vitality so essential to jazz: "Especially on the blues, one has the impression that Taylor lets us in on the workings of his mind, but not his soul."[17] For a formalist so clearly deferential to the Western classical tradition, Schuller didn't quite know how to assess Taylor's seemingly odd and abstract style, and he foresaw Taylor's listeners questioning whether his music was jazz or not. Whitney Balliett, reviewing "abstract" jazz records for the *New Yorker* magazine in 1961, described Taylor and Ornette Coleman as "unofficial leaders of abstract jazz" working from "opposite quarters": "Taylor is a well-schooled classical pianist whose use of atonality and free improvisation is conscious and academic; Coleman is a self-taught alto saxophonist whose methods are mostly intuitive."[18]

Adherence to an apparent form in an intelligent, coherent, and artful way was a primary concern for critics interested in identifying and predicting future directions in modern jazz. Martin Williams, Schuller's colleague at *The Jazz Review*, published "Extended Improvisation and Form: Some Solutions" in 1958 on the "problem" of longer and more abstract improvisation emerging in modern jazz.[19] Improvisation in jazz evolved, according to Williams, through three historical stages: variations on a composition's melody, variations on a composition's harmony, and, currently, freer improvisation that breached the limits of conventional melody and form. Skilled musicians developed motivic material intelligibly within the bounds of form, and the formal "flights-of-fancy" of younger musicians, Williams insisted, still had to be intelligible. In this Williams shared Schuller's criteria for improvisation in modern jazz rooted in intelligible design (through motivic development) and chided the "less ordered efforts of many young modernists" who could not meet that challenge.

Was Taylor's style revolutionary? To answer yes would imply that, like the Cuban guerrillas, there was a clear revolutionary objective in mind that necessitated the overthrow of a reigning political order. There is nothing in the archive of Taylor's public statements where the pianist articulates a desire to overturn a political or aesthetic regime, but he is adamant about the historicity of his style: the influence that the jazz and black vernacular music of the past had in shaping his sound. Abstraction in Taylor's recorded work in this period manifests in how improvisation permeates all aspects of a performance, including how predetermined and spontaneous musical events unfold, which begins with the minimal and nonverbal parameters that Taylor offered collaborators as ways to incite their deep listening and intuition within a performance.

Motifs, sometimes presented as lyrical, song-like melodies and other times as punctuated chromatic sets of pitches, are like the towers of a suspension bridge that anchor and sustain—with tension—the action and movement that passes in between. Sound, in the collective improvisations Taylor designed, is a volatile and fluid substance; it fluctuates in density and velocity, explodes outward to a wall of dissonant sound, and collapses down to a murmuring heterophonic stream. The endurance and focus necessary for musicians to remain engaged and attentive during the long, intuited sessions of improvisatory co-creation lends to Taylor's performances captured on record a palpable and exhausting sonic energy that can have a dramatic or sublime effect on the listener. Cathartic, overwhelming, unpleasant, disturbing, transportive, and transcendent, Taylor and his collaborators developed by the mid-1960s an abstract and potent performance practice that, like a current of electricity, could elicit strong, impulsive reactions from their audiences.

The "revolution" represented by Taylor's style went beyond melodic and formal abstractions. Critics also made note of his percussive approach to the piano during improvisations and accompaniment, which contributed to the busy, dissonant, and dense textures of his music. It would take over a decade for the literary public to gain a better understanding of Taylor's creative vision and expressive methods. His was a highly kinetic approach to the instrument; he utilized his entire body in the act of performing, leveraging his body weight to strike the keys with force and momentum, producing a pronounced and arresting sound. That physicality functioned, Taylor later professed, as a catalyst "feeding material to soloists in all registers," their aggregate sounds congealing into a heterogeneous flow of sonic energy (a "rhythm-sound energy") typically expressed, Andrew Bartlett observes, in Afro-diasporic dance traditions.[20]

The corporeal force behind Taylor's playing was channeled into the instrument through his fingers, which he used individually and tightly bound together, but in the mid-1960s he also incorporated his palms and forearms, thereby fully exploiting the piano's hammer action. Taylor approached the piano like a percussion instrument, like "eighty-eight tuned drums" wrote Valerie Wilmer in 1977.[21] Extrapolating on this point, Taylor's abstract pianism might be what happens when reimagining the instrument as a balafon or other West African idiophone, where each wooden key (under which there is a resonator made out of gourd or, in the case of a piano, a highly reflective wooden soundboard) vibrates with a fundamental pitch when struck but also resounds with a prism of overtones. In the act of improvisation, Taylor, with his stiffened, bundled fingers, flattened palms, and forearms, strikes the keyboard in tone clusters and alternates this with single-note chromatic torrents played with individual fingers. This interest in the drum, Taylor recounted in the mid-1960s, began in childhood with a timpani and drum set, and the drum's central role in driving action—the movements of dancers on the dance floor, for instance—was apparent to him in the orchestras of Duke Ellington and Jimmy Lunceford and the fluid, rhythmically sophisticated acrobatics of tap dancers like the Four Step Brothers and Baby Laurence.[22] Like a dancer on a marley or wooden floor, Taylor traversed the keyboard's range in skips and leaps, moving quickly between its different registral planes in a flow-like sonic "choreography" achieved in collaboration with other musicians. Theater too, Taylor divulged, shaped his performance method, informed by his close relationships with actors, directors, and playwrights in New York's downtown experimental theater scene.[23]

In 1958, Taylor began experimenting with a modular approach to form, where precomposed pitch collections—cells or melodic shapes—are played either with exactitude or more loosely (improvisationally) gestured by musicians in sequences or moments that would also be determined improvisationally. Collaborators were expected to learn these motifs largely by ear, memorizing/internalizing them so that they can be organically and intuitively recalled during performance.[24] An early recorded example of this method is "Of What" on *Looking Ahead!*, which Taylor's ensemble recorded in June of that year—a tune that bassist Buell Neidlinger called the "original free piece" of Taylor's repertoire.[25] It begins with Denis Charles's cymbal crash and a series of short motifs played by Taylor on piano, as Neidlinger interjects with melodic ideas in response, sometimes in direct imitation. After a short, possibly precomposed figure (▶ 00:28), Charles establishes a steady pulse on the hi-hat that remains for the length of the performance as the other two musicians improvise, vacillating in and out of phase with the pulse.

The sum of their collective improvisation is a heterophonic lattice where each musician creates with a great degree of autonomy. Cohesion is achieved through conventional means when the musicians lock into a centralized pulse and general tonal/key area (D Lydian), but also more abstractly through an intuited synergy that is dialogic and gestural when the musicians are out of phase with the pulse. Taylor offers few clues to its design in the liner notes (written by Nat Hentoff) apart from its being a thirty-two-bar tune "with some interesting things happening in it."[26] The second half of the track (▶ 4:18–8:08), after Charles's drum solo, is where Taylor more forcefully directs the loose, freely improvised dialog; Neidlinger spontaneously breaks out into a walking bass line which he interrupts with small melodic fragments that hang suspended in the air, all while Taylor plays in a perpetual stream of consciousness across the keyboard. Taylor's piano is mixed by the studio engineer to be at the foreground of the recording, but despite Taylor's prominence in the stereo image, Neidlinger and Charles are also always "soloing." The quartet, with Earl Griffiths on vibraphone, applies this collective method on the LP's last track, "Excursion on a Wobbly Rail," Taylor's homage to Billy Strayhorn and Duke Ellington's signature tune "Take the 'A' Train."

This kind of free group improvisation secured Taylor's reputation as an avant-gardist, but the abstraction and opacity of his sound led to unfavorable coverage by the press and diminishing opportunities in venues across New York, a fallout that Taylor recounted with dismay to Spellman in *Four Jazz Lives*. Developing an experimental practice, Taylor found, made it difficult to survive, and being a black experimentalist seemed only to heighten that difficulty. While some, like Baraka, described his sound and methods as revolutionary, the cultural paternalism of writers who insisted that his style was derivative of modern classical music and the racial violence, economic exploitation, and political struggle of black people in American society at large would provoke Taylor to voice his thoughts on these matters out loud. There was, Taylor would insist, a direct connection between the social and political world and his creative practice as a black man living and (barely) working in the United States.

Cecil Taylor: Bartók in Reverse

Spellman's profile of and dialog with Taylor, printed in *Four Lives in the Bebop Business* of 1966, captures Taylor reflecting on his career and the machinations of the industry he's been working in. He expresses resentment about the way his music was being explained in magazines and newspapers as an aspiration toward modern classical music, something that he frequently confronted in interviews. This characterization, he thought, alienated him from black listeners and distanced him from a culture and community that he deeply identified with. It also seemed to reinforce the presumed superiority of classical music and white composers. Western music aesthetics and formal technique, Taylor believed, could neither adequately explain nor fully capture Black American musical sensibilities, and the intrinsic cultural chauvinism of European and Euro-American music epistemology prevented white composers and musicians from genuinely engaging with and understanding jazz's roots in black vernacular culture. He referenced his own experiences as a student in Boston to illustrate how de facto segregation upheld a physical and psychological barrier between white and black Americans such that the former knew nothing of the lives and experiences of those communities ghettoized across the bridge.[27] Since "serious" (classical) music was at the top of the aesthetic hierarchy in the United States, and the colleges and conservatories that canonized Western music history, theory, and instrumental and vocal technique set the standards "serious" people subscribed to, his music was received and scrutinized within that paradigm—a limitation abetted by the constant highlighting of his conservatory training in the press.

Baraka was the first writer to explain Taylor's abstract style as being rooted in the black vernacular, and the blues specifically. In a 1961 review of *The World of Cecil Taylor*, Baraka argues that Taylor's interpretations of popular songs—like Rogers and Hammerstein's "This Nearly Was Mine" from the 1958 Hollywood film *South Pacific*—is evidence that he was not as much of an outlier as other writers made him out to be. Taylor, like other improvising musicians, reconfigures "maudlin" popular songs and show tunes into a more interesting musical statement because he "completely rearranges the melodic, harmonic and rhythmic devices of that tune" into something idiosyncratic, "personal and intimate." His ability to "go to old forms and old nightmares and make his own music" speaks of a kind of experimentalism that eschews more systematic and academic methods for a resourceful "*use* of materials and ideas that are perhaps [his] cultural inheritances."[28] This is the kind of abstraction that led Baraka to herald Taylor as a leading avant-gardist alongside Coleman in his 1961 *Metronome* article "The Jazz Avant Garde."[29]

In Taylor's abstractions are a deep and esoteric kind of blues, argues Baraka, that is found beyond his choice of notes; in the context of the form, it exists more holistically as a matter of Taylor's unapologetically original style. Like Coleman and Eric Dolphy, Taylor made "melody out of rhythmic elements of the music," thereby prioritizing, in Baraka's view, black vernacular musical elements in an otherwise experimentalist, "avant-garde" creative practice. Baraka also critiques the notion that Taylor's music doesn't swing and is therefore lacking: "There's a little group of irregulars walking around nowadays saying that they can't 'pop their fingers' to Taylor's music (or to Ornette Coleman's, etc.). To them I can only say: there's definitely something wrong with your fingers." While Baraka seems to insist here that the music has its own kind of presumably abstract swing that he and other "insiders" can detect, another way to understand the rhythms and overall sense of musical time in Taylor's music is that they are more fluid and less rigidly defined and felt.

Baraka's insistence that Taylor's style was rooted in the black vernacular was part of his larger investment in a black musical avant-garde grounded in that vernacular, one that stood counterpoised to the presumed supremacy of classical music, and by extension European and Euro-American culture. That claim of ownership over the black vernacular in the context of musical abstraction is also present in Spellman's interview with Taylor. He celebrates Taylor's original style and sound and the fact that he's persisted despite the incredible adversity faced by "avant-gardist" freelancers in New York's jazz industry. He shares Taylor's grievances against writers like Schuller who defer to classical European music aesthetics to characterize his style. Taylor is different from other modern black musicians "such as John Lewis . . . involved in what has been called Third Stream music [who] have been decidedly nineteenth century in their European derivations."[30] Spellman carefully points out that Taylor is not ashamed of his conservatory background but that he does value the cultural education he received outside of his formal studies, on the streets of Harlem and Brooklyn, two large black enclaves in New York City. Spellman agrees with Baraka that black vernacular culture—epitomized, secularly, by the blues—is the essence of musical expression in Black American life and that Taylor, as a composer, sources its expressive powers. This is why, Spellman writes, Taylor insists that listeners should focus on the blues content in his music instead of the "forms and devices he may have brought over from the conservatory."[31]

In Spellman's and presumably Taylor's view, the third stream is symptomatic of a long-standing, pernicious condition where jazz (improvising) musicians feel that they must prove themselves to be capable of playing classical music as a signifier of musical erudition and prestige, thereby demonstrating that "playing the blues was a matter of choice":

> There is only one musician who has, by general agreement even among those who have disliked his music, been able to incorporate all that he wants to take from classical and modern Western composition into his own distinctly individual kind of blues without in the least compromising those blues, and that is Cecil Taylor, a kind of Bartók in reverse.
>
> Cecil believes that his problem is to utilize "the energies of the European composers, their technique, consciously, and blend this with the traditional music of the American Negro, and to create a new energy. And was it unique? No. Historically not. This is what has always happened. Ellington did it."[32]

Spellman calling Taylor a "Bartók in reverse" is an evocative inversion of the conventional modernist aesthetic hierarchy. Béla Bartók (1881–1945), the Hungarian ethnomusicologist and composer recorded and notated Hungarian, Romanian, Slovak, Bulgarian, and Serbian folksongs, interpolating some of their elements in his own abstract "modern" compositions. Gesturing toward Bartók's concert music for orchestra, solo instruments, and voice, suffused with what outsiders might hear as a Hungarian musical vernacular—a detail that resonated in the era's folk revivalism, which popular black artists like Harry Belafonte seized upon—Spellman suggests that Taylor instead interpolated abstract modern techniques into an idiosyncratic style rooted in the black vernacular.[33] The implications here seem to be a subversion of the orthodox aesthetic hierarchy that privileges elite culture and notated compositions over oral/aural musical traditions and improvisation.

The "fact" of Taylor's style being derived from European musical modernists circulating in the music press distorted his influences, leading to, according to Spellman and Taylor, a fundamental misunderstanding of his process.[34] Spellman tries to dispel this misunderstanding by invoking Taylor's insistence that his sound and style are the sum of his creative proclivities and lived, subjective experience as a Black American navigating a racist society and an exploitative music industry. Spellman's "Bartók in reverse" analogy also plays into the nationalistic overtones of Bartók's appropriation of his own "native" cultural vernacular. A conservatory-trained pianist and composer who toured Europe frequently, Bartók wrote concert music that projected the sounds of a Hungarian national identity during and after the collapse of the Austro-Hungarian Empire and the drawing of new national borders in 1920. Neidlinger, Taylor's longtime collaborator, remarked to Bill Coss (who otherwise classicized Taylor's music) that while Taylor's music may sound to some like Stravinsky, his ultimate source was the blues. Taylor expands on Neidlinger's point in Spellman's profile by explaining in his own words (which Spellman quotes) that his sound reflects the kinetic energy of life on the streets of New York City: energy "that built these ugly buildings. Well, they're dirty, so they look ugly—I never realized how lovely Carnegie Hall was until they cleaned it. And the tempo and the people . . . well, they're here, but most of them have been beaten by the system."

> In any case, the greatness in jazz occurs because it includes all the mores and folk-ways of Negroes during the last 50 years. No, don't tell me that living in the same kind of environment is enough. *You* don't have the same kind of cultural difficulties I do. I admire someone like Zoot Sims [a white saxophonist], because he accepts himself. He is unique. He tries to come to grips with *everything*, musically, not so-cially. But even Zoot, and Lennie Tristano, only simulate the feeling of the American Negro—the way American composers concern themselves with Stravinsky, Webern, and such.
>
> Jazz is a Negro feeling. It is African, but changed to a new environment. It begins in the Negro community, and it is the only place for Negro hero worship.
>
> The reality is that what I play is jazz. Anything happening after is fine. Somehow my comping has become a matter of put-down. It's not nervous. I try to provide a full orchestral background. That causes a horn player to really play. He'll respond, if he can. You look at the reviews. See what happens when Coltrane and I play to-gether. He and Dolphy can hear me.[35]

Taylor makes his investment in black vernacular culture abundantly clear, and his blunt identification as a "jazz musician" a bulwark against his reputation as a classically oriented "third stream" musician.

Bartók was not, however, the only reference for Taylor's modern abstractions. Starting in the early 1960s Taylor began "preparing" the piano (strategically affixing rigid and resonant objects to piano strings to alter the sound) and playing directly on the instrument's strings and soundboard with his fingers, mallets, or other objects. For this he was compared to John Cage (b. 1912), the Los Angeles–born white American composer who used prepared piano and other technical distortions and misuses of the instrument in works like the *Sonatas and Interludes* cycle of the late 1940s. Cage's *Music of Changes*, premiered by pianist David Tudor in 1952, was the composer's first piece to rely fully on chance elements in its composition; Cage drew up charts for various parameters—tempo, dynamics, pitch, silence, duration, and superimpositions—and tossed coins to determine the value of each, notating the result in conventional Western music notation. In contrast to Taylor's improvisatory, modular style, Cage's score "determined" the performer's musical action with specificity. Cage was a faculty member of the New School for Social Research in Downtown Manhattan from 1956 to 1960, and he and his life partner and collaborator, choreographer Merce Cunningham, held workshops and performed work in and through the Judson Memorial Church in Greenwich Village in the 1960s. In or adjacent to that milieu, Taylor collaborated with choreographer Fred Herko to set the piece *Like Most People—For Soren* at Judson in 1962.[36] Spellman quotes Neidlinger's description of Taylor's prepared piano playing at the December 1963 Jazz Composers' Guild concert at Judson Hall in Midtown Manhattan as being markedly different from Cage's approach: "I don't find any of the sounds Cecil makes on the inside of the piano at all similar to John Cage or Christian Wolff or Stockhausen or Kagel. I know he's heard all that music, but the implements that he uses to play the inside of the piano are nothing like the ones that they use. For instance, he uses bed springs, steel mesh cloth, things that he lives around. And like those cats are using rubber erasers, corks, and felt mallets. Cecil's is a much more metallic sound, very brilliant, but the Western cats soften the piano down."[37] (Cage did indeed use hard, metallic objects such as bolts, screws, and nuts in addition to rubber erasers and other softer, pliable objects.)

Taylor took issue with the ideal of depersonalization that Cage pursued in his indeterminate music. "David Tudor is supposed to be the great pianist of the modern Western music [*sic*] because he's so detached," Taylor is quoted saying. "You're damned right he's detached. He's so detached he ain't even there. Like, he would never get emotionally involved with music. It's a theory, it's a mental exercise in which the body is there as an attribute to complement that exercise. The body is in no way supposed to get involved in it."[38] He explained his style, by contrast, as embodied and emotive, as is the convention in black vernacular music.[39]

Spellman emphasizes that immediacy and kinesis are fundamental to Taylor's style. Sound, in this regard, is the end product of kinetic activity, so there's an unbroken circuit between energy coursing through the performer's body—exerted in the act of performing—and the sound produced and projected outward by their activity, which reaches the listener. Taylor, in Spellman's description, equates sound energy and its variable intensities with affective power, such that the potency of sound has a visceral and psychological effect on the performer and listener alike. In this way, the performance, as it unfolds in the moment through collaboration by like-minded musicians—not melody or form—is the "content" of the music.

Taylor made a distinction between form and structure in his group's performance practice: "The emphasis in each piece is on building a whole, totally integrated structure. In doing this, we try to carry on—in ensemble as well as solo sections—the mood of a jazz soloist." He continues, "I mean that principle of kinetic improvisation that keeps a jazz solo building. What makes jazz unique is the compression of that energy into a short period of time, and that, in turn, reflects what the machine has done to our lives in metropolitan areas in America. . . . When they [the European modernists] come to the point where everything happens, where the development, the climax is, that's good. Why not just give me that? That's music; that should stand by itself."[40] In an interview published in *Down Beat* in 1965, he told Hentoff that he was "continually involved in using different types of forms and in working out different kinds of sound problems. . . . I have pieces composed of four or five parts and not one of them is concerned with 32-measure frameworks or that sort of thing. Similarly, I'm involved with pieces that have no chords at all. The harmonic foundation is made of clusters on which various scales are superimposed. You just don't have to be hamstrung by thirds and that kind of nonsense, just as you don't have to be hamstrung by the 'song form' to have a great deal of order."[41] Spellman expands on this point with a quote by Archie Shepp, the saxophonist on *The World of Cecil Taylor*:

> Taylor has found that even the idea of written composition often hampers the communication of ideas among the musicians. The tune and the structure must often be transmitted in the same oral fashion that marked the difference between mulatto Jelly Roll Morton and the illiterate black musicians from around the docks. According to Archie Shepp, who played tenor saxophone with Cecil in 1959, "Cecil has returned to natural music. At that point, Cecil stopped writing his music out and started to teach the cats the tunes by ear. He would play the line, and we would repeat it. That way we got a more natural feeling for the tune and we got to understand what Cecil wanted."
>
> "Now a lot of musicians don't want to do that because they have a bourgeois hangup about the whole status of being a competent reader. . . . That was the way jazz was written before—by ear; and now Taylor has trouble finding musicians who can meet that challenge. The black man has come full circle."[42]

In the same 1965 interview with Hentoff, Taylor says, "I write my pieces, but I communicate them to the musicians orally. This way, we cut down on the superfluous, and we communicate on a much deeper level. Furthermore, since I have to actually write so *I* can understand it on paper, I can write much more quickly. In the middle of a session, for instance, I can write down things immediately. . . . I'm right now very interested in problems of sound, in the interrelations between the textures possible on various instruments."[43]

I reprint these long quotes to illustrate how Taylor understood his style in his own terms, which contrasts with the composer- and score-centric dynamic in modern European classical music. The performer's intuition was important in Taylor's group dynamic, and he encouraged his collaborators to play beyond his written music or verbal instructions. Drummer Sonny Murray recalled his first experience playing with Taylor, in October 1961, when he asked Taylor what to play on one tune: "He said, 'Just play.' I said, 'What do you mean? Like a drum solo?' 'No, I mean just let yourself play your drums, but listen too.' And it happened."[44] Murray confesses that he had just started to read music notation in a reliable way and that Taylor's invitation to create music away from the page was liberating. On this sense of trust between the musicians—to co-create sympathetically—Spellman adds, "The implication of all this is that the composition is begun when the musicians are chosen."[45]

Taylor's embodied, kinetic practice stems from his deep, long-standing interest in dance. Neidlinger told Spellman, "The dance, I think, had its results on his playing because a lot of his playing depends on body motion, especially the fast playing. He does things with a speed that most pianists, if they heard it on record, would say, 'How does he do that.' It has a lot to do with the rhythmic flailing of his arms or his ability to move his body back and forth like a pendulum from one end of the piano to the other so that he can put his hands in the proper position, and I think his interest in the dance has a lot to do with that."[46] Writing about Taylor as the "prophet of the new jazz radicals" in a 1965 issue of *Status* magazine, Hentoff includes a similar quote by Neidlinger, adding, "Energy—leaping, enormous energy—is one of the characteristics of a Taylor performance. He plays with such force and such total immersion in the music that he leaves the listener exhausted."[47]

Rather than taking on institutions or aesthetic orthodoxies in a direct and antagonistic way, Spellman's profile of Taylor portrays him and his collaborators as artists endeavoring to develop new material—new modes of expression—and to work regularly in an unpredictable and austere industry. The hardships Taylor experienced playing in local clubs is the most persistent trope in his early 1960s interviews.

Insisting that there was an audience for his group's abstract sound, Taylor put the onus on club owners for prioritizing profit over art. Spellman spoke to Joe Termini, the proprietor of the Five Spot Café, about his hiring of Taylor in the past and his reluctance to do so at that time, a decision that Termini insisted was nothing personal. But there was no money in experimental jazz because the young, bohemian crowd eventually moved on to popular music: "I might not have jazz in the future. People seem to like dancing, and I might go into that. The jazz following is just not a commercial popular following. There are well over five hundred jazz musicians in New York, and maybe five clubs that hire jazz musicians. . . . I don't know. If I lose money, I won't have jazz anymore. Giving up the jazz policy would be throwing away the last ten years."[48] That same profit motive is why, Taylor insists, he could not find regular work in black clubs. He recounts an incident at the Coronet, a white-owned club in Bedford-Stuyvesant, Brooklyn, with a largely black clientele, where the black manager fired Taylor's group on the bandstand despite an otherwise receptive audience. The lack of financial support for experimental improvised music and the self-preservation of club owners made keeping a band together extremely difficult, Neidlinger remarked.[49]

Lack of work not only deprived the musicians of a livable wage but also, according to Neidlinger, diminished the cohesion of the band. Worse, when there was work, the clubs' backline and equipment were in various states of disrepair; both Neidlinger and Taylor commented on the sheer number of out-of-tune pianos the group had to endure, and how this neglect negatively affected their performances. Taylor also placed blame on the cabaret laws in New York and around the country ("which taxed and harassed cabarets nearly out of existence"), union wage demands for venues that small bars could not afford, and the meddling of booking agents and radio DJs that deprived new experimental music of a wider, less elitist audience and musicians like himself of a living wage: "What jazz jobs there are in the Harlems of America go invariably to the safest performers. And the young musicians who are interested in the new music almost always have to take their music 'downtown,' in order to find a receptive atmosphere."[50] Taylor's grievances with the industry were related to the near impossibility he and his collaborators faced in maintaining a livelihood while developing experimental work.

In addition to the economic exploitation and profit motives of the radio stations and clubs was the inescapable racism in the United States which, to Taylor, made Europe a better place for the new music. His position on Europe was likely informed by his months-long Scandinavian tour in 1962, when, like some of his professional peers, he found European audiences to be more receptive and supportive of the new music and black musicians.[51] Still, Spellman warns, "neither the universities nor Europe can solve the basic dilemma with which Cecil, like every serious black musician, is now faced: how to maintain those roots within the community that fructify and justify the music. The racial awareness that the Negro is expressing now is certainly not lost on the jazz musician. The problem, then, is how to live in this society that seems to despise both a black man and an artist, and stay the same man all day long."[52]

Responses to that kind of exploitation led Taylor to the Jazz Composers' Guild, a cooperative that trumpeter Bill Dixon formed with several other composer/musicians after his four-day "October Revolution" concert series in 1964 at the Cellar Café, a bar on the Upper West Side of Manhattan. The Guild, comprising Taylor, Shepp, Sun Ra, Paul Bley, Roswell Rudd, John Tchicai, Burton Greene, Michael Mantler, Carla Bley, Alan Silva, and Jon Winter, was organized to foster mutual aid between members, who were to negotiate on behalf of and redistribute opportunities to each other. The group disbanded six months later after significant internal disagreements.[53]

Though Taylor emphasized throughout Spellman's text his strong connection to black vernacular culture and black audiences, Spellman maintains that Taylor's reception was more mixed and unpredictable than he claimed.[54] His alienation from black audiences and the young bohemian crowd of the East and West Village, Spellman speculates, left only one viable solution for Taylor's lack of work: to "mine the affluent sections of American cities—where they probably will find only frustration and even further alienation."[55] That he was such an outsider—to modern jazz, black vernacular culture, and the white worlds of classical music and Cage's downtown avant-garde scene—confirmed for Taylor that the price for developing an original style was prohibitively high. The way to make it, it would seem, was to assimilate: "I've known Negro musicians who've gotten grants, but it's very interesting that no Negro *jazz* musician has ever gotten a grant. If you're a black pianist who wants to learn to play Beethoven, you have a pretty good chance of getting a grant. That's the fucked-up liberal idea of uplifting the black man by destroying his culture. But if you want to enlarge on culture, forget it; your money will have to come from bars and that cutthroat record industry."[56]

Spellman's interview with Taylor is a poignant account of the pianist's struggles in and grievances about a fickle industry with no infrastructure of support for black experimentalists. But Taylor felt his animus about lacking material support was distorted in music journalism, which depicted him as angry and resentful of a white music industry and white audiences. As they had in their criticism of Coleman, some writers alleged that Taylor's relevance was itself manufactured by sympathetic critics and record producers looking to cash in on a new fad. But the source of his outsider status, Taylor confided to Coss in 1961, was the disparagement of musicians in the field which seemed to affect the opinions of club owners and record producers: "The sad thing is the fact of how much nonmusical forces have to do with the music. Not only in the business itself, but the musicians themselves reflect the greedy society. Contemporaries impose on you, impress you with the futility of doing things.

Really, they are emphasizing death as such. Our whole society seems to be based on cutting down flight."[57]

Their discomfort, Taylor insists, is not an inherently negative or undesirable response and could potentially serve as a catalyst for change: "I think we frighten some people. I know that they work harder when we are playing opposite them. You know, music isn't only supposed to satisfy you. It's also work. If it intimidates you, that's good, too. That makes you work harder. But I haven't heard anything for a long time that intimidated me, frightened me. I should explain that. Music that does that is my fault. It means I've forgotten my ears. It makes me angry, not afraid—angry because *I* couldn't hear it."[58] For some younger musicians, Taylor was not just a conceptualist of an emotionally jarring and immediate kind of improvised music but also a symbol of nonconformity. Jeanne Phillips, one of Spellman's interlocutors ("a black woman who has devoted much of her adult life to modern jazz") and witness to Taylor's performances recounts the gaggle of young musicians that would hang around Taylor's bandstand who had since gone "as musically far out as Taylor":

> You look at the situation. Certain musicians were hostile to Cecil, but certain others dug him. An interesting thing is that someone like Monk has Cecil's records. Who knows whether Miles does or not? When Miles first heard Cecil, back in the Fifties, he put him down, right? Well, it's an interesting thing that Miles's present piano player, Herbie Hancock, is trying to go in Cecil's direction, because he thinks that's where the music has to go. And these musicians dig Cecil. Miles's drummer, Tony Williams, does. Tony would rather play with Cecil than with Miles. That would sound strange wouldn't it? But it's a fact.[59]

New Units, Same Structures

Taylor's group was thoroughly enmeshed in Manhattan's downtown art scene in the early 1960s. For three weeks starting in January 1961, they substituted for Freddie Redd's quartet in the Living Theatre's production of *The Connection*, an experimental veritas play written by Jack Gelber that depicts a group of heroin-addicted jazz musicians waiting for their connection to return with the dope; in the drama of the play, they are simultaneously being filmed by a documentary film crew. Redd—a pianist and composer of *The Connection*'s music—and his ensemble were also cast members, and they played music, at Gelber's request, in the style of Charlie Parker.[60] Taylor's group played his original music, their abstract sound possibly more aligned with Gelber's experimentalism and the Living Theater's decade-long programming of avant-garde works.[61]

They were concurrently, on January 9–10, at Tommy Nola's Penthouse Sound Studios in Midtown Manhattan for a session coproduced by Hentoff and Neidlinger that would be released decades later.[62] Each date had a different ensemble configuration; on January 9 it was Shepp, Taylor, Neidlinger, and Denis Charles, and on the 10th it was veteran trumpeter Clark Terry, saxophonist Steve Lacy, trombonist Roswell Rudd, baritone saxophonist Charles Davis, Neidlinger, and Billy Higgins. This would be the last recording of Taylor's original trio, their disbanding after five years of collaboration brought about by months without work and Neidlinger's legal troubles. Neidlinger remembered "Cell Walk for Celeste," one of the tracks from the January 9 date, as best capturing the group's creative peak because of the level of cohesion they achieved and Taylor's compositional prowess. "This is not just a regular jazz chart," Neidlinger remembered. "[There] are real *parts* for everyone. Cecil, as a matter of fact, taught the drum part by rote to Denis Charles. They play in unison a lot in this piece, and at the time Denis didn't read music."[63]

That unison can be heard in the first three minutes of "Cell Walk for Celeste," where the group collectively play through a series of discrete motivic cells that function as abstract melodic shapes or gestures, where contour and direction take precedent over specific and individual note choice. The synchronicity here is not perfect: Taylor and Neidlinger improvise antiphonally against Shepp and Charles, blurring any perceivable distinction between predetermined (or precomposed) material and improvisation. At just over three minutes into the track the group transitions into a lengthy episode of collective heterophonic improvisation (▶ 03:13) over a common pulse (i.e., *time, no changes*), slipping in and out of phase. Toward the end (▶ 09:30) Neidlinger and Charles "trade eights" with each other, a call-and-response technique that, in conventional modern jazz performance, signals the end of the solo section and a return to the head melody. Taylor's group does not return to the opening material and instead plays through a series of closing precomposed motifs (▶ 10:46) distinct from the ideas introduced at the top. This is an example of Taylor's modular approach to asymmetrical structural design, where a performance is composed of cells or segments of thematic or motivic material that are plotted out and played through in variable and improvisatory fashion. "Cindy's Main Mood" is the clearest example of the group's heterophonic collective improvisation in fluid, unmetered musical time; the musicians spontaneously invent melodic sound in dynamic motion around each other in a way that mimics dancers traversing a stage. According to Hentoff's liner notes, the performance was extemporized at the session, and Neidlinger later noted that it was dedicated to Cynthia Clark, a "great American dancer" who worked with Erick Hawkins, a former member of the Martha Graham Company.[64]

By the end of summer, Taylor's regular trio had dissolved. Neidlinger, struggling with addiction, had been arrested and had his cabaret card revoked, which prevented him from working in nightclubs, and Charles eventually moved on for lack of work. "For Cecil, the breakup of a band is a far more serious matter than it is for any other leader, with the exception of such similarly individualistic composers as Thelonious Monk and Ornette Coleman," wrote Spellman. "Most of his sidemen admit that it takes a minimum of three years of steady rehearsal to fully assimilate his music. Cecil's approach to group improvisation is so demanding that it usually requires a thorough re-evaluation for the musicians." Neidlinger remembered the group's disbanding coming at a time when they were just beginning to relax on the bandstand, "to really make music with Cecil instead of just following along. We were just getting to the point where we could make a real contribution. If we'd been together for the whole summer, the results would have been fantastic."[65]

Taylor was invited to record a session for Impulse!, a subsidiary of Atlantic Records, on October 10, 1961. He recorded three pieces with two slightly different groups, "Pots" and "Bulbs" with a quintet and "Mixed" with a septet; the quintet had Jimmy Lyons on alto saxophone, Shepp on tenor, Henry Grimes on bass, and Sunny Murray on drums, and the septet had the addition of Ted Curson on trumpet and Rudd on trombone. "Pots" begins like "Cell Walk for Celeste" recorded months earlier: a series of precomposed shapes or gestures played by Taylor and the two saxophonists, which, according to Shepp, he had them learn by ear.[66] Afterward the quartet transitions into heterophonic collective improvisation over a pulse (i.e., *time, no changes*). The kinetic interplay between Grimes, the bassist, and Murray, the drummer, builds upon the fluid playing methods of Taylor's former trio, and the intensity of the overlayed activity of the ensemble creates the illusion of a fast tempo. However, in the absence of metric time, the density of the aggregate texture is more a fluid mass of surging and receding waves of instrumental sound.

"Mixed" is a series of predetermined, orchestrated sections—labeled (for the reader's listening purposes) ABB^{1}C—played through and returned to in reverse (CB^{1}BA) after two episodes of collective improvisation that vary in orchestration. The series of four cells in "A" foreground the two brass instruments and the rhythm section: each cell has its own unique shape (contour and character), and the group repeats each cell several times before moving on. Notably, Grimes plays through the entire performance on his bow (*arco*), which lends to the overall fluid sensibility of the performance—an un-metered slurry of free and coordinated sound. The next part, "B," begins for the saxophones (at ▶ 01:15) with Lyons's rhapsodic melody and, following this, Shepp with one of his own. After Shepp (▶ 01:52), the two saxophones play an orchestrated passage ("B1") that resembles the previous section, har-monically and gesturally. Then suddenly, at "C" (▶ 02:43), the full ensemble plays through a series of four orchestrated cells, each repeated several times, and Murray maintains the pulse. Following that are two episodes of collec-tive improvisation (▶ 04:02), the first featuring one pair of "mixed" horns, Lyons and Rudd, with the rhythm section and then (▶ 05:21) with Shepp and Curson. Underneath the collective improvisation, Grimes and Taylor whisper each cell of "C" underneath the freer improvisations of the other four musicians, thus maintaining a faint outline of an underlying organizational structure.

Episodes of heterophonic collective improvisations in "Mixed" are a sonic texture of fluid heterogeneous simultaneity. They end (at ▶ 06:44) when the whole septet returns to the fully orchestrated cells of "C." The remaining sections introduced at the start are then played in reverse order. These dif-ferent modules presumably can be reordered for every new performance—they are swappable parts of a structure in which their sequence can be arrived at in the moment, improvisationally. "Mixed" is an example of the "extended form" that Williams and other writers identified as characteristic of jazz's *new thing.* "Pots," "Bulbs," and "Mixed" were compiled into an LP titled *Into the Hot* and credited to the Gil Evans Orchestra along with three other tracks—Evans's arrangements of pieces by John Carisi—that were recorded in September and early October 1961. Lyons, speaking to Spellman, remarked:

> Sometimes Cecil writes his charts out, sometimes not. I dig it more when he doesn't. I don't know how to say this, but we get like a singing thing going when he teaches us the tunes off the piano. It has to do with the way Cecil accompanies. He has scales, patterns, and tunes that he uses, and the soloist is supposed to use these things. But you can take it out. If you go into your own thing Cecil will follow you there. But you have to know where the tune is supposed to go, and if you take it there another way than the way Cecil outlined it, then that's cool with Cecil. That's the main thing I've learned with Cecil, the music has to come from within and not from any charts.[67]

Taylor spent the next year with only sporadic local gigs, but in November 1962 he embarked on his first European tour with a new quartet that he began calling his Unit. They spent seven weeks abroad, mostly in Scandinavia, performing in Stockholm's Gyllene Cirkeln (Golden Circle) on November 2.[68] Bassist Grimes, who had been playing with Taylor since Neidlinger's departure, is absent from this and subsequent dates on the tour, replaced by Kurt Lindgren. The extant bootleg recording of this date contains only three tracks: "Flamingo" and "What's New," two frequently recorded popular songs from the 1940s that the group approaches abstractly, and a fully heterophonic fourteen-minute performance titled "Spontaneous Improvisation" that begins with Lyons, Taylor, Lindgren, and Murray that, about halfway through, reduces to only the rhythm section. The piano that Taylor is playing is conspicuously out of tune, and though his improvisation with Lindgren and Murray is characteristically kinetic and stream of consciousness, he frequently hammers out tone clusters in the most out-of-tune areas on the piano, as if to make a point.

Weeks later the group was in Copenhagen, performing at the Café Montmartre without a bassist (probably because no viable replacement for Grimes was available) and with Taylor on another out-of-tune piano. A recording of one night at the Montmartre, November 23, was commercially released by the Danish label Debut and captures performances of five of Taylor's original pieces: "Trance," "Lena," "Call," "D Trad, That's What," and "Nefertiti, the Beautiful One Has Come." The group plays through the standard "What's New" as they did "Flamingo" in Sweden: Lyons abstracts the familiar melody, and Taylor and the other musicians improvise around it, collectively exploding the tune's conventional thirty-two-bar structure into a charged flight of fancy. After a vamp at just over a minute into the recording, the group transitions into an episode of heterophonic improvisation over a central pulse (i.e., *time, no changes*).

Spontaneity and emotional immediacy—the freedom for musicians to play something based on how they feel—within the structural parameters of a piece is one of the directives that apparently guided Taylor's Unit, and "Lena" from the Montmartre recording is a clear example of this. Taylor begins the performance solo, playing each of the piece's three motivic cells before repeating the entire sequence as Lyons and Murray begin to improvise. Traces of the cell-sequence structure are heard in Taylor's playing as Lyons carries on. Afterward, when Taylor is left to improvise with Murray (▶ 02:28), which they do in a close heterophonic exchange, traces of the cells can still be heard in the piano's middle register, played by Taylor's left hand. The performance ends with a completely new motif (▶ 05:34) that the trio plays through and repeats once before dissolving to a close with a small coda. The audience's applause heard at the end is tepid and cautious.

"An Outlaw Art"

Taylor's group returned to New York from their European tour in January 1963. Work was still sparse; apart from a high-profile concert in Lincoln Center's Philharmonic Hall in December, the group scraped by with occasional jobs in Manhattan's downtown cafés and were virtually ignored by the city's better-paying venues. Taylor took advantage of these inadvertent breaks from performing and recording to study and work on his poetry, supporting himself, as so many other musicians did, with various odd jobs.[69]

When Taylor's work did receive coverage in the press, writers continued to emphasize modern classical music's influence on his style. Saxophonist Don Heckman, *Down Beat*'s de facto avant-garde jazz analyst, wrote about Taylor's unique ability "to shift from music with the textural densities of Debussy's *Preludes* to a scattershot pointillism like Schoenberg's *Five Piano Pieces* (Op. 23) and just as easily return to down-home, barrelhouse playing. Displaced rhythmic motives and accents, dramatic ostinatos, frequent polytonality and Cowell-like tone clusters, [nontonal] rhythmic punctuations in the style of Stravinsky—all these are part of Taylor's improvisatory style."[70] This particular vein of musical modernism is what makes Taylor different from other jazz avant-gardists, Heckman argues, and Taylor's erudition has only contributed to his lack of popularity. Like other avant-gardists, Heckman writes, Taylor's rejection of tonal harmony simply will not attract audiences to nightclubs, making his commercial prospects quite grim. That sentiment of aesthetic failure was echoed by Whitney Balliett, who reviewed Taylor's appearance at Philharmonic Hall in early January 1964 on a bill shared with Coltrane's quintet and Art Blakey's Jazz Messengers. Coltrane's and Taylor's groups displayed "a wildness and passion that came close to holocaust; in places their playing was supramusical, or perhaps amusical, for it took on distinct and disturbing human characteristics—defiance, anger, and bitterness." Taylor's Unit, with Albert Ayler on tenor saxophone, played "just one number," which lasted close to an hour, an experience Balliett found "abrasive."[71]

In April 1964, the Unit performed in Vermont at Bennington College's "Jazz Weekend" as part of a program that included a poetry reading by Baraka and various musical performances. Taylor was invited to participate in a panel discussion on the concluding day, and moderating that panel was Frederick Koenig, a professor of social science, and composer Louis Calabro—both faculty at Bennington—in conversation with Taylor and the composer and arranger Hall Overton. The discussion, which was captured on tape, for which there is a transcript, is charged. Taylor spars with Calabro and Overton for what he perceived to be their bias against nonnotated and free improvised music that stemmed from their subconscious Western cultural chauvinism. Overton insists that notation is more rigorous than improvisation because it entails forethought and revision, while the latter requires only intuition, albeit one that is unique to every musician because of their personal background and lived experience that they channel "in the moment," through improvisation.

Taylor then interrupts Overton. "That's what we are and all we can ever be: what we are at the moment," he scolds, and argues that there is no audible difference between notated and nonnotated music. "So that if a cat chooses to improvise, which is, you know, a technical mastery of certain materials put in the framework of certain forms . . . [you] cannot tell me—you'll have to prove it to me—that, when after twenty years of playing, that Charlie Parker didn't play the Blues as many ways as was possible within his experience. And if he had sat down to write this it wouldn't have been any more valid, because, in the final analysis, what we heard was what we heard." Taylor accuses Overton of claiming that improvisers do not use their intelligence as much or as rigorously as composers of notated music, and that this kind of bias is endemic among white composers, musicians, and listeners whose only reference for musical erudition is classical music.[72]

Taylor tries to explain to the panel that his music has form, but not the kind that they would find in nineteenth-century European music or a popular song. Like Coleman, Taylor insists, he draws from black vernacular forms like the blues for inspiration and ultimately seeks to create new, expansive forms that push musicians beyond their ingrained, reflexive musical knowledge and toward a raw and more intuitive kind of sonic invention. "In other words, we're no longer thinking in terms of [common melodic intervals], we're thinking in terms of all combinations of notes—whether they be seconds, groups of seconds, groups of fourths, groups of fifths, or just a-musical [*sic*] sounds. Like this [bangs on table], perhaps making that music." Calabro responds dismissively, saying that Coleman's concept of form is actually quite simple: "[Coleman's ensemble] play some kind of riffs together and then go off on a long improvisation and then maybe come back to give it some kind of semblance of a form." He asserts that composers of "serious music" have been writing music with unconventional intervals, harmony, and sounds for "a very long time," and that these elements have only recently made their way into jazz. "You see you can't help it," Taylor replies with justified indignation. "You just can't help it. Now, in serious music, he says. Ah, you mean I'm not serious. . . . [You] mean Ornette isn't serious in what he's doing?"

To drive his point home, Taylor lists the educational barriers faced by black musicians and points out that, were it not for prohibitive social and economic factors, such concepts might not have taken forty years to cross over. He insists that black experimentalist musicians like himself use these abstract devices differently from European and Euro-American modernists because of a different cultural "impetus": "We are the inheritors of all the great civilizations before us—and we are just building on them, that's all. We're doing our job. What I'm saying is: let me do my job, but don't shackle me with your social and your thought prejudices by saying things are semantic—when they are really socially-oriented." According to the transcript, Taylor's comments elicited hostile shouts from the audience, and the event seems to unravel after that. Inadvertently serving as spokesman for the jazz avant-garde, Taylor, whose style was explained in music periodicals as a product of his conservatory training and classical influences, is put in a position to defend the legitimacy of free improvisation and more intuitive playing—as a creative process not devoid of intelligence and forethought. This discussion, like so much of Taylor's coverage in the press, illustrates the kind of confusion around—and acrimony directed at—Taylor's nonnormative sound, which occupied a vexed intermediary space between the abstract and the vernacular, jazz and classical, black and white. It also documents Taylor's indignation and fury.

The Unit continued to perform for the next year mostly in Downtown Manhattan in lieu of recordings or tours, but prospects slowly began to improve. He brought his Unit and a separate group (a quintet featuring his former bassist, Neidlinger) to perform at Judson Hall in late December 1965. The Unit performed in Manhattan's Town Hall in March 1966 and then the Newport Jazz Festival and the Village Vanguard (one of New York's most renowned jazz clubs) in July. In September, Taylor's Unit had a series of engagements at the Village Gate, another prominent New York club, one of which was scheduled to be filmed as part of a television program titled *Jazz: The Experimenters*, produced by Jerome Toobin, James Perrin, and Clair Roskam for the New Jersey public television network WNET.[73] Art D'Lugoff, proprietor of the Village Gate, author Albert Murray, and Martin Williams served as musical consultants. Featured in the film are the ensembles of bassist/composer Charles Mingus and Taylor's Unit. The program's hosts were author Ralph Ellison (whose novel *Invisible Man* won the 1953 National Book Award for Fiction), who co-wrote the script, and Williams.

The film opens with Mingus's group playing his piece "The Art of Art Tatum and Frederick Webster." After the band plays a few bars, a male voice-over is heard:

> Charles Mingus is one of the most highly regarded creators of modern jazz. But this program is about a controversial music, sometimes strange in sound, unusual in structure, intellectual, often un-danceable, un-singable, serious. It is considered by

some critics a new flowering of jazz and by others a dead-end in the art. It is the jazz that came to prominence in the 1950s.

In addition to Charles Mingus, this program will present Cecil Taylor, one of the most radical jazzmen to gain international attention. Our host is the distinguished novelist and social critic Ralph Ellison, author of *Invisible Man*. Jazz critic Martin Williams will comment on the new jazz and the experimenters. This program takes place at the Village Gate, a New York nightclub that specializes in contemporary jazz.

Mingus's ensemble stops and Ellison begins a monologue in which he contextualizes the new experimental music represented by Mingus and Taylor within the arc of jazz history:

In the beginning, jazz has [*sic*] been nothing if not experimental, and the experimental attitude sprang from its very creators. As practitioners of an outlaw art, jazz musicians could create free of the concerns of status and respectability. This freedom was expressed in their choice of instruments, and their playful manipulation of sound, and a wild freedom with harmony and counterpoint, and a ceaseless search for rhythmical variety.

Jazz grew from an attempt to express with musical instruments the sound and the style of the Negro American voice, as raised in prayer, protest, shout, and song. It was an attempt to humanize the world in terms of sound: an effort made with musical means to impose the Negro American sense of time upon the larger society and upon the world of nature. Early jazz was by no means an intellectual music; it was, however, marked by a highly-conscious sense of its sources and its own tradition. While it drew from the European musical tradition, it was instinctively aware that its goals were different.

How does a new experimentalism differ from the old? For one thing, jazz today exists in a climate wherein a certain piety has developed towards the goals of so-called serious music; wherein experimentation is less a means towards achieving expressiveness than a value in itself. And for some Negro musicians it has become a musical route to social respectability, and to a wide acceptance among the cult of jazz intellectuals. For the most serious of these composers, however, the breaking down of the wall between jazz and modern European music has posed a problem of absorbing that music without losing touch with their own tradition. This has created a clash of styles, and one may say that the main motive of the experimentalism [*sic*] is to absorb—to Americanize—the most recent developments of European classical music. The music of Cecil Taylor is, I think, the most interesting illustration of that struggle.

Here again, Taylor's experimentalism is understood in terms of its proximity to European classical music. Furthermore, Ellison explains jazz as an outgrowth of a uniquely African American experience and culture, but that essence runs the risk of dilution in the new experimenters' apparent embrace and interpolation of modern classical techniques. Despite Taylor's insistence elsewhere that his music was firmly rooted in the black vernacular, Ellison believed the source of abstraction was clear. Ellison's take on Taylor contrasts with Williams's comments just minutes later, after Taylor's group performs "Number One"—a freely improvised (heterophonic) piece with Lyons, Grimes, and Murray where Taylor, while standing, plays the piano strings directly with his fingers, a vibraphone mallet, and a small metallic wire basket (Figure 4.4).

Williams provides brief comments on the new music as he introduces each group:

> By now, the radical innovations of the 1940s in jazz—the music of Charlie Parker and Dizzy Gillespie, which sounded so startling when one first heard it—is a part of the mainstream of the music. And it's quite evident now, in the 60s, that there is a new kind of jazz—that jazz has its avant-garde just like any other art. It was evident, actually, in the music of Cecil Taylor; quite evident by 1958. And Taylor's music has certainly continued to develop since then. Cecil Taylor has attended an American academy of music, he knows twentieth-century European composition, but he also knows the jazz tradition thoroughly and he approaches the music of Duke Ellington and Thelonious Monk with a real reverence. His is not typical of the avant-garde at all because Cecil Taylor's is a very individual music, and many players in the avant-garde are equally individual. But if I were to say anything about what they all have in common, it would be something like this: jazz players today approach improvisation with a new kind of freedom, if you will.

Williams goes on to explain that what separates avant-gardists like Taylor from their predecessors is their free invention, which they accomplish without any reference to an overarching melody or chord progression. Players of the new music, Williams concludes, wish to be freed from these inhibiting things.

In the next scene Taylor is standing behind the piano, sunglasses obscuring his eyes and a small microphone hanging from his neck. He begins a monologue before the group begins to play "Octagonal Skirt and Fancy Pants," a piece designed like his other originals, with motivic cells bookending an episode of collective improvisation. Staring directly into the camera, Taylor explains his process in his own words. He introduces the term "anacrusis"

Figure 4.4 Two screenshots from WNET's *Jazz: The Experimenters*, shot in 1965. (Above) Cecil Taylor playing the harp of the piano directly with his fingers, a mallet, and a metallic basket. (Below) Taylor with his ensemble, featuring Jimmy Lyons (alto saxophone), Henry Grimes (bass), and Sunny Murray (drums). Courtesy of WNET/ THIRTEEN Productions, LLC.

(used in both poetry and music to describe unstressed syllables or notes before the formal start of a piece) to describe an aspect of the piece's formal design: the motivic cells that buttress the ensemble's collective heterophonic improvisation. With prosaic and performative flair, Taylor's introduction is itself an anacrusis that precedes the musical action:

> Music is the building of sound structures. The piece that you're about to hear contains an anacrusis complex: the first statement, the shape of what is to be—its form, the possibility of the other. We will then proceed through areas which contain melodic and percussive divisions. The unifying link of the piece will be its rhythm, which will consist of regular and irregular measurements of coexisting bodies of sound. The philosophical premise [that] this music is based on is that man begins a transliteration of the mean fact towards symbolic representation when mind and body move, recognizing their singularity, therefore their unity, and therefore their sanity. The question is: were the economic and social factors determining an artist's existence—those which permit the expression of time, through time—to one whose consumption is unlimited, or were they the producers for others?

The Unit then plays "Octagonal Skirt and Fancy Pants," after which Williams, without missing a beat, reintroduces Mingus's group.

5

Anti Jazz, Anti Music

On the cold afternoon of February 21, 1965, El-Hajj Malik El-Shabazz, formerly known as Malcolm X, was murdered as he stood on the stage of the Audubon Ballroom in Harlem. He was delivering a speech as the spokesperson for the Association for Afro-American Unity, a role he assumed after his turn away, in exile, from the Nation of Islam. His notoriety as the NOI's firebrand minister was cemented in the public sphere after the national scandal caused by his comments on John F. Kennedy's assassination, which he referred to as a case of "the chickens . . .[coming] home to roost" in a rally at the Manhattan Center only a week after the incident. Reprinted by *The New York Times* in December 1963, the remark was part of a bigger critique of the violent U.S. campaign in Africa and Asia.[1] El-Shabazz focused specifically on Vietnam and Kennedy's silence about the assassination of South Vietnamese president Ngô Đình Diệm and his brother, as well as that of Patrice Lumumba and African American activist Medgar Evers in Mississippi. His callous sardonicism about the president's death ("Being an old farm boy myself, chickens coming home to roost never did make me sad; they've always made me glad") and his public renunciations of other black leaders, including Dr. Martin Luther King, Jr., for their seemingly meek responses to racist and imperialist violence made El-Shabazz a folk hero among disaffected black urban dwellers in and outside of the Islamic community. In his death, El-Hajj Malik El-Shabazz became a martyr: a symbol of fearless indignation in the face of white supremacy and its integral place in American state apparatuses, of liberation, self-determination, resistance, and black pride. More specific still, El-Shabazz embodied an uncompromising and heroic kind of black masculinity, one that was perhaps most poignantly articulated by actor and activist Ossie Davis's eulogy, delivered at El-Shabazz's funeral, in which he extolled the former minister as "our own black shining Prince."[2]

Only two weeks after El-Shabazz's murder, Archie Shepp also eulogized him. "Malcolm, Malcolm, Semper Malcolm" was one of two last tracks for his next album for Impulse! Records, *Fire Music*, which Shepp had almost completed. Shepp begins the piece by reciting an unmetered poem, and bassist David Izenzon freely improvises along with the text:

Change. Kwami Coleman, Oxford University Press. © Oxford University Press 2025.
DOI: 10.1093/9780197780121.003.0006

> It's not what it seems
> A tune perhaps
> Burned, whistled while even America
> listened
> We play
> but we aren't always
> dumb
> We are murdered
> in amphitheaters
> on the podium of the Audubon.

The remainder of the recording is a collective free improvisation shared between Shepp on tenor saxophone, Izenzon on bass, and J. C. Moses on drums. The trio's momentum jolts backward and forward, rushing and receding in fluid and unmetered time, and they occasionally build tension with a shared unison riff before slipping apart again to something more disjointed and fragmented. Shepp plays long, languid melodies that are interrupted with short swoops, yelps, and squeals. The performance ends with a short riff of a few punctuated notes—a few gunshots, maybe—played by the three musicians in unison that disappear as suddenly as they appeared. Then the sound stops. "Malcolm, Malcolm, Semper Malcolm" is less a dirge or mournful homage than a blunt and defiant statement. It's not pleasant, nor is it beautiful, but it is raw and potent and gets cut short, just like the life of the incendiary black messiah that El-Shabazz had now become only days after his death.

This chapter explores free improvisation as a method for cathartic and affectively charged performances in the work of more established black improvising musicians who collaborated with younger or less professionally established experimentalist musicians. My goal is to show that intergenerational collaborative experimentation—with new sounds and techniques— pushed these established musicians into increasingly abstract and uncharted creative territory. These forays into the *new thing* (free heterophonic improvisation) went beyond the aesthetic and ideological borders that self-appointed guardians of modern jazz erected around the *new thing* at a particularly charged political moment. Musicians like Sonny Rollins, Miles Davis, and John Coltrane each developed new works by experimenting with and hiring "avant-garde" musicians. I explain how these experiments were largely maligned in the music press of the mid-1960s because of musicians' evocation of and overt statements on political issues. Shepp, Cecil Taylor, Abbey Lincoln, and Max Roach, to name only a few, did not shy away from commenting on race and racism, economic exploitation in the music industry, and the ways in which these forces shaped their creative work and lives. Consequently, by 1966 factions in the national and international music press interpreted the *new thing*'s abstraction and discordancy as a protest against jazz modernity and white people at large.

This new perspective on the *new thing* in print media emerged at a historical moment when American liberalism and all its purported cultural and political triumphs were perceived as being under threat. The "Great Society" policies that Kennedy's successor Lyndon B. Johnson pursued to support free market capitalism and liberal democracy—the bedrock of American postwar modernity—were being "attacked" by unruly urban blacks and multiracial student coalitions on college campuses while the nation was suspended in a nuclear stalemate with the Soviet Union. Johnson pressed Congress to increase funding for education, healthcare, nature conservation, urban renewal, and infrastructure (his "War on Poverty" campaign) while J. Edgar Hoover's FBI and its secret counterintelligence program (COINTELPRO) targeted individuals and dismantled organizations deemed to be enemies of the state. Student antiwar groups, community and mutual aid groups, civil rights activists, and "Mohammadian" sects like the Nation of Islam were infiltrated, plowing a deep division between the status quo, represented by the American state, and "the people." I argue that the backlash against the *new thing* in print media was paralleled in the state's pushback against the rebellion and dissent signified by the race riots conflagrating across the United States. For some of these writers, modern jazz (just like American liberalism itself) was under siege, and their critique of the *new thing* reflected that defensive position. However, for musicians, like those engaged in the struggle for a new and more just world, change was inevitable.

Rollins Finds Cherry

Seemingly out of nowhere, star saxophonist Sonny Rollins (b. 1930) decided in 1959, at the height of his critical acclaim, to go on hiatus. He had recently become something of a standard-bearer in modern jazz; Gunther Schuller had praised his "logical" solos in the inaugural issue of the short-lived *Jazz Review* the previous year, and all the hard work he put into recording, performing, and touring after surmounting addiction and the 1955 prison sentence it led to had paid off.[3] Still, Rollins's personal journals from this period divulge his search for creative influences and strategies that would lead not only to artistic growth but also to becoming a better human being.[4] He devoted himself in these years away from public performances to spiritual introspection and musical experimentation. He was preoccupied with how new concepts and techniques might alter the way sound is produced on his instrument, the metaphysics of timbre, and the impact that mental and physical fitness has on a musician's sound. In this quest for a more holistic and creatively fertile creative practice and a break from New York's unrelenting and unhealthy nightlife and club scene, Rollins pivoted from a modern jazz insider to a deliberate (if temporary) outsider.

It was during this hiatus that Rollins maintained a daily routine of practicing over a watery void on the Williamsburg Bridge, close to his apartment in the Lower East Side of Manhattan—a ritual that quickly became a topic of jazz lore in magazines.[5] Rollins's hiatus also overlapped with Ornette Coleman's residency at the Five Spot and John Coltrane's rise as a star soloist and bandleader outside of Miles Davis's quintet. Coltrane, to whom Rollins was often compared, recorded an album for Atlantic Records with Don Cherry, Charlie Haden, and Ed Blackwell (three members of Coleman's quartet) in 1960, the same year that Coleman recorded *Free Jazz*. It was released years later under the title *John Coltrane & Don Cherry: The Avant-Garde*. Coltrane's work with Cherry draws an interesting parallel to Rollins's collaboration with the younger trumpeter in the following years.

Rollins effectively ended his hiatus by securing a coveted $90,000 royalty contract with RCA-Victor in early 1962, recording first *The Bridge*, an homage to his special practice space, with a new quartet.[6] After several gigs and another album, *What's New*, Rollins formed a new quartet with bassist Bob Cranshaw and Coleman collaborators Billy Higgins and Cherry for a series of gigs at the Village Gate in July 1962. Proprietor Art D'Lugoff had just renovated the venue to accommodate live recordings, an upgrade that RCA-Victor took advantage of by taping the first night of Rollins's run, Friday, July 27, releasing it commercially as *Sonny Rollins: Our Man in Jazz*.[7] Rollins's intent for these shows seems to have been fundamentally experimental, an opportunity to test out some of the new concepts that he had spent the previous two years exploring.

My understanding of Rollins's self-directed study during those two years comes from his manuscript archives deposited in Harlem at the New York Public Library's Schomburg Center for Research in Black Culture. These papers—a collection of song manuscripts and lead sheets, study notes, literary references, thought fragments scrawled on note and manuscript paper, notated melodic patterns, and inspirational and often philosophical quotes written on scraps of looseleaf, notepad, and manuscript paper—offer a partial glimpse into Rollins's dedicated creative routine fueled by curiosity and autodidacticism. He wrote out unconventional and highly chromatic melodic patterns to practice and harmonic superimpositions to be deployed while improvising, stockpiling a mental arsenal of improvisational methods and possibilities to keep at the ready.[8] He also wrote instructive passages directed at technical improvement and to enhancing his creative thinking; strategies that ultimately stemmed from an improvement in his mental and physical health. Taken as a whole, this archive serves as a "vision board" of the ideas and aspirations behind the new creative turn Rollins took with Cherry by his side in 1962.

Rollins's *new thing* was focused on sound in the abstract, as an esoteric material with different properties and characteristics depending on the musician's inflection and intent. The "color" (timbre) of the sound has synesthetic equivalences in optics as a property of light, and it is contingent on the pitch and register by which it is emitted. Rollins, in his personal notes, appears to have been deeply committed to developing a synesthetic approach to improvisation whereby each of the twelve tones of the chromatic scale corresponds to a color, but his notes don't make clear the extent to which that correspondence is literal or metaphorical (Figure 5.1).[9] This synesthetic sound concept seems to have served Rollins and Cherry mostly as a source of inspiration to draw from in the flow of improvisation, based on the vibe or energy of that moment—an expansive, chromatic spectrum of sonic possibility that exists beyond the boundaries of a singular key. This ethos of transcendence extended to Rollins's affinity for the Japanese Shakuhachi flute (which he drew illustrations of and wrote about in his personal notes), his investigations into Eastern philosophy and culture, and attention to cosmic transcendence:

ALL TIME RHYTHM AND HARMONY ARE PULSATING SOUNDING RESOUNDING AND HAPPENING ACCORDING TO THE GRAND SYMPHONY WHICH IS CONSTANTLY BEING PLAYED . . . ALL SOUNDS WHEN DISCERNED IN THIS CONTEXT ARE RHYTHMICALLY AND HARMONICALLY INVOLVED AND FIT.[10]

Given the conceptual space that Rollins's archival materials suggests he was in, his collaboration with musicians exploring a more abstract approach to musical sound and improvisation for his dates at the Village Gate comes as no surprise.

The recordings of those gigs capture Rollins and the ensemble engaging in free, heterophonic improvisation. The band's rendition of Rollins's original "Oleo" during their opening set at the Gate, on July 27, is an example of this approach. It begins with a heterophonic dialog between Rollins and Cherry with no discernible key or meter, then they quickly stammer through the familiar

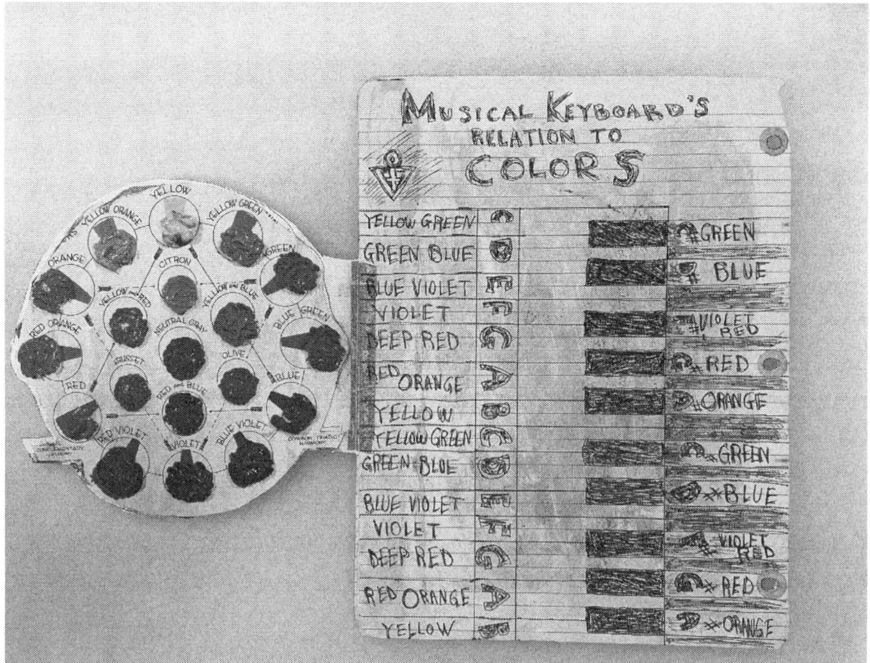

Figure 5.1 An illustration showing a correspondence between a nineteen-tone color wheel and a twelve-tone chromatic scale delineated across a two-octave keyboard. From Sonny Rollins's notebook archive at the Schomburg Center for Black Culture, Manuscripts, Archives, and Rare Books Division, New York Public Library.

melody as if to get it out of the way and resume their collective improvisation. Cherry drops out and leaves Rollins to improvise freely above Cranshaw (as the bassist plays through the tune's form) and Higgins (maintaining the pulse). Higgins stokes the intensity of the other musicians' playing with propulsive energy from the drum set. The three drift in and out of phase with each other and, while aligned in an intuited, synergistic way, they do not always coalesce around the centralized pulse, thus giving the performance a fluid-like quality. Their collectivized free playing on a recognizable tune defamiliarizes it for the musicians and audience alike, and they employ this same strategy in each performance of "Oleo" over the four nights at the Gate. Rollins commented on the last take on the Sunday night set in his personal notes: "[W]e played Oleo and we thus concluded that set—short - but - sweet.—the lessons to be learned are that we as a group were able to function in a collective intuitive effort. Producing improvised music, or rather <u>LOGICAL</u> <u>MUSIC</u>.—SUNDAY EVE. 1 complete composition was performed in the INTUITIVE, LOGICAL MANNER." The "complete composition" Rollins mentions was one of several unnamed originals the group performed that evening, for which Rollins drew up a detailed set of directions:

FORMAT OF COMPOSITION:
1. ALL BEGIN TOGETHER
2. THROUGHOUT COMPOSITION 2 INSTRUMENTS PLAY TOGETHER. E.G., SONNY + BOB PLAY TOGETHER AFTER START. THEN SONNY + BOB ARE JOINED FOR A DISSONANCE BY DONALD WHICH THEN LEADS TO THE DONALD SONNY DUET WHICH INCIDENTALLY SHOULD SUGGEST A DIFFERENT TIMBRE THAN THE 'DISSONANT "CARRY OVER" 3-PART SECTION.'

The term <u>RELEASE</u> of the music presupposes the <u>fact</u> that the music is [already] in existence. We then attune ourselves by intuition and a form of meditation into and with the music so that we become absorbed into its essence. Closing of the eyes is a form of shutting out the objective faculties (seeing) which helps to increase the other faculties such as those necessary to produce our music.—Keep each timbre started by someone complete onto itself before changing sound. Donald was guilty of joining in with a different timbre than that which was already in progress.[11]

Here, Rollins expands on a point he makes elsewhere in his personal notes, that sound—and thus music—are everywhere and ever-present, and that the musician needs only to channel this universe of sound in the act of performance. Rollins's approach here is no doubt influenced by the Coleman quartet's loose and spontaneous performance method; now working with those same musicians, Rollins seeks a deeply intuited music that draws from esoteric knowledge existing beyond tonal harmony. However, that spiritual connection, Rollins insists in his notes, should extend beyond the individual and toward a more metaphysical harmony construed by the collective. Because of this, musicians in the group must find and match each other's sound/color and creative energy before shifting into something new: that is what he felt Cherry did not do at some point on the Sunday gig.

Rollins's quartet played several free-improvised pieces in their sets at the Gate. The half-hour-long "Untitled Original B," from their fourth recorded set, begins with Rollins playing arpeggios that climb into the upper range of his horn, with Cherry following by stringing together fragmentary bursts of sound that spill through the air like rushed and incomplete sentences. The bass and drums enter after the horns with a vamp; Cranshaw orbits around on F-sharp, and Higgins, using his ride cymbal, establishes a firm, swinging pulse. In this tune, each of the four musicians has a moment to improvise "a cappella" for a length of time before the others enter and initiate an episode of collective improvisation—one that may build from the previous musician's vibe. Sometimes an individual's solo spontaneously evolves into a duet, as when Higgins's march motif is jumped on by Cherry, who almost imitates a bugle call (▶ 24:34). This alternating solo-collective arrangement brings into relief the generative potential of free improvisation, where musicians engage in an abstract sonic dialog based in mutual deep listening and synergy. The freely improvised originals like this one, or "Untitled Original A #1" from the first night—where the musicians play freely and spontaneously over a bossa nova groove—are experiments in close, empathetic listening with the goal of producing a more unpredictable and intuited musical performance. Rollins also implodes other familiar tunes in his repertoire, including "Oleo," "Doxy" and "Love Walked In," and well-known originals like the calypso-tinged "St. Thomas."

Unsurprisingly, the critical establishment received Rollins's heterophonic sound/color music like the rest of the *new thing*: with reluctance and bewilderment. *Down Beat* critic and record producer Pete Welding, who championed Coleman's album *Free Jazz* upon its release, reviewed *Our Man in Jazz* for the magazine, noting that Rollins and the ensemble, in "an attempt to achieve the notable goal of complete spontaneity and collective freedom … have jettisoned order and formal discipline in favor of an approach stressing emotional continuity."[12] He underscored what he believed to be their "purposeless" musical meandering, which he found to be a chore to listen to. The magazine's readers subsequently pushed back against Welding's opinions in letters to the editor, but Welding's outsized platform as a staff writer overshadowed their concerns. His disregard of the veteran saxophonist's new sound is illustrative of how critics easily mistook or overlooked a process of sonic experimentation as inchoate and irrational music.[13] For Rollins's new band in 1962, improvisation was integrated into every part of the performance as part of a strategy of abstraction and defamiliarization in the service of new expressive possibilities.

Rollins's new band played a similar set a few days later, on August 7, after their engagement at the Gate concluded, in a public outdoor concert produced by the Lower Eastside Neighborhood Association and New York's local chapter of the American Federation of Musicians. It was the final concert in the series held at the East River Park Amphitheater, only a short walk from Rollins's Grand Street apartment. In January 1963, the band began a month-long European tour where they performed in this "freer" mode of collectively improvised performance in what Ekkehard Jost referred to as a "spontaneously evolving suite."[14] Rollins returned to New York in February, playing and recording with other younger experimentalist improvisers like bassist Henry

Grimes, drummer Charles Moffett, pianists Paul Bley and McCoy Tyner, and the veteran Coleman Hawkins in different group configurations.[15] "Rollins caused a stir at the recent benefit for the Village Aid and Service Center at the Village Gate," the editors of *Down Beat* wrote in early June 1963; "he appeared with Prince Lasha and altoist Sonny Simmons, along with Grimes and Moffett. The group played free, new thing collective jazz."[16] His personnel continued to change, recording with bassist David Izenzon, who was part of Coleman's trio, and Herbie Hancock and Ron Carter of Davis's quintet in 1964, and he explored further the possibilities of a collectively improvised "spontaneously evolving suite" in the following few years.

Coltrane's "Anti-Jazz" and *Ascension*

In the early 1960s, John Coltrane had been compared to Sonny Rollins often. Though he was four years younger, Rollins preceded Coltrane as Davis's star tenor player (working with the trumpeter from 1951 to 1957, with Coltrane from 1955 to 1960), and had gained recognition in the press as a virtuoso modernist slightly earlier.[17] After the release of *Giant Steps* in 1960, his first LP for Atlantic Records, critics began to take notice of the density—of notes and harmonies—and abstraction in Coltrane's music. In 1958, Bill Coss, then an editor at *Metronome* magazine reviewing the Newport Jazz Festival, referred to Coltrane's playing with Davis's group, somewhat contemptuously, as "mere sheets of sound" as a way to describe the torrent of notes the saxophonist draped over the songs' forms—a turn of phrase that critics would use repeatedly in the next several years as they struggled to grasp the saxophonist's maximalism.[18] The negative reception of Coltrane's increasing abstraction is epitomized by John Tynan, one of *Down Beat*'s editors. After catching Coltrane with Eric Dolphy in Los Angeles, Tynan questioned whether his abstract playing was instead evidence of an intent to create an anarchic "anti-jazz":

> Go ahead, call me reactionary. I happen to object to the musical nonsense currently being peddled in the name of jazz by John Coltrane and his acolyte, Eric Dolphy.
>
> At Hollywood's Renaissance Club recently, I listened to a horrifying demonstration of what appears to be a growing anti-jazz trend exemplified by these foremost proponents of what is termed avant-garde music. . . .
>
> It is my old-fashioned notion that there should be discernible rapport between soloist and rhythm section, that each should complement the other, transforming individual effort into a collective blend delivering what I have come to expect from good jazz—the elusive element, swing. Coltrane and Dolphy seem intent on

deliberately destroying this essence, this vital ingredient. They seem bent on pursuing an anarchistic course in their music that can best be termed anti-jazz.[19]

Whitney Balliett struck a similar tone in a 1963 piece titled "Anti-Music" for the *New Yorker,* where he lambastes the abstract music of the "talented" but misdirected reedist Jimmy Giuffre at a concert at Manhattan's Town Hall, sniping, "The avant-garde is the last refuge of the untalented. But it can also be a quicksand for the talented."[20]

These were years of searching and experimentation for Coltrane. Like Rollins, he studied and developed new approaches to improvisation that extended beyond tonal and harmonic conventions, a practice of exploration that was inspired or sustained by a devout spirituality and cosmological attunement. Coltrane was striving for a new creative plateau directed toward a transcendent music driven by a deeply intuitive and cathartic improvisatory group dynamic that might also inspire spiritual uplift in the listener. Since Coltrane's passing in 1967, these spiritual strivings have become a topic of research, liturgy, and deep lore, with the LP *A Love Supreme* of 1964 often cited as an apotheosis.[21] But an important step in Coltrane's latter heterophonic abstractions was his recording session for Atlantic Records with three members of Coleman's quartet (Cherry, Haden, and Blackwell) and bassist Percy Heath (who introduced Coleman to John Lewis in Los Angeles) in late June 1960.

Coltrane had just returned from Europe in what were his final shows as a member of Davis's small group, and this would be the first of two recording sessions (the second in early July) that Atlantic would release commercially seven years later under the retrospective title *The Avant-Garde.*[22] The music they recorded is heterophonic, where the musicians engage in a more decentralized ensemble texture driven by improvisatory exchange. A. B. Spellman wrote the LP's liner notes. The portentous significance of the session is, for Spellman, what makes it special: it's "important because it brings together musicians who do not ordinarily play together, representing as they do different corners of modern jazz," and it "catches these men and these ideas at a time when all the freshness of discovery was on them, with all the electricity of the exchange of genuinely new concepts of group and solo playing."[23]

Spellman highlights 1960 as a year that marks an important aesthetic turning point in jazz, when Thelonious Monk's abstractions had, it seemed, been internalized by a new crop of avant-gardists intent on "assaulting" the old guard on three major fronts—"harmonic (Coltrane), tonal (Cecil Taylor), and rhythmic-harmonic (Ornette Coleman)"—an apropos association given Coltrane's stint with Monk at the Five Spot Café in 1957.[24] That Spellman sees

Coltrane following in the path of avant-gardists like Taylor and Coleman speaks to the paradigm shift occurring in New York City after Coleman's premiere at the Five Spot the previous year, an event Spellman claims Coltrane attended. Coleman's impact on New York's scene opened new "possibilities in the liberation of the rhythm section [and] in the elimination of the gap between soloist and accompanist," a quality that Spellman sees Coltrane and the other musicians intent on re-creating in the studio.

Spellman's liner notes illuminate the exploratory nature of this session, where the veteran players (Coltrane and Heath, each a decade older than Cherry, born in 1936) sought out younger experimentalists. In the recollection of Reggie Workman (b. 1937), a bassist who recorded with Coltrane in 1961, musicians with similar or complementary artistic interests found each other on the road or working in New York and clustered together, studying, socializing, and collaborating with each other.[25] This exchange was mutually beneficial for both emergent and more established improvising musicians, and this exploratory kind of creative exchange was the generative force behind the *new thing*—an experimentalist ethos and sound that would direct the aesthetic paths of other established jazz modernists.

The Avant-Garde is a recording that documents an encounter between musicians of complementary, overlapping interests: for Coltrane and Heath, an opportunity to work with emergent musicians exploring new concepts in improvisation, and for Cherry, Haden, and Blackwell, a chance to record with two highly regarded, open-minded veterans. Reflective of the convergences that arose through intersecting networks of musicians in New York City and beyond, sessions like these are also the product of creative solidarity forged among musicians exploring new conceptual terrain.

Heath is singled out as the sole representation of the "old-guard" in Spellman's notes, though he mentions his appearance on Coleman's early Los Angeles recordings, where two of the tunes present on the current LP, "The Invisible" and "The Blessing," were first commercially released.[26] For Spellman, Heath, like Coltrane, was after "new patterns, structures and sounds which could provide an ever-opening release," and Spellman sees his collaboration with the younger members of Coleman's quartet as his catalyst. Despite this, Cherry, according to Spellman, still hears in Heath's playing a musician focusing more on chords, unlike the younger bassist Haden, who plays "more melody" and "tells a story." That transition from a more chordal to a more purely "melodic" approach to improvisational thinking is, for Spellman in retrospect, what makes the recording important, and is something that he sees Cherry playing a significant role in fomenting. He quotes Cherry's thoughts on their version of his original tune "Cherryco" to provide insight into their process: "*Cherryco* is the only really freely improvised tune on this date. We didn't play with any set chords, even though 'Trane went back to the changes in his solo."

The group plays through the tune's peculiar nine-bar melody three times before the first solo, with Blackwell's swung beat providing the pulse that scaffolds the arc of the melody. Both Cherry (▶ 00:32) and Coltrane (▶ 02:09) improvise with great melodic freedom while loosely aligning with the quick and steady pulse. Contrary to Cherry's comment, Coltrane is just as "free" from chords as he was. The musicians adhere to the steady pulse as the primary, centripetal force tethering them together, and the pulse is most faithfully maintained by Haden on bass and Blackwell's ride cymbal. (Blackwell's unaccompanied solo, ▶ 05:09, is partially metrically free.) This is the technique later called *time, no changes* by drummer Tony Williams, and it appears again on the LP's second track, "Focus on Sanity," where Coltrane, in the opening solo, intersperses tonal motifs with bursts of chromatic sound. Cherry, according to Spellman, explains this performance by stating, somewhat confusingly, that "[the chords are] everything, because the form sets up the whole chromatic scale; all twelve notes, up and down. And the form permits full exploration." Monk's abstraction was an important common ground for the musicians on the session, inspiring their choice to record his original "Bemsha Swing." "I dig to play Monk because Monk's tunes make you improvise on melody and not on chords," Cherry quips. "They have you thinking without thinking, like some kind of conscious unconscious. Or vice versa. Or something."

A transcendent creative plane was a goal that Coltrane sought with the musicians he hired for his new quartet, formed in 1960. One of them was McCoy Tyner, a young pianist from Philadelphia who met the saxophonist when he was seventeen on one of Coltrane's visits to town; Coltrane's friend Calvin Massey, Tyner's bandleader and a trumpeter ten years his senior, introduced them. Tyner adopted Ahmadiyya Islam that same year and was involved in Philadelphia's local Islamic community; he saw in Coltrane (a former Philadelphia resident) a musician of deep spiritual conviction who had an impulse to experiment, and this had an impact on him early on in their relationship: "John was like a big brother to me. He was such a kind and humble person. His music was so strong, melodically, harmonically, spiritually, it taught me so much."[27] Tyner left Philadelphia for New York in 1959, joining Coltrane's group shortly thereafter and finding that explicit discussions about music theory or conceptual positions were kept to a minimum; instead, Coltrane's method was to encourage musicians to find their own unique sound and approach, channeling it in an intuitive and organic way within the collective. Theirs, Tyner recalled, was a deeply felt and almost telepathic exchange where all that the musicians were learning and developing musically was to be applied to the repertoire:

> That period of time was a milestone in my life and had a tremendous influence on me. It was good for all of us. This was not "just his band" but it was a unit of men with a variety of ideas playing together. He was like the conductor. There wasn't an overemphasis of leadership, but we each gave our all.
>
> The unit was like a train; its parts make it what it is. Of course, 'Trane had more experience than the rest of us, that's why he was the conductor, the leader. He was like an everflowing [*sic*] spring. Always giving. People like him are the ones who have contributed great things to music.[28]

The abstract and potent sound of Coltrane's quartet—with Tyner, bassists Reggie Workman and/or Jimmy Garrison, and drummers Elvin Jones and Roy Haynes—held great symbolic power in an era of rebellion, and it inspired writers to draw a close association between their sound and an impending political revolution after Coltrane's death in 1967. Frank Kofsky's 1970 *Black Nationalism and the Revolution in Music* (later expanded and republished in 1998 as *John Coltrane and the Jazz Revolution of the 1960s*) was the first monograph to do so, followed in 1971 by the French publication *Free Jazz/Black Power* by Philippe Carles and Jean-Louis Comolli, and Valerie Wilmer's *As Serious as Your Life: John Coltrane and Beyond* of 1977, all instilling a trope of revolution that subsequent narratives on Coltrane's life and work reproduce.[29]

Thematic references to African and South Asian cultural folkways and cosmologies in several recording projects of the early 1960s also cemented Coltrane's position in the black cultural vanguard—a creative orientation that likely informed Amiri Baraka's view of Coltrane in 1961 as a leading avant-gardist. It was during his engagement at the Village Vanguard in November of that year that Coltrane invited bassist Ahmed Abdul-Malik to play tanpura, the long-necked lute of the Indian subcontinent that can sustain a drone, on a few tunes. Recordings from the last set on November 5 were released by Creed Taylor's Impulse! Records over a decade later, and Abdul-Malik's playing can be heard on "Spiritual" and "India," where the band engages in *time, no changes* free improvisation.[30] The younger reedist Dolphy was also on stage with Coltrane at the Vanguard and would go on to record the LPs *Africa/Brass* and *Olé*, joining the quartet on several live performances in New York and Europe in 1961–1962. Archie Shepp, who would work with Coltrane a few years later, spoke of his generosity with younger musicians and his encouragement of their creative development: "He was a marvelous man. He was very accessible to younger musicians at the time. Guys like Pharoah Sanders and Wayne Shorter . . . we were all around John. He was like an older brother in a sense because he was so accessible and generous with his time. . . . John was so open to exchanging ideas with younger, lesser known musicians."[31]

"Drum Thing," the final track of the LP *Crescent*, recorded in April 1964 just before *A Love Supreme*, is another example of Coltrane's overt reference to Africa and, possibly, Islam. It begins with Jones playing on his drumheads with soft mallets in a way that emulates the hand drums of West Africa and their diasporic proliferation through the Americas. Coltrane plays a solemn melody while Garrison keeps a steady, two-note drone on the bass in metric time; the three musicians slip in and out of metric alignment with each other during this melodic statement, endowing the performance with fluidity. But the centerpiece of the performance is Jones's solo (▶ 02:11). In it, he accelerates and decelerates over Garrison's pulse in waves of percussive sound delivered in a dense, heterophonic duet that ends as he swells in energy, completely taking over in a bombastic solo episode. Coltrane and Garrison reenter afterward, ending the performance with the melody over Garrison's two-note drone/vamp and Jones's wall of percussive sound, all slipping in and out of sync with each other.

Ascension was Coltrane's unprecedented large-scale experiment in free improvisation. Recorded on June 28, 1965, it was likely modeled after Coleman's *Free Jazz* in that both performances feature a large ensemble cycling through episodes of heterophonic collective improvisation in a large ensemble texture ostensibly led (or revolving around) a single musician at a time. According to Tyner, the musicians had no clue what to expect in the studio that day; Coltrane provided no advance instruction or direction in the studio, "[n]othing like that at all. Just 'play.' No details, no structures. He had a line, which he would call a melody line, that he opened with. That was all. We'd just build."[32] Unlike Coleman's double quartet on *Free Jazz*, Coltrane utilizes piano on *Ascension* along with two bassists, a drummer, and a frontline of six horns.[33] There are two trumpeters, Freddie Hubbard (who was also on Coleman's *Free Jazz*) and Dewey Johnson; two alto saxophonists, John Tchicai and Marion Brown; three tenor saxophones, Coltrane, Shepp, and Sanders; and Coltrane's quartet members—Tyner, Garrison, and Jones—as the rhythm section.

Ascension is a lengthy, approximately forty-minute suite of heterophonous collective improvisation. The LP features each of the two takes on either side, mirroring the other in the sequence of its formal parts and the order of soloists. Despite Tyner's recollection of its formlessness and lack of instruction from Coltrane, *Ascension* contains three formal parts: (1) a melodic refrain that opens and closes the performance, (2) solos where each musician improvises within a reduced rhythm-section texture (like *Free Jazz*), and (3) heterophonic episodes by the full ensemble in between each featured soloist's turn. The performance opens with a short, blues-inflected motif that the ensemble restates like a mantra, and they allow it to unspool as each musician inflects upon it with heterophonic improvisatory variation. The motif eventually dissipates as the eleven-piece ensemble's heterophonic collective improvisation takes over in a mass of instrumental sound that expands and contracts as soloists "ascend" toward the front of the texture, the first being Coltrane (▶ 04:00 in Part I). The intensity of the performance remains high throughout, even as the ensemble's density expands ("3") and contracts ("2") from eleven to five or fewer musicians and back again. Jones plays an important role in stoking and driving that intensity by virtue of the relative loudness and sharp, potent attack of the drum set; his is an almost inexhaustible source of sound energy that drives the other ten musicians to play beyond their limits.

Spellman wrote the liner notes for this album too, and in them discloses important details about how the piece was executed based on commentary by saxophonists Shepp and Brown. They explain what they understand to be Coltrane's creative goals for the session and reflect how the recording was a test of both their endurance and their courage:

> Speaking of the total effect of *Ascension*, Archie Shepp said, "It achieves a certain kind of unity; it starts at a high level of intensity with the horns playing high and the other pieces playing low. This gets a quality of like male and female voices. It builds in intensity through all the solo passages, brass and reeds, until it gets to the final section where the rhythm section takes over and brings it back down to the level it started at. . . . The idea is similar to what the action painters do in that it creates various surfaces of color which push into each other, creates tensions and counter tensions, and various fields of energy."
>
> Marion Brown approached it another way: "In the ensemble sections you get a different idea of what harmony is, or can be. Certain chords were used, but they were stretched out and orchestrated." . . . Again, quoting Archie Shepp: "The ensemble passages were based on chords, but these chords were optional. What Trane did was to relate or juxtapose tonally centered ideas and atonal elements, along with the melodic and non-melodic elements. In those descending chords there is a definite tonal center, like a B flat minor. But there are different roads to that center. . . . In the solo plus quartet parts there are no specified chords. These sections were to be dialogues between the soloists and the rhythm section. The whole work, beginning with Trane's solo, was keyed, especially in McCoy's playing to a minor blues."

Spellman emphasizes the high spirits and camaraderie felt among and between the musicians, engineers, and studio guests during and after the recording:

> Marion Brown described the session as "wildly exciting. We did two takes, and they both had that kind of thing in them that makes people scream. The people who were in the studio *were* screaming. I don't know how the engineers kept the screams out of the record."
>
> "Spontaneity was the thing. Trane had obviously thought a lot about what he wanted to do, but he wrote most of it out in the studio. Then he told everybody what he wanted: he played this line and he said that everybody would play that line in the [ensemble]. Then he said he wanted crescendi and decrescendi after every solo. We ran thru [*sic*] some things together, and then we got into it."
>
> Archie added, "The emphasis was on textures rather than the making of an organizational entity. There was unity, but it was a unity of sounds and textures rather than like an A B A [common song form] approach. You can hear, in the saxophones especially, a reaching for sound and an exploration of the possibilities of sound."

Shepp acknowledged the precedent and influence that Coleman's *Free Jazz* had on Coltrane's vision for *Ascension*: he was more interested in "a group concept of playing—you'll notice that he took no more solo time than anybody else. That's because he didn't want any stars on this record, he wanted a group effect." This collectivity was a central feature in the work of other bandleaders like Sun Ra and Cecil Taylor, and Shepp traces this dynamic to the tradition of collective improvisation in New Orleans jazz adapted and transformed by "1965 people." When asked about how the musicians figured out what to play in such a free-form environment, Tyner remarked, "If you're used to talking to a cat, you get familiar with his mode of expression. You get to know his vocabulary. That's the same thing in our music—you have a general idea of the man's mode of expression and you kind of know certain things. You know how to respond."[34]

Like Coleman's *Free Jazz*, the "harmony" in Coltrane's *Ascension* is that of dense and opaque decentralized simultaneity. In both, "unity," Shepp explains, is a composite of heterogeneous sounds that collide and diverge. Though Coltrane is the nominal ensemble leader, *Ascension* blurs the distinction between soloist and accompanist in pursuit of a cooperative and unwieldly musical experience. The saxophonists play at the extremities of their instruments in *Ascension*, utilizing "extended" (unconventional) techniques like multiphonics and slap tonguing, mimicking the sounds of human voices driven to their expressive edge by an ecstatic and transcendent catharsis. Pharoah Sanders (▶ 11:54–12:35 in Part 1 and ▶ 11:16–13:31 in Part 2) approximates the hollers, whoops, and guttural yells of someone in an altered state. Considered in the context of the U.S. war in Vietnam and Malcolm X/El-Shabazz's recent assassination, Sanders's intense and arresting sound might also represent the pain and rage that many in the United States felt on an existential level. While there is no evidence that *Ascension* contained any overt political messaging, it didn't have to for its sound to have political meaning.

"It is a vast maelstrom of sound which at first appears to be the wildest kind of anarchy," writes John S. Wilson about *Ascension* in *The New York Times*. "But in it Coltrane has found an amazingly effective framework for two elements which have sorely needed both organization and a complementary setting; his own experiments with cumulative effects of a long, long, repetitious performance, and the avant gardists' urge to produce outlandish noises. With only the four members of his quartet at his disposal, Coltrane's efforts at extensive repetition have, all too often, turned into monotony. On the other hand," Wilson continues, "with 11 men and using a pattern in which the full ensemble not only alternates with soloists but continues to provide strong support behind [them], there is so much boiling activity that the kind of boredom engendered by seemingly endless solos is swept completely aside." Coltrane's *Ascension* was a measure, for critics like Wilson, of how far the avant-garde strayed from modern jazz convention, creating instead noises he could only describe as "squawk and shriek."[35] Its revolutionary significance was not lost on Bill Mathieu, who, in reviewing the LP for *Down Beat*, rated *Ascension* five of five stars: "Present time has always been most crucial to jazz. Yet nowadays, as a revolution crystalizes, what was once merely crucial is now the thing itself. This revolution, this black one, has a vested interest in 'now' as *opposed* to 'then.' The forces that spawned it are wasting no love on old things. The old order was 'then.' It passeth to 'now.' No one alive today can remember a more concerted cry for a new social being. *Ascension* is (among other things) at the center of this cry."[36]

Tony Williams's "Anti-Music"

In the winter of 1965, Miles Davis agreed to record the band's annual Christmas engagement in his home state of Illinois, probably as a means to fulfill his contractual obligations at Columbia Records. His quintet was still new; he'd just hired the composer and saxophonist Wayne Shorter to join him on the frontline of an ensemble that included pianist Herbie Hancock, bassist Ron Carter, and drummer Tony Williams, all of whom had been recording and touring with Davis since 1963 with other saxophonists. Davis's quintet was scheduled for a two-week nightly engagement at Chicago's Plugged Nickel nightclub to start on November 24, but the dates were pushed back to the first week of December, then later in the month, and ultimately canceled because of Davis's health.[37] Just shy of thirty-nine years old, he had undergone surgery in April for calcium deposits on his left hip bone, and the intensive procedure left him incapacitated for weeks.[38] Davis did not want to perform and would have preferred to cancel completely, but he relented, and Teo Macero, his producer at Columbia Records, arranged to record the quintet's sets on December 22 and 23, installing microphones and tape machines in the club and hiring engineers to operate the equipment.[39] This would be the quintet's first performance after their bandleader's hiatus.

These Plugged Nickel recordings illustrate the extent to which Davis's quintet embraced and experimented with some of the abstract methods associated with the jazz avant-garde. They played on these nights mostly Davis's repertoire from the 1950s—tunes his audience would likely recognize—in an abstracted, defamiliarizing way: fragmentation or deconstructions of the melody, spontaneous formal digressions, and speedy, frantic tempos that promoted reactive, intuitive, and energetically intense improvisation. Williams, only twenty years old, referred to this approach as "anti-music"; according to Michelle Mercer, Wayne Shorter's biographer, the young drummer came up with the idea to use the gig as a pretext for experimental playing, and the term "anti-music" was his way of imploring the other musicians to avoid convention and cliché by following their intuition and pursuing a more collectively improvised dynamic—a directive the band agreed to before the first set without telling Davis.[40] In opting to step into unfamiliar creative territory and forcing their unsuspecting and beleaguered bandleader to do the same, Davis's quintet used the familiar repertoire as a catalyst for improvisation in a performance mode that Hancock referred to as "controlled freedom."[41] He elaborated further in an interview decades later:

What I was trying to do and what I feel they were trying to do was to combine [or] take these influences that were happening to all of us at that time and amalgamate them, personalize them in such a way that when people were hearing us, they were hearing the avant-garde on the one hand, and they were hearing the history of jazz that led up [to] it on the other hand, because Miles was that history. He was that link. We were sort of walking a tightrope with the kind of experimenting we were doing in music, not total experimentation, but we used to call it "controlled freedom."[42]

The Plugged Nickel sessions were a catalyzing moment for the quintet that presaged the more experimental, "free" music that they would record and perform for the next several years that culminated with Davis's 1969 LP *Bitches Brew*, which was recorded with a new ensemble that did not include Williams (seen below in Figure 5.2), considered today in American music historiography as the urtext of jazz's experimental fusion period.

Williams's "anti-music" dictum summarized a set of improvisational strategies that music theorist Garrett Michaelsen describes as experimental, interactive, and yet "divergent" that, in sum, still relied on perceptible traces of those conventions as a common reference.[43] One such technique grounding the quintet's "controlled freedom" was what Williams, Hancock, Carter, and Shorter called *time, no* [chord] *changes*—free melodic improvisation synced with or flowing above a steady pulse—that Coleman had pioneered in the late 1950s. In their digressions of *time, no changes*, the musicians maintained the centripetal force of meter as a common reference point upon which to affix improvisatory flights and also negotiate returns to the underlying form of the familiar tune.[44] Williams's "anti-music" approach was inspired by the mutable,

Figure 5.2 Tony Williams, ca. 1966. Photo credit: Riccardo Schwamenthal—N.Y. Jazz Museum/Schomburg Center for Research in Black Culture, Photographs and Prints Division, New York Public Library.

heterophonic methods referred to as jazz's *new thing*, and his recorded work outside of Davis's band illustrates his commitment to an experimentalism beyond well-rehearsed patterns and modern jazz clichés.

Heterophonic textures like those pioneered by Coleman and Taylor permeate Williams's original music on the LP *Life Time*—his first as a band leader—recorded on two separate dates with two different quartets in August 1964.[45] The opening tracks are a diptych, "Two Pieces of One: Red" and "Two Pieces of One: Green," and feature Sam Rivers on tenor saxophone and two bassists, Richard Davis and Gary Peacock—a piano-less ensemble primed for heterophonic improvisation. "Red" begins with a somber melody in free meter played by the group homophonically (led by Rivers with the two bassists harmonizing in lockstep) while Williams provides strokes of sound color with brushes on the snare drum. Rivers and Williams play a transient unison figure before the two bassists embark on an improvised heterophonic duet (▶ 00:58), with one bassist in arco and the other with his fingers. One of the bassists (panned in the left channel on the stereo recording) begins a walking bassline (▶ 02:25), establishing a steady pulse for the remaining three musicians to improvise heterophonically (▶ 02:37): *time, no changes.* Though their phrasing over the pulse hints at a quarter-note duple meter (4/4 time), their phrasing is loose and fluid in a way that displaces metric regularity. The bassists utilize extended techniques—noise elements—in their duet (▶ 05:08), slowing the momentum of the performance before the opening melody reappears (▶ 07:12) and the piece ends. The first half of "Green" is a "free," interactive heterophonic duet between Rivers and Williams, after which the two bassists enter, leading the quartet through a brief, dirge-like motif before Williams's intense and exhaustive solo (▶ 04:57), where the drummer builds peaks of dense activity and more sparse and quiet moments of percussive color. The piece concludes with the full quartet collectively improvising (▶ 08:17) in a brief digression from Williams's free-flowing solo, which he resumes until the sudden end of the track.

Life Time's "Tomorrow Afternoon" is explicit in its reference to Coleman: it's an up-tempo, extended *time, no changes* collective improvisation where the musicians are only tenuously tethered to a steady pulse. The ensemble density fluctuates as one or more of the four musicians drop out, throttling the momentum of the performance into suspended moments that are most acute when Williams stops playing. The nifty, singsong melody that bookends the heterophonic collective improvisation is led by Rivers on the saxophone and played in a loose "unison" by the other three musicians in the style of Coleman's quartet. "Tomorrow Afternoon" is a spirited ode to Coleman's *Tomorrow Is the Question!*–era piano-less quartet, and it invokes the same spirit of creative adventure that Williams and other improvising musicians entering the professional field in the 1960s were surely inspired by.

Sam Rivers had just returned from a tour of Japan when he recorded Williams's *Life Time* as the interim saxophonist of Davis's quintet before Shorter's hire. His relationship with Williams, however, went back further as one of the young drummer's earliest mentors in his native city, Boston. The spirit of experimentalism that Rivers brought to Davis's group in Japan— recordings of which were later released commercially by Columbia as *Miles in Tokyo*—was a great inspiration to Williams, and the abstract approach Rivers took to Davis's repertoire might have had an influence on Williams's "anti-music" concept.[46] Rivers's embrace of abstraction and intuitive, expressively potent improvisation stemmed from a deep sense of creative conviction. "[I was] never deliberately avant-garde. I do what's natural to me," Rivers explained to Nat Hentoff in 1964. "Within my sense of the form of any particular piece, I go where my emotions lead me, and if rising intensity calls for 'human' sounds and other departures from conventional jazz practice, that's what I'll do.[47]"

Davis was open to the change introduced by his band and followed their voyage into the creative unknown.[48] Joined by native Chicagoan Hancock, Carter (also a Midwesterner, from Detroit), Shorter, and Williams, Davis was coerced into "anti-music" at the Plugged Nickel by his younger bandmates. These recorded performances document the quintet's aesthetic of controlled abandon, where familiar melodies and rhythms serve as a pretext for excursions into the abstract realms of heterophonic collective action and sound energy. This daring is particularly evident in a less familiar tune; Davis starts the melody of "Agitation," which the band only just recorded in January, with abrupt aplomb in the middle of the band's second set of December 22. They barely finished the final strain of "I Fall in Love Too Easily," a saccharine ballad that had been part of Davis's repertoire since the 1950s, and it is Davis who catches the other musicians off-guard. The group stammers through the tune disjointedly because of this, already foreshadowing the barely controlled chaos to follow. Davis is first to improvise over the form (▶ 00:28), and he sputters out fragments of phrases that are choked, buzzy, and full of indiscernible pitches, falling in and out of sync with the other four musicians. The band takes the tune's title literally, thrusting forward to peaks of tension that recede with only a faint reference to the stable beat. Shorter's solo begins as the rest of the band sustains a pedal point pulse (▶ 03:12), but, as this happens, Williams slowly slips out of sync with the other musicians, destabilizing the centrality of the meter and distorting the field of musical time (▶ 04:30). Moments later, Carter joins Williams's distortion field, and the band slips into heterophony, elevating the already mounting tension enveloping the listeners in the club.

"Agitation" reaches its first climax six minutes in, when Hancock reaches into the body of the piano to pluck and strum the strings with his fingers (à la Cecil Taylor), prompting Williams to shift down and drop in volume, thinning the texture and almost bringing time to a halt. Now seven minutes in, the band snaps back into the form by finding a common pulse, but Shorter thwarts that brief stability with short bursts of chromaticism and noise: squawks, bleats, and squeaks (▶ 7:20–7:37). Then, close to eight minutes in, Hancock joins Davis's and Shorter's torrential outbursts while Carter and Williams play *time, no changes*—a feat of coordinated sonic acrobatics that rouses enthusiastic applause from the audience. At the ninth minute, the steady pulse dissolves yet again, and Hancock, Carter, and Williams burn out, finding a common pulse at the end of Hancock's solo (▶ 11:36). After this, Williams begins to improvise by using the full orchestral potential of the drum set, exploring the instrument's full range of tone color in a virtuosic manipulation of the drumheads and cymbals that maintains momentum and drive. Davis comes back in with the melody almost thirteen minutes after his sudden start of the tune, and the band ends "Agitation" by fizzling out like a spent fuse, collectively landing on its final cadence.

Davis's quintet carried on with their "anti-music" experiment for the rest of the night. The audience, for their part, is audibly enthralled by their intensity and chance-taking. After a particularly tender, almost fragile rendition of "I Thought about You" in their third and last set of the evening, an audience member voices his solidarity by shouting loudly, "Take your time, Miles." Listeners today might imagine what it was like to see the iconic modern jazz musician so deliberately and unexpectedly deconstructing and distorting some of his best-known material. For example, the quintet's take on "So What," from Davis critically acclaimed 1959 LP *Kind of Blue*—his most popular recording to date—is performed in a raw and uninhibited way at the Plugged Nickel in sharp contrast to the original's minimalist modern aesthetic. Williams's "anti-music" concept was the portal through which Davis's quintet stepped into the abstract *new thing*.

While Davis's quintet did not go as far "out" as a group compared to Taylor's Unit, they shared with them, Coleman's quartet, and other experimentalists a desire to create beyond the bounds of musical knowledge, ability, and the conventions of jazz practice. They, like these peers, privileged moments of free (heterophonic) collective improvisation, and the Plugged Nickel recordings demonstrate how diffuse these new concepts were in an era of modern jazz orthodoxy.

The "Anti-Traditional Art"

Music critics in the United States writing in various music, culture, and lifestyle magazines and newspapers in the mid-1960s identified an emergent schism between modern jazz and the *new thing*. The latter, some claimed, was hype upheld by a cadre of passionate if not sycophantic advocates—record producers and other writers—like Amiri Baraka and Nat Hentoff. Their insistence that such abstract and bewildering music was not only at the cutting edge of modern jazz but that it was legitimate music at all was fodder for editorials. Coverage of jazz's *new thing* in print media peaked in 1966, when writers in *Down Beat,* the *New Yorker, Status,* and the short-run progressive music magazine *Sounds & Fury* speculated on the possibility that the music was cover for more reactionary and insurgent motives. For some, its abstract sound was noisy, aggressive, and illogical: a bellwether of a rising tide of political and antiestablishment fervor in jazz.

The notion that the *new thing* was discordant protest music became more widespread by 1965. "For a number of reasons having to do with major economic, social, and political developments relating to the status of the Negro in this country in the recent period, young Negro musicians, many of them brilliant and very well trained musically, have turned away from the traditional melodic, harmonic, and rhythmic bases of jazz to seek new ways of expressing their tensions, hostilities, and aspirations," spills Nat Shapiro in *Status*. "This musical counterpart of and counterpoint to the black revolution is often pretentious, naïve, amateurish, and, we fear, occasionally fraudulent."[49] Hentoff wrote a profile of the jazz avant-garde for *The New York Times* in 1966 titled "The New Jazz—Black, Angry, and Hard to Understand," using descriptive adjectives like "sulphurous [*sic*]" and "bristling" to describe the music and musicians' commentary on race in the United States, concluding, "Among black musicians with new dimensions of self-respect come new depths of anger. Anger at the still low status of jazz in America."[50] Hentoff wants readers of the *Times* to know that the abrasive sound of the music has parity in the experiences of black musicians living under dire racial and economic oppression.

Don Heckman, hitherto an impartial theorist concerned with the music alone, accepted the possibility that social politics was the best explanation for the sound of the new music: "Some of today's players conceive of jazz as a symbol of a natural change—even social revolution. They feel that the contribution made by the Negro to jazz and the [broader] entertainment arts in general has been inadequately recognized by the public and subject to [continuing] economic exploitation by the music industry. There can be little doubt of the accuracy of these views." The kind of commercial success that a "popularizer" like Dave Brubeck enjoyed exists, for Heckman, in sharp contrast to the hardships faced by a "creator" like Cecil Taylor, whose difficulties were "far greater than those experienced by any white musician." Heckman adds, "The problem of art as a symbol of social commentary is an extremely knotty one. Inevitably, the artist encounters inconsistencies between means and ends, artistic and social objectives. I am not suggesting that art is, or should be, detached from the surrounding community. . . . More often artistic elements are subordinated to social message, and we are left with little more than proselytizing tracts."[51]

Heckman's comment alludes to the modernist bias against any direct reference of controversial political topics in significant art, which, in post-Enlightenment aesthetics, was understood as a corruption of its higher aesthetic purpose.[52] The roots of modern jazz's "enlightened" aesthetics are, as I explained in Chapter 1, in the European music aesthetics inculcated by institutionalized music education (especially at the college level) in the United States that filtered into "middlebrow" music writing.[53] A trained musician with sympathies for civil rights causes, Heckman's reluctant acknowledgment of politically charged music was, in an increasingly caustic war of words, enough for him to be viewed as a proselyte as debates on the merits of the *new thing* became more polarized.

Jazz musicians, for Heckman and other writers in the mid-1960s, were skilled, erudite musicians who had attained technical mastery of their instrument and "modern" improvisation (i.e., chordal and within the bounds of discernible form). That erudition is what made modern jazz a *modern* art, but its "authenticity" was determined by writers using a different rubric. For Baraka, jazz was black music with roots in black vernacular culture, and as such reflected—and should reflect—the Black American experience. Though eclipsed by the popularity of rhythm-and-blues in black communities, Baraka argued that the *new thing* and the avant-gardists at its helm were, as I discuss in this book's Interlude, the black musical vanguard. Critical writing on the *new thing* bifurcated along these lines: between an ideal of abstract and apolitical modern art, and a revolutionary, politically charged music that reflected a radical new black subjectivity. If the abstract *new thing* was indeed rooted in the African American experience, as Baraka argued, its cacophony, other writers thought, must have a connection to the protest and unrest enveloping American society.

Two pieces published by *Down Beat* in 1965 focused on saxophonist Shepp were flashpoints for the controversy surrounding the *new thing*: Baraka's "Voice from the Avant-garde: Archie Shepp" published in January, and

"An Artist Speaks Bluntly" by Shepp, published in December, months after he recorded "Malcolm, Malcolm, Semper Malcolm."[54] These two essays helped set the terms by which the *new thing* was politicized and, as such, an impetus for critical scorn. In the first piece, Baraka offers an earnest profile of the saxophonist, describing him as a black artist of uncompromising originality well beyond the tastes of the average jazz listener. Shepp, Baraka writes, had become a fixture in the East Village scene, the epicenter of New York's artistic avant-garde.

It was his mentorship by Coltrane and Taylor, Baraka writes, that most profoundly shaped Shepp's latest work, and these musicians served as the impetus for his embrace of Coleman's music. He quotes Shepp saying, "The reason Ornette wasn't such a big influence on me was because when I first heard him, I wasn't prepared to listen. There was nothing wrong with his music; there was something wrong with my listening. After Cecil, I dug Ornette because I'd grown musically."[55] Taylor expanded Shepp's musical consciousness and prepared him for the rejection that comes with creative experimentation: "Cecil freed me from the doldrums. I thought I'd heard all that jazz could do. It was like a door being opened to go into something else. Many people don't like our music because it's not conventional." In embracing abstraction and approaching the piano like a percussion instrument, Taylor, according to Shepp, was making a political statement with his art; his style was a "rebellion against the ultrasophistication of jazz" and a reorientation toward pure tone color and rhythm. This was important to Shepp, Baraka underscores, because of "the weight of black in his thinking, which is also, of course, in his playing," adding from Shepp that the "Negro musician is a reflection of the Negro people as a social and cultural phenomenon. . . . His purpose ought to be to liberate America esthetically and socially from its inhumanity." He quotes Shepp saying:

> The inhumanity of the white American to the black American as well as the inhumanity of the white American to the white American is not basic to America and can be exorcised. I think the Negro people through the force of their struggles are the only hope of saving America, the political or cultural America.
>
> Culturally, America is a backward country; Americans are backward. But jazz is American reality—total reality. The jazz musician is like a reporter, an aesthetic journalist of America. Those white people who used to go to those bistros in New Orleans thought they were listening to nigger music, but they weren't. They were listening to American music. But they didn't know it. Even today, those white people who go slumming on the east side may not know it, but they are listening to American music . . . the Negro's contribution, his gift to America. Some whites

seem to think that they have a right to jazz. Perhaps that's true, but they should feel thankful for jazz. It has been a gift that the Negro has given, but they can't accept that.[56]

Baraka ends his profile of Shepp with the saxophonist's blunt critique of white musicians' troubled place within jazz, which Shepp sees as a microcosm of race relations in the United States. He attributes this trouble to white musicians not finding (or being unwilling to find) "their true roots" in the music, and their ignorance or denial of its black cultural origins. Shepp cites the problematic comments made by Lennie Tristano in an earlier issue of *Down Beat*, where the white pianist expressed disdain, among other sentiments, at what he saw as undue praise being lobbed at Coleman. Shepp paraphrases Tristano saying that "just because a Negro plays jazz it doesn't necessarily make him a man," but the full comment, reprinted here, is far worse:

It's a curious thing that everyone forgets what we did [on his Capitol recording "Intuition"]; but, after all, we were white. . . . Ninety-nine percent of the words written about jazz in the last 40 years are garbage. That wasn't so in other arts, particularly many years ago. . . . No white man could ever get away with the things a Negro does today. So many people are exploiting the negative popularity of the Negro. . . .

It's wrong, you know. A Negro may think jazz makes a man out of him, but nobody has a corner on music. Let's be logical. There are Negroes and/or slaves all over the world, but nothing like jazz ever happened anywhere but here in this country. There is nothing African about jazz. Jewish cantors and gypsys [*sic*] sound more like it than anything from Africa. . . . It's about time people realized jazz is an American thing, only possible here, and that a persecuted minority should realize it does no good to affect another minority prejudice.[57]

Shepp lambastes Tristano for having "that much gall" and for his ingratitude toward a "music that has been given to him, rather graciously—in light of [the] oppression" faced by black people, which he should treat as a "marvelous gift."[58] His denouncement of Tristano and candor on race, racism, and jazz's black cultural context, in addition to Baraka's endorsement, made Shepp an unwitting spokesperson for the *new thing*, but his commentary inadvertently helped to shift the critical discourse to one of racial grievances.

Shepp's second controversial piece for *Down Beat* that year, "An Artist Speaks Bluntly," published in December, goes further on the points he raised in Baraka's essay. He addresses his commentary directly to the "bigots" and "those 'in' white hipsters who think niggers never had it so good (Crow Jim)," and flouts the "negative attention" black musicians like him received for speaking out against racism and exploitation. Shepp understands the defensiveness of white critics and musicians as betraying their desire to retain their privilege, and he disagrees with the assertion that politicized art can't be "universal" in its appeal. Black men like him, Shepp concludes, simply wish to regain the dignity stolen from them, starting with the institution of slavery, and that he, like any true artist, seeks to pursue his creative goals and dreams. In the meantime, he warns, whites should not be surprised by the unleashing of blacks' "collective rage."[59]

In the months between the two essays, critics in several publications opined on the merits and politics of the *new thing*, some denouncing the sensational coverage it was generating. Herm Schoenfeld, writing for *Variety* in April 1965, mourns the slow, agonizing death of commercially viable jazz, which became "enfeebled" by the increasing "complexities and obscurities" that have taken hold in the past several years. Jazz's "finishing blow," Schoenfeld adds, is the *new thing*, which he sees as an "all-out assault on every musical form" that, because of its repellant "esoteric" sound, has forced venues that would otherwise feature jazz artists to turn to rock 'n' roll bands and function as discotheques, which is "the equivalent of the Metropolitan Opera turning into a burlesque house." For him, the *new thing* is an "authentic underground movement" that some quarters of the intelligentsia believe to be a music "that cannot be listened to, but only talked about," and because musicians strive for "spontaneous composition" instead of improvisations on a recognizable melody, the *new thing* can be nothing but a commercial flop. Coleman is the *new thing*'s leader, and the others from "outer space," like Archie Shepp, John Tchicai, and (white) trombonist and composer Roswell Rudd, conform to a philosophy that amounts to a "total rejection of society and its traditions," like "the most ultra wing of the civil rights movement."[60]

Schoenfeld singles out Heckman because of his two deeply analytical articles on Coleman's music and a more general essay on avant-garde techniques of music notation published in December 1965. He also mentions Martin Williams because, as discussed in Chapter 2, he was one of Coleman's first critical supporters and wrote several of his album liner notes.[61] Like Schoenfeld, Leonard Feather, long the most prominent critical voice in jazz, lamented in *Down Beat*'s penultimate issue of 1965 the "painful self-consciousness in jazz." Gone, in his view, were the days of natural expression and universalism, when the average listener might derive pleasure from this new music—both expectations are incompatible with the radicalism of the times. He calls the *new thing* jazz's "cosa nova" (i.e., its mafia) and insists that while it is neither "box-office gold" nor "poison," it has penetrated and corrupted modern jazz. A critique by such a prominent, trusted voice likely only validated listeners' distaste for jazz's *new thing* despite Feather's later entreaty that writers should remain objective and stop fighting among themselves.[62]

Questions about the *new thing* were posed to a broader audience in more general publications. Whitney Balliett, the long-standing critic for the *New Yorker*, called the *new thing* "hard sell music" motivated by an "armored passion. It grits its teeth, seizes the listener, shakes him, and hisses 'Damn you, *listen* to this!" That affect and effect, Balliett contends, is what feeds the *new thing*'s "confusions and shortcomings. The new-thing musicians play too loudly and appear never to have heard of dynamics. . . . [T]hey play too long . . . and they often become so caught up in their own musical gales that they completely forget their compatriots (good jazz rests on collective individualism)." In what is otherwise a flattering review of Taylor's performance at Town Hall in March ("Taylor is an extraordinary pianist. He is a hammer and the keyboard is an anvil"), he informs the listener, "At its worst, then, the new thing is long-winded, dull, and almost physically abrasive. At its best—in the hand of Ornette Coleman or Taylor—it howls through the mind and heart, filling them with an honest ferocity that is new in jazz and perhaps any music. (Some observers have suggested that the new thing is primarily a social-protest music, that its sledging is still another anti-white Negro shout. If that is so, it will date as quickly as the proletarian novel.)"[63]

The jazz avant-garde, writes British historian Eric Hobsbawm (using the nom de plume Francis Newton) for the London-based *New Statesman* in May 1965, officially began five years earlier, with its "masters," Coleman, Taylor, and the late Eric Dolphy, all of whom had influenced an emergent crop of musicians. Those up-and-comers attracted a fair number of skeptics among other musicians, critics, "and some non-playing champions like the militant writer LeRoi Jones," whose book *Blues People* Hobsbawm praises.

Hobsbawm is a self-described skeptic of the *new thing* because he doesn't understand what the *new thing* "rebellion" is about, aesthetically speaking. To him, it's a nihilistic movement that "rejects and seems to hold in disdain tonality, the unwavering beat, the conventional chord structure, and improvisation that is chiefly based on chord progressions." Hobsbawm surmises that while there is undoubtedly a prominent New York jazz avant-garde, the problem is that the public doesn't want to pay to hear them: "There is at best an ability to find genuinely original and suitable noises for a recognizable human predicament: so much so that the 'new thing' has been called (wrongly) a music of social protest—a musical equivalent of, maybe, Harlem Maoism."[64]

Magazines ran with the narrative that the *new thing* was a harbinger of modern jazz's decline in 1966. Writers placed blame on the *new thing* for the corrosive effect it had on jazz's already waning listenership and the undeniable commercial vitality of rock 'n' roll, which eclipsed jazz record sales. That the new thing was both anti-jazz and anti-white was beginning to settle as consensus, as did the belief that its discordancy was the sonification of the political upheaval of the day. "The proponents of this noise seem to fall into two main groups: Rhapsodists and Threateners," writes Ralph Berton, editor of the short-lived jazz magazine *Sounds & Fury* in its April 1966 issue. "The former explain that the noises indicate Cosmic Love; the latter decode the message somewhat differently, as warning the rest of us in no uncertain terms (though in no particular key) that we had better learn to dig it or prepare to be forcibly liquidated as soon as LeRoi Jones and Archie Shepp take over the universe."[65]

Berton's targeting of Baraka and Shepp is part of the larger scapegoating of the *new thing* as the source of jazz's decline, but this critical consensus overlooked or dismissed the structural decline affecting the livelihoods of the musicians in question. The commercial music industry was shifting its priorities to an untapped and lucrative consumer base: teenagers.[66] Deindustrialization and urban renewal programs in New York City and Chicago transformed infrastructure and culture in profound ways, with "slum clearance" initiatives, redlining, and suburban white flight exacerbating racial segregation, social inequity, and wealth disparity. While the *new thing* became a useful bête noire for self-appointed defenders of modern jazz and good music aesthetics, New York City and other urban areas entered an unprecedented era of economic decline and political neglect that would have a deep and deleterious effect on the arts, artists, and marginalized communities.

But framing the *new thing* as the music of racial grievance played handily into the omnipresent paranoia among white Americans during the Cold War of black revolution and retribution and the lurking threat of communism. These fears are evident in writers' preoccupation with how noisy and incomprehensible the *new thing* was. *Down Beat*'s critical roundtable on the "pros & cons" of the *new thing*—an edited transcription of a discussion organized by associate editor Dan Morgenstern that included Don Heckman, Ira Gitler, Martin Williams, and photographer and album art designer Don Schlitten, published in early 1966, illustrates this fixation.

Because of its perceived lack of discernible melody, chords, and coherent form, Morgenstern, Gitler, and Schlitten argue, the *new thing* rejects beauty which, the discussants all agree, is art's primary objective. The *new thing*'s abstraction makes it difficult to listen to, thus denying the listener (in this case, a well-informed jazz critic) a pleasurable experience. Morgenstern finds that "in the new music, there is very often, I think, a conscious rejection of standards, of esthetic principles which apply to the older forms of jazz. Such as getting a good and beautiful sound, a sound, which by the musician's intention, is pleasing to the ear." The *new thing*, Morgenstern continues, "just does not provide pleasure. It provides, in some sense, an amplification of the agony of modern existence, which is an extremely legitimate and worthwhile thing, but which does set it apart," and, in 1965, was already passé.[67] Schlitten concludes that music should fundamentally induce some kind of pleasure and evoke "a feeling of love . . . that can communicate [to the listener]. Art is a means of communication. But it doesn't try to communicate anguish, horror, hate, and war; it tries to communicate beauty. If you want to look at pictures of war, look at *Life* magazine. But in art we're trying to create out of the havoc of living and of the world something beautiful, something that's outstanding."[68] Schlitten's mention of *Life* magazine is a reference to their graphic and uncensored photographic coverage of the Vietnam War.[69]

Williams insists that the sheer innovativeness of the new music qualifies it as being important in modern jazz, but Morgenstern and the others demur, questioning how much the *new thing*'s notoriety is owed to its overzealous and sycophantic proselytizers. The new music, Morgenstern asserts, is just too opaque and unpalatable to reach jazz's ideal—presumably white—audience. "There has been a problem in reaching a wider audience for this new music, and I think . . . that a lot of the guilt for that lies with the musicians, because they refused to let the audience in on what's going on," he opines. "Take a man who plays as uncomplicated music as Dave Brubeck. I think one of the reasons he has such a big audience is that he always explains to people what the group is doing. . . . And that makes people feel very good, because then they feel that the artist is interested in communicating with them, and they also feel that they have some kind of guidelines to go by."[70]

Morgenstern's last remarks summarized the new critical consensus: "The attack on tradition, which has now been going on for a good 65 years or so, was initially a response to the overwhelming force of academic art in all fields. Today the anti-traditional art has itself become the academy—because there is no academy to attack. And much of what is in the minds of young jazz players who are coming out today is really an attack on an idol that has already fallen."[71] Like the writers discussed previously in this chapter, he predicts that the *new thing* will not remain relevant among "serious" jazz musicians. For these critics, the *new thing* has a future only if, as Hobsbawm wrote, the "ordinary non-avant-garde players absorb its innovations."[72] As this chapter demonstrated, the irony in this statement is that some extraordinary improvising musicians already had.

Closing: Black Power

In late 1966, *Down Beat* published an essay by Don Heckman in their annual year-in-review issue on the impact of the jazz avant-garde. Amid a rising tide of derision and debate, Heckman celebrates the aesthetic achievement of what seemed like a growing movement:

> It was the year of the breakthrough for the jazz avant-garde. Small and imperceptible as it sometimes appeared, it was a breakthrough nonetheless, one that provided the most significant impetus the new music of the '60s has yet received.
>
> New York is teeming with fine young players, and every trip I've taken outside the New York area underlines the fact that the new-jazz movement is the dominant style among the youngest generation of players.[1]

Heckman, a saxophonist engaged in avant-garde and new music circles in New York City, celebrates the heterogeneity of the new music, a quality he claims was missing in earlier eras in jazz. He sees something unique in Abert Ayler's style, acknowledging the saxophonist's interpolation of vernacular sources, "simple spiritual-like tunes, march themes, all the varieties of melodies that recur in folk cultures throughout the world," that are singable, which vividly convey the saxophonist's feeling and spirit. Perceptively, Heckman pinpoints an important quality in Ayler's playing that seems to be a common and distinguishing feature of jazz's avant-garde at large: an understanding of sound as a potent form of energy. This idea—that musicians of the *new thing* channel and transmit sound as beams of energy encoded with a raw emotion and visceral affective power—is both interesting and abstruse. After all, what does it mean to say that musicians are "playing" with and projecting energy? Descriptions of Cecil Taylor's music as having "kinetic" properties, for instance, appeared in the pianist's album liner notes and more sparingly in the music press, but the way Heckman describes Ayler's music as something more ineffable and electric reflects a new musical phenomenology based in sound, its intense affective power, and its potential for the transcendent:

Change. Kwami Coleman, Oxford University Press. © Oxford University Press 2025.
DOI: 10.1093/9780197780121.003.0007

Ayler starts with melodies and somehow—mostly in a way that cannot be described in words—transforms them into nonmelodic sounds that follow naturally and feelingly. . . . That is, his "charge," the emotional (he would probably call it "spiritual") energy that bursts forth in such astonishingly powerful fashion, seems to build up during the tireless examination and re-examination of these "simple" melodies.

In this respect, Ayler's rediscovery of the non-cadential aspects of harmonic densities is a major artistic achievement. He has shown that harmonies can be storage points of energy.[2]

It is the jazz avant-garde's experiments in sound as energy, in Heckman's view, that will have a lasting effect on jazz's future. Even though the *new thing*'s abstraction does tend to alienate listeners, preventing it from fully "arriving" as a genre and from being embraced by the general public, the musicians Heckman cites in his essay—Ayler, Coltrane, Taylor, Sun Ra—have achieved something that has, thus far, only confirmed the avant-garde's "growing eminence as the jazz of the decade" as an energy-based, viscerally charged kind of music.[3] Heckman's attention to this new sound phenomenology was, he believes, lost on most critics writing about jazz in 1966. He sees their unfounded critiques of the jazz avant-garde as based in their fundamental misunderstandings of the music, their refusal to acknowledge the aesthetic change it represents, and technical trifles in recording (like subpar audio mixes, the culprit usually being a fledgling indie label with a limited budget) which simply can't reproduce for the listener the full intensity of a live performance. To truly appreciate the potency of the *new thing*, he believes, one must experience it—feel it—in person.

Heckman's focus on the significance of sound—the fundamental yet esoteric medium of the new music—draws on the aesthetic change that many in the critical and record-buying milieu found to be radical and disconcerting. Like the thunderous, electrified sound of rock music, the noisiness of the *new thing* was largely represented in the print culture of the 1960s as a sign of decline, like the social and political unrest then so common in the United States. Heckman was one of the few white critics in 1966 who seemed to acknowledge the possibility of something else.

For the previous several years Amiri Baraka had been the reactionary music press's scapegoat for jazz's aesthetic decline because of his insistence that the *new thing*'s abstract sound was that of "[a] people and an energy, harnessed and not harnessed by America." He remained a target in 1966.[4] Taylor Castell, the publisher of *Sounds & Fury*, a magazine devoted to the cutting edge of modern music, called out Baraka (then LeRoi Jones) directly in the front matter of their April issue. In "Some Thoughts on Publishing, or . . . Yes, LeRoi, There Is a White Power Structure," Castell justifies the editor's decision to have the magazine focus less on jazz as a matter of necessity given the *new thing*'s divisiveness, and he underscores that the editors would never waver in delivering good judgment in the face of a new or popular fad. The critical roundtable printed in this issue, "The New Thing: Those in Favor," is prefaced by editor Ralph Burton, who condemns what he hears as unmistakable noise regardless of the "floods of rhetoric, such unbridled verbal folly, as have been called forth by the assorted brayings, squealings, hammerings, etc., of the heroes of the New Music."[5] "These and all the other 'new jazz' musicians subscribe to a particular view of society," writes Bruce Cook for the *Chicago Tribune* in May 1967. "All those named and nearly all the rest involved in the so-called 'free form' new jazz movement are Negroes. The harsh, strident, angry music they create has been closely identified by them with the 'black power' cry of the militant Negro Left."[6]

The literary discourse on the *new thing*, I've tried to show, was largely molded by white American critics' rejection of its presumed noisiness, illogicality, and rejection of beauty, which represented, for them, black defiance and a sonic protest of jazz and America's "white power structure." As I mentioned at the start, my goal in this book is not to depoliticize the *new thing* but rather to show that abstract experiments in sound by black artists in the 1960s—and the claim of creative agency that drove those experiments—could not and should not be reduced to reactionary politics, and that the *new thing* was indeed a robust and diverse creative practice. Nat Hentoff argued that the *new thing*'s unapologetic blackness was precisely the reason for its censure and that the music's sonic freedom had real-world implications:

> [T]he consciousness of being black, the pride in black, has never been more acute than now because jazz could not be isolated from the resumption in the 1960s of the unfinished revolution that began with the first slave revolts.
>
> What, however, is the function of the music emerging from this black consciousness? In this respect, many of those in the new jazz—though otherwise disparate in their philosophies and in their music—are convinced that music can be a unifying and liberating force.
>
> For [Archie] Shepp, it seems to me, the music has two imperatives. One is to confront those in the white society who will listen with as full and deep a spectrum as possible of black feelings, from rage to pride, so that there can be much less misunderstanding of black convictions, black needs, and black strength. The other imperative is to reach into and invigorate as many of the black masses as possible with the sustenance of a music that, after all, is an essential element in their

heritage and in their way of opposing total conquest by the white society through
its destruction of their culture (see LeRoi Jones's book *Blues People*).[7]

For Hentoff, like Baraka and other advocates of the new music, the *new thing*
was the sonification of an emergent black revolutionary consciousness, and
avant-gardist musicians at the vanguard of that revolution.

The *new thing* as sonified black power is a trope that also circulated in
Western European music literature, and in France especially as the country
was set ablaze with rebellion and social unrest. The revolts of May 1968 that
brought the French state to a halt were a culmination of anti-authoritarian
activism initiated by leftist artists, students, and laborers in response to consumer capitalism, governmental inertia, and the Vietnam War. In this atmosphere, the freedom of jazz's *new thing* and its revolutionary black musicians
served as symbols of resistance. That resonance is the undertone of Alain
Corneau's 1966 interview with saxophonist Marion Brown, who had participated in John Coltrane's *Ascension* sessions the previous year, for the Parisian
Jazz Magazine. Corneau asks Brown about the freedom of the new music and
its revolutionary significance vis-à-vis race relations in the United States, and
Brown responds by denouncing violent acts, clarifying that he doesn't believe
that true revolutions are based only in anger.[8] Despite this, the trope of the
new thing as being, fundamentally, the discordant sonification of black anger
was becoming entrenched in the literary media of the later 1960s.

That justified anger—at the expropriation of jazz from black culture and
the economic exploitation of the musicians—is an angle that forms the core
thesis of the 1971 book *Free Jazz/Black Power* by Philippe Carles (the editor-
in-chief of *Jazz Magazine*) and writer Jean-Louis Comolli. "Free jazz resists . . .
expropriation," they write. "[It] rejects the musical and extra-musical values
of dominant ideology—which in the United States is capitalist and white—
and attempts to achieve cultural freedom, echoing the struggles of black
Americans for their political and economic freedom."[9] Carles and Comolli
emphasize the indelible link between political struggle and cultural production, underscoring that to ignore politics in or excise it from the *new thing* is
to obfuscate its revolutionary potency. However, their focus on black discontent, rebellion, and free jazz as a political project ignored questions of craft
and creativity in the work of the artists they upheld as revolutionaries. More
recent scholarship explores free jazz's complicated reception in France and
Western Europe, and offers further context for Carles and Comolli's positions.
Saxophonist, composer, and scholar Steve Lehman underscores the French
press's preoccupation with the *new thing* and the exoticization of nonconformist black musicians starting in the late 1960s. Theirs was, Lehman writes,

a "genuine fascination . . . tempered by received notions about race and musical idiom" that essentialized the music with primitivist tropes like virility, naturalness, and impulsiveness.[10] Musicologist Eric Drott sees French and broader Western European interest in jazz avant-gardists of the late 1960s and onward being fed by the presence of Black American musicians as émigrés, touring and settling in Western European cities like Paris and Copenhagen. Their status as de facto political and/or economic refugees searching for a more tolerant society, better and more regular employment, and respect only reinforced free jazz's fugitivity.[11] To summarize, the *new thing* was being essentialized as the sound of black discontent on both sides of the Atlantic by the late 1960s.

This book sheds light on registers unheard, overlooked, and otherwise ignored by these narrow (mis)hearings. I propose here, in the book's closing, that changes in how Black American improvising musicians understood themselves and their place in the world and universe fed into the intense creative focus by some on sound energy, for which the more intuitive heterophonic collective improvisation method served as an optimal vehicle. Those changes stemmed from what they learned and imagined of Asia, Africa, and Black America, and they (re)claimed new identities and modes of expression attuned to the cosmos and fed by esoteric knowledge. Given the historical moment, imbued with a sense that revolution was imminent and inevitable, the experimentalist ethos behind jazz's *new thing* and the intensity of heterophonic musical performance did indeed conjure the possibility of new worlds.

In engaging with the archive of jazz criticism, I've tried to unpack how the lore surrounding jazz's *new thing* was erected by record and concert reviews, analytical essays, artist profiles, articles, editorials, letters to editors, and critical debates. My focus on the design and anatomy of recorded performances (and their manifestation of musicians' bold creative agency) is not to deny that these artists were also activists. Music scholars have long since revisited and contextualized the many overt acts of protest musicians engaged in, from the alternative Newport "Rebels" Festival in 1960, to benefit concerts supporting the Student Nonviolent Coordinating Committee (SNCC) and the March on Washington in 1963, to the 1964 "October Revolution" series at Manhattan's Cellar Café.[12] For black artists, asserting the right to be abstract, opaque, irreducible, and provocative was, in a racialized and economically exploitative society, a radical act. Refusing to conform to a predetermined and depoliticized modernity was a radical act. Efforts by experimentalist improvising musicians to find, in the words of poet Jayne Cortez, "somewhere in advance of nowhere" manifested as what critics called jazz's *new thing*, and the musicians leading this charge jazz's avant-gardists.[13]

The *new thing*/free jazz was not simply a rejection of Western harmony; it was an embrace of a new heterogeneous and decentralized kind of harmony: heterophony. This book is in loose "unison" with Robin D. G. Kelley's concept of "freedom dreams" as a framework for understanding social and political revolutions as fundamentally creative acts. I understand the heterophony of the *new thing*/free jazz as conjuring a new set of social relations between improvisers and their audience in the act of creative performance. This is because, as I describe throughout this text, the music has a jarring and decentering effect, which the listener can choose to engage with but cannot so easily decide to not be affected by. This transformational power can potentially unlock or induce a new way of listening, feeling, and being—it can spark a new consciousness—in the listener, like a sonic shock to their system.

Electrifying Sound

Sound is a phenomenon dependent on energy and motion. Humans, as with many other of earth's terrestrial organisms, are endowed with ears—complex organs that pick up the amplitude and frequencies of particle oscillations in the air. The ear contains a vibrating membrane (the tympanic membrane, or eardrum) that transmits those energetic vibrations through small bones that contain nerves connected to the cochlea, the fluid-filled inner chamber of the ear. It's the cochlea that beams those electrical signals to the brain for decoding and interpretation. Humans also feel sound energy with the rest of our bodies, from the outer layer of our skin's nerve endings to the inner core of our body's viscera as they travel through material and air. Sound is a haptic energy, and what we take that energy to mean, cognitively and subconsciously, as well as the pleasure or lack thereof that we derive from that energy, is manifest in subsequent stages of our experience of auditory phenomena. The peripheral nerves in the skin spool outward from the spine and brain toward the outer limbs and extremities, and they perceive waves of sound and relay that sensory data back to the central nervous system via electrical signals transmitted through axons (nerve fibers). Thus our "felt" experience of sound is an embodied information-retrieval process powered by electricity. The effects of sound on our circulatory and immunological health—how it makes us move and function—is a topic in biological science, and the bidirectional relationship between sound and cognition underpins the entire academic field of music aesthetics.[14]

How we interpret sound and music is shaped by our cultural contexts, which can be as narrow as the customs and behavioral expectations of our family, community, and social networks. French sociologist Pierre Bourdieu, in the canonical study *Distinction: A Social Critique of the Judgment of Taste* of 1979, underscores the determining power of class, privilege, and access on an individual's understanding and assessment of art, including judgments of whether the work or performance is "good" or "bad," legitimate (i.e., "serious"), and important. Bourdieu describes the web of ideas and behaviors—including discourse—that enables this kind of discernment as the *habitus*, an epistemology and cultural domain. What I'm trying to say is that, in the 1960s, modern jazz became a habitus that the *new thing*/free jazz, in its sonic abstraction and opacity, disrupted. In the modern jazz habitus, musicians' heterophonic sounds were heard as *noise*: discord and chaos. This perceived noisiness only increased the more the *new thing* became synonymous with black power.

Noise, in the 1960s, was political and politicized. Civil rights activism and urban rebellions electrified cities in the United States with defiant sounds and violent noises. The student-led Berkeley Free Speech Movement of 1964, where students sat in, marched, chanted, and shouted their demands to end the university's policies aimed at curbing open dissent on campus, was one such noisy disturbance. It followed years of student-led direct action in the southern American states by SNCC, amplifying the youth-driven rebellion against the status quo. Loud acts of dissent on college and university campuses transformed them into "stages" where cooperative world-building was enacted and "performed." The Watts Rebellion in the summer of 1965, sparked by the arrest of Marquette Frye, a black Angelino pulled over for suspected drunk driving by the California Highway Patrol, and the ensuing police altercation set the city of Los Angeles ablaze after mounting tensions erupted between the city's black residents and the police. This was one of several destructive, chaotic, and indeed cacophonous acts of cynicism, defiance, and retribution that sparked protests in more than 150 cities across the United States in the "long hot summer" of 1967. And in January 1966, Fidel Castro hosted the Tricontinental Conference in Havana, which gathered hundreds of delegates from more than eighty countries across Asia, Africa, and Latin America to forge a multinational front against global capitalism and American imperialism (Figure C.1). Larger than the Bandung Conference held in Indonesia a decade earlier, the aims of the Tricontinental included solidarity among revolutionaries across the globe in a roar of political insurgency.

Making noise, Algerian French economic theorist Jacques Attali argues, symbolizes an individual's "affirmation of the right to be different," and creating/performing noisy music can be a process driven by the desire "to create one's own code and work" to challenge, supplant, or supersede existing

Figure C.1 Billboard promoting the Tricontinental Conference, Havana, 1966. Photo12/ Universal Images Group via Getty Images.

epistemes and structures of power.[15] He writes in *Noise: The Political Economy of Music*:

> More than colors and forms, it is sounds and their arrangements that fashion societies. With noise is born disorder and its opposite: the world. With music is born power and its opposite: subversion. In noise can be read the codes of life, the relations among men. Clamor, Melody, Dissonance, Harmony; when it is fashioned by [human beings] with specific tools, when it invades [modern human clock] time, when it becomes sound, noise is the source of purpose and power, of the dream— Music. It is at the heart of the progressive rationalization of aesthetics, and it is a refuge for residual irrationality; it is a means of power and a form of entertainment. . . . I would like to trace the political economy of music as a succession of orders (in other words, differences) done violence by noises (in other words, the calling into question of differences) that are prophetic because they create new orders, unstable and changing.[16]

No surprise that Attali turns to the example of free jazz as the sonification of political struggle, and he essentializes it in much the same way as Carles and Comolli before him. What I think is useful about Attali's theorization of the *new thing*'s noisiness is its being the condition and active negotiation of a radically new reality—one that may not make sense in the context of the current world but, instead, can be dreamed about and aspired to through the act of performance.

Sun Ra, the cosmic, world-conjuring pianist, composer, and band-leader, was born in 1914 as Herman Poole "Sonny" Blount in Birmingham, Alabama. A precocious learner, Blount was awarded a scholarship to attend Alabama Agricultural and Mechanical (A&M) University, where he studied as a music education major for only a year before migrating to Chicago in 1946 to freelance as a pianist and arranger. There, he gained some of his earliest professional experience in the Fletcher Henderson Orchestra. He began using electric instruments as early as 1948, beginning with the Solovox keyboard attachment for piano and organ, which produced a distinctive, otherworldly, space-age sound not unlike the Theremin (thus priming it for use in the emergent film genres of horror and science fiction).[17] Years later, Blount began playing and recording with a Wurlitzer electric piano, and it can be heard on some of his first extant recordings as a bandleader and arranger, such as "India" and "Medicine for a Nightmare," both recorded in 1956. While in Chicago, he organized a big band he came to call the Myth-Science Arkestra (later simply the Arkestra), which would serve as a laboratory and vehicle for his ethereal compositions, sound design, and performance art.

Blount (Figure C.2) was a prodigious and compulsive reader with a deep interest in philosophy, science, technology, religion, Egyptology, the cosmos, and the occult. He and the Arkestra—in sound and appearance—were, for the 1950s, *far out*. He even claimed to have interstellar knowledge attained during his studies at Alabama A&M, where he was contacted by "space men" impressed by his intelligence. Those benevolent extraterrestrials offered him the opportunity to travel with them on their spacecraft into outer space—a voyage that began with a beam of energy:

> They said it was quite dangerous because you had to have perfect discipline. . . . I'd have to go up with no part of my body touching outside of the beam, because if I did, going through different time zones, I wouldn't be able to get that far back. So that's what I did. And it's like, well, it looked like a giant spotlight shining down on me, and I call it transmolecularization, my whole body was changed into something else. I could see through myself. And I went up. Now, I call that an energy transformation because I wasn't in human form. I thought I was there, but I could see through myself. Then I landed on a planet that I identified as Saturn.[18]

Sonny Blount officially changed his name to Le Sony'r Ra (after the Egyptian sun god Ra) in 1952, but it was during his abduction that the name Sun Ra was given to him by his alien tour guides, who subsequently sent him back to Earth with a mission to impart his cosmic wisdom to his earthly kin. According to his biographer, anthropologist John Szwed, Ra would recount this fantastical

Figure C.2 Pianist and composer Sun Ra on the piano at the Village Gate, ca. March 1965. Photo credit: Chuck Stewart.

origin story to anyone, and it became a kind of creative manifesto that amalgamated science fiction, contemporary UFO reports in print media, biblical parable, and a messianic calling to enlighten the masses with esoteric knowledge and advanced technology.[19] "He was," Szwed observes, "prophesizing his future and his past with a single act of personal mythology."[20]

Ra's long-standing interest in electronic music technology was crucial to the success of his mission. He procured recording equipment to capture the Arkestra without having to rely on a record label and sold those recordings independently and on his own terms—a rare feat for a black experimentalist musician in the 1950s. He founded his own record label, Saturn Records, in 1957 with the intention, former Arkestra member and Sun Ra archivist Michael D. Anderson notes, to promote his musical message of spiritual uplift for all humans, black people in particular.[21] An enhanced sonic experience might, in Ra's original lore, provoke a shift in consciousness within the listener, enlightening and possibly liberating them from earthly maladies. Given the hostilities and deprivations that were common in Black American life, Ra's message of deliverance identified Saturn—because of its advanced technology and more enlightened civilization—as a viable alternative to Earth for black people. Blending the past (Ancient Egypt) and the far-off future (civilization on Saturn), existing musical styles and new, abstract sounds, acoustic with electric, and the political with the mythological, Ra's Arkestra was an avant-garde performance art troupe aimed at transporting the observer beyond the known world. This lore can be understood as an example or application of Maulana Karenga's Kawaida concept—the necessity for Black Americans to create new myths or repurpose older folklore in the context of the current liberation movement, thereby empowering Black Americans with the agency to author or alter their culture and identity. Baraka evokes Kawaida in his "changing same" theory of a black musical vanguard, but Ra's Arkestra was putting that concept into practice years earlier with their ancient-abstract cosmic music.

The Arkestra relayed ancient and intergalactic messages to curious, unsuspecting, and bewildered audiences in Chicago. Albums from around 1960 capture their otherworldliness: *Sun Ra Visits Planet Earth* (1957–1958), *We Travel the Spaceways* (1959), *Rocket Number Nine Takeoff for the Planet Venus* (1959), *Music from Tomorrow's World* (1960), and *Angels and Demons at Play* (1960). Seeking bigger and better professional opportunities, Ra and some members of the Arkestra moved from Chicago to New York City in 1961. Ra traversed the city—from Harlem down to the Village—recruiting musicians for mostly sporadic performances.[22] In October of that year, the new Arkestra recorded their first LP, *The Futuristic Sounds of Sun Ra*, for Savoy Records.

Several of the tunes on *Futuristic Sounds* feature heterophonic textures in moments of free collective improvisation. In the up-tempo "What's That," the third track, Ra plays a short solo introduction on the piano that evokes (or possibly pays homage to) Thelonious Monk, and the Arkestra whips into a riff that they play in lockstep afterward. The head melody is divided into several short motifs arranged into asymmetrical groups of bars: an "A" section of three bars repeats (3 + 3), and a "B" section of nine bars follows, containing three consecutively smaller phrases (4 + 3+2). Disappearing as quickly as it appeared, the head melody gives way to Bernard McKinney (who later assumed the name Kiane Zawadi) on the euphonium already improvising over the swinging duple pulse (▶ 00:22). McKinney's solo is then followed by several bars of collective improvisation (▶ 00:46) that includes the Arkestra's three saxophonists—Marshall Allen on alto, John Gilmore on tenor, and Pat Patrick on baritone—and the rhythm section. The musicians all play freely while abiding by the common pulse (*time, no changes*) producing a dense and lively heterophonic texture, then Ra takes over (▶ 01:23) to improvise freely with the bassist Ronnie Boykins and drummer Willie Jones. The Arkestra reprises only the "A" section of the head melody (▶ 01:52), and the tune ends with a long, sizzling, sustained final note.

The fifth track of *Futuristic Sounds*, "The Beginning," features the Arkestra engaged in a full-ensemble free (heterophonic) improvisation without a centralized pulse for the length of the six-and-a-half-minute performance. Perhaps the sonification of a cosmic creation myth, it begins with the ringing of bells and cymbals—a shimmering haze of sound that Leah Ananda, the *conguero*, punctures through with muted tones from his lower drum. Boykins strums an open-fifth pedal (a drone) on the bass throughout, and the rattle of a maraca and jingling metal (▶ 00:27) lead into Jones's swinging ride pattern complemented by a steady snapping hi-hat (▶ 00:34). Gilmore begins a loping, mesmeric melody on the clarinet (▶ 01:11), and Allen, on flute, and McKinney, on trombone, interject with short bursts of sound. All the while Ra—with an arsenal of percussion listed in the liner notes as "bells from India, Chinese wind chimes, wood blocks, maracas, claves, scratchers, gongs, cow bells, Turkish cymbals, and castanets"—discharges darts of sound through the texture, like asteroids in the pitched ether of outer space. The musicians play together with an intense sensitivity and cooperation, and they achieve a spacey kind of "harmony" in an otherworldly heterophonic conversation using cosmic tones. Ra interjects with tone clusters (▶ 03:57) in the instrument's middle and lower registers, thickening the already opaque texture, switching back to percussion (▶ 05:10) and cueing the ensemble to begin a proverbial descent. The horns drop out after a sustained note (▶ 05:06) and the drummers and bassist gradually fade away, leaving Ra and McKinney alone (▶ 06:01) to shimmer and fade into the darkness.

The Arkestra's sound and appearance provoked fear and wonder in their New York audiences:

[The] Arkestra was scary in a different way. White people had never seen black performers in such assertive, unpredictable roles, even though some of their performances—marching through the audience, the vocal call-and-response between the leader and the band, and musical "battles" among singers and musicians—had deep roots in church services and in earlier jazz. But black people, too, could find the band frightening, and even some of the Arkestra's musicians feared what might be coming next. Not everyone got into the spirit of these "space rituals": some black musicians thought Ra was conning white people into taking him seriously, others thought he was Tomming, playing to whites' stereotypes.[23]

We might easily identify the aesthetic of Ra's cosmic *new thing* as "Afrofuturism" today—a concept and creative methodology that, Szwed notes, "draws on history, art, science fiction, music, technoculture, African diasporic experiences, and contemporary politics, and operates free of the constraints that often separate those fields." Afrofuturism as an aesthetic concept offers the possibility of a more promising future by first stepping into the African past.[24] But the Arkestra's kind of mythological world-building was lost on those expecting modern jazz. "If gimmickry were all, the 'space age jazz' of a group led by a pianist, philosopher, and poet who calls himself Le Sun Ra would be assured success," wrote John Wilson for the *New York Times* in a review of the Arkestra's downtown debut in February 1962 at the East Village's Charles Theater. Puzzled by the Arkestra's exotic instruments and sound, and amused if not impressed by Ra's wardrobe, mythological lore, and use of props (he mentions that Ra would silently glide a flashing model flying saucer through the air periodically), Wilson could not get past the dissonance of the music, which he heard as lackluster and noisy improvisation. Their unusual equipment and instruments, which "produce scraping, scratching, swishing and ringing noises, create music that usually has a strong rhythmic propulsion but tends to be drab melodically and harmonically." This so-called space music, Wilson concludes, contains too much "keening dissonance" ("keen" meaning a lament or grief-filled wail for a dead person). What does it mean that Wilson, writing for the *New York Times*'s readership, heard death wails in Ra's music, not a cosmic future?

This book is a long-form, process-oriented rebuttal of dismissals like these, which became routine for critics like Wilson, who, with their formidable platforms and influence, shaped how large swaths of a literary and record-buying public came to understand the *new thing*. Sun Ra and the Arkestra's use of heterophony, electric, African and Asian instruments, mythology, and folklore did indeed become the future of improvised and black music, evident in "far-out" groups like the Art Ensemble of Chicago and Parliament-Funkadelic. It is hard to imagine the abstract, electrified musical sorcery of Miles Davis's *Bitches Brew* without the precedent set by the Arkestra. Ra's use of an electric piano more than a decade before almost all his professional peers is a precedent for the relentless search for new sonic resources that many improvising musicians in the 1960s embarked upon; their impulse to experiment with new sounds, ensemble configurations, and strategies for improvisation represented a strength of conviction in their creative choices in the face of abject rejection. The experimentalist practice known as the *new thing* was not the novelty or fringe reactionary movement that staunch jazz modernists claimed it to be. In tracing the genealogy of this experimental improvisatory milieu throughout this book, and cataloging artists' setbacks and resoluteness, I, as a composer and improvising musician myself, appreciate their struggle to assert their creative agency in an industry and society that viewed such ambitions—especially for black artists—as irrational. If there is one takeaway to this story, it may be that any hope of arriving at a potentially better and liberated future for us all requires that we experiment, cooperate, and collectively improvise now. Saturn awaits.

Acknowledgments

One of the most important things I wanted to clarify for myself as I embarked on this project was *why* I chose to write a book on the jazz avant-garde of the 1960s. There's a pragmatic and somewhat superficial answer: the topic was born from my doctoral dissertation on Miles Davis's "second great" quintet of the mid-1960s. My interest in that band and their music stemmed not from my graduate-level musicological studies but instead from the conversations, listening sessions, and shows I bore witness to with and by musician peers and elders, starting in my high school—the Fiorello H. LaGuardia High School of Music and Art and Performing Arts—and intensifying during my uneven efforts afterward to establish myself as a professional musician in New York City. In pursuit of a doctorate at Stanford University and granted an opportunity to conduct original research on a chosen topic, it was important to me (as it was for the musicians I respected and admired back home) to understand the forces behind that lauded band's distinguished and cutting-edge sound. Fateful advice from my dissertation adviser, the composer, multi-instrumentalist, and ethnomusicologist Michael E. Veal, directed my attention to the experimentalist milieu that Davis and especially his younger bandmates were immersed in during those years as a way to find an answer, which brought me to artists, recorded music (commercial and bootleg), and indeed sounds that I'd known since childhood but did not—and was perhaps too intimidated to—fully grasp.

My musical upbringing was shaped by my father's hefty record collection, which contained LPs by Ornette Coleman, Cecil Taylor, and plenty of John Coltrane. He was a pianist and composer, and, as I write in the introduction, I'd learned, through osmosis and the sticky ears of a young child overhearing stories not meant for him, that he had been around these musicians in the early 1960s and paid close attention to what they were doing. I'd wait until he left the house to thumb through the stacks, eventually choosing an evocatively worded or illustrated sleeve from the shelf to play on our turntable. My father had a habit of playing his records and tapes loudly in the house, so, intruding on my mother's few moments of aural peace, I dutifully did the same. The mass of sound that surged from those "avant-garde" records was overwhelming and intimidating; already struggling to gain proficiency on the piano through my formal studies, I couldn't make sense of how and what these musicians were playing. The "why" part, though, was a forgone conclusion: I'd gathered, from what I heard at home, that they simply *had* to create and play that way. My doctoral dissertation presented the first opportunity for me to consciously and critically explore the compulsion, reasons, and circumstances that provoked these musicians to create these disruptive sounds and to ponder how much they informed the generations of improvising musicians that followed, including my own. I've since learned while writing that their "why" was not unlike my own: *I had to because I was compelled to.*

So I acknowledge all the music creators, practitioners, and thinkers whose commitments and generosity informed my own thinking and methods. As an improvising musician who came of age at the turn of the twenty-first century, I recognize and wish to honor those before me whose passion, work, and creative offerings have touched the lives of many and inspired some of us to create work too. I send thanks into the cosmic ether to the artists named in this book—the band leaders, ensemble members, and many other collaborators inside and outside of the studio sessions and live performances—who have transcended this earthly plane and whose recordings I take as objects of study. I honor the memory of Wayne Shorter and Wallace Roney, who took the time to talk with me about the music and world that it emerged from. And Olly Wilson, who invited me into his home in Berkeley as a curious and still unmoored graduate student and spoke to me at great length about music creation, bravery, and life's simple pleasures; he showed me the kind of validation and kindness that a master shows a precocious young novice. Thank you, Olly.

Thank you to Reggie Workman, Denardo Coleman, Archie Shepp, and A. B. Spellman for the time they selflessly offered in their interviews for this project. To the composers, musicians, and artists who have contributed to this book—directly and indirectly—through the knowledge and experience they've shared with me, thank you: Bob Stewart, Jimmy Owens, Wynton Marsalis, Wycliffe Gordon, Eric Lewis, Farid Barron, Mike Longo, Barry Harris, Vijay Iyer, Rich Medina, Roscoe Mitchell, Geri Allen, Muhal Richard Abrams, Nicholas Payton, John Santos, Jeff "Tain" Watts, Lenny White, and Miguel Zenon.

To my brothers, sisters, and family in music, thank you for being my community and sustaining me as I figured this and many other things out: Marcus Gilmore, Vicente Archer, Rashaan Carter, Burniss Earl Travis II, Yosvany Terry, Yunior Terry, Melvis Santa, Justin Brown, Brandee Younger, Rajna Swaminathan, Anjna Swaminathan, Jake Goldbas, Abdul Shakoor Hakeem, X. Hill, Sean Lewis, Mtendere Mandowa, Drew Kim, Corey King, Myron Walden, Russell Holzman, Calvin Johnson, Marina Rosenfeld, Steve Lehman, Omar Little, Malik Abdul-Rahmaan, Courtney Bryan, Rafiq Bhatia, Nina

Moffitt, Azikiwe Muhammad, Roy Nathanson, DJ OBAH, David Virelles, Dayna Stephens, Valerie Trout, Imani Uzuri, Curtis Stewart, and Alicyn Yaffe. Thank you, Paulo Rafael, for designing an early draft of this book's beautiful cover.

To those who've helped shaped my thinking on music history through encouragement and by placing me in the middle of things, thereby helping me figure out my next steps, thank you: Ruth DeFord Kotecha, Ben Bierman, Genevieve Stewart, Erika Floreska, Mary Fiance Fuss, Andre Guess, Cat Henry, Hughlyn F. Fierce, Roland Chassagne, Susan John, and Ms. Jackie Harris. A special thanks to Nyala Wright and the late Albert Murray, who, through the Essentially Ellington High School Jazz Band Competition, presented me with my first national award for writing. Cool to see where that's led to, huh, Ny?

This book would not exist were it not for the generous and consistent moral and material support of my colleagues and community at the Gallatin School of Individualized Study at New York University. This project has benefited profoundly from various faculty grants, research leaves and sabbaticals, and the enthusiasm and grace of award committees and administration. I thank my fellow faculty, our staff, and our students for helping to create the generative environment I needed to get it done. I thank our former dean, Susanne Wofford, for her steadfast and enthusiastic support from my postdoc days all the way to my tenure case; and our current dean, Victoria Rosner, for seeing, among other things, the significance of the artist-scholar model—the peculiar professional path that I have chosen and have been able to nurture at the Gallatin School. I thank our former associate dean Millery Polyné for his guidance, friendship, and counsel which made the not great times less awful. I thank our current associate dean Alejandro Velasco for his encouragement, strategic advice, and vision.

Thank you, in no particular order of course, Greg Erickson, Angelina Tallaj, Nina Katchadourian, Stephen Duncombe, Kim DaCosta, Eugene Vydrin, Roseanne Kennedy, Michael Dinwiddie, Hallie Franks, Eugenia Kisin, Sinan Antoon, Andrea Gadberry, Ben Ratliff, Kristin Horton, Duncan Yoon, Julie Malnig, Linda Wheeler Reiss, Rachel Plutzer, Theresa Anderson, Mehmet Darakçıoğlu, Jen Birge, Tracy Clapper, Joey Betances, Cynthia Allen (thank you for that gem of a documentary on the Music Inn), Rae Georges Navarro, Amy Spellacy, Jaime Berthe, Noah K., Rosalie Kaplan, Jenny Kijowski, Nick Likos, Keith Miller, Roy Nathanson, Kathryn Posin, Bill Rayner, Leslie Satin, Eugene Cittadino, Sharon Friedman, George Shulman, Tahesha Atkins, Sharice Burroughs Maureen Bannon, Anna Brown, Gil Cruz, Tess Derby, Bobby Peñaherrera, Melissa Davis, Ivy Garcia, Gisela Humphreys, Marissa

Mattes, Monique Sorel-Dominguez, Chris Streeks, Jason Yi, Jessica Pavone, Leo de Rothschild, Kent Underwood, Alex Kennedy-Grant, the Avery Fischer Center and Downtown Special Collections divisions of NYU Libraries, and those I haven't named for their help, kindness, amicability, and friendship. A special thank you to Aliya Jones and Scott Chupp, whose interest and labor as student research assistants at Gallatin helped me to complete some of the more tedious parts of the research and editing processes.

A shout-out to my colleagues across NYU and scholars in the fields of music, the arts, and culture for their help and support as well—folks who set precedents, offered templates, and gave me valuable feedback: Suzanne Cusick, Brigid Cohen, Martin Daughtry, Robert Rowe, Scott DeVeaux, Guthrie Ramsey Jr., Michael Gallope, Steve Swayne, Deborah "Deb" Willis, Lewis Porter, Peter Katz, Charlie Kronengold, Tracy McMullen, D'Angela Duff, Eric Porter, Raquel Z. Rivera, Bryan Wagner, Chrissy J. Wells, Jade Conlee, Tatiana Koike, Erica Lorraine Williams, James Gordon Williams, Ryan Mahoney, Tamar Barzel, James Downham, and Mary B. Paddock. This book would not be possible were it not for the singular archival collections at the Institute of Jazz Studies at Rutgers University–Newark; thank you, Wayne Winborne, Adriana Cuervo, Dianne Biunno, Vincent (Vinny) Pelote, and Adriana Surles. The RIPM (Répertoire international de la presse musicale) Jazz Periodicals database, https://ripmjazz.org, has been indispensable in locating and accessing some of this book's most important primary source material. For allowing me to be a somewhat errant—if still committed—member, I thank Kimberly Hannon Teal and the Jazz Studies Group of the American Musicological Society. Thank you also to Bob O'Meally, Farah Jasmine Griffin, Brent Hayes Edwards, and Yulanda Mckenzie at Columbia University's Center for Jazz Studies, and Nick Patterson and the staff at Columbia's Music & Arts Library.

I owe Shana Redmond, George E. Lewis, and Fred Moten a very special and profound thanks for participating in and helping me finalize my manuscript in the book development workshop sponsored and hosted by the Dean's Office of the Gallatin School. Shana, I hope I answered your paradigmatic question—which I can paraphrase as *Why are you writing this story in this particular way?*—in the introduction.

Thank you to Rachel Ruisard, my editor at Oxford University Press, who saw this project through, as well as Lauralee Yearly, whose early enthusiasm and efforts brought a much earlier version of the manuscript to the press. This text would not have reached completion were it not for the copyeditor, and Shenbagavalli Saravanan, project manager at Newgen—thank you. And thank you to this series' editor, Philip Ewell, whose belief in this book preceded its completion by a measure of years. To both Anne Moebes and Kim Stewart, thank you for granting me permission to reprint your fathers' iconic photos in my telling of this story. The Michael Rosenfeld Gallery and Wadsworth Atheneum Museum of Art are to thank for their permission to use Bob Thompson's painting *Garden of Music* (1960) on the book's cover. Thompson (1937–1966) was an expressive figurative painter, a drummer, a friend or acquaintance of several of the musicians discussed in this book's narrative, and a denizen of the Lower Manhattan bohemian art scene.

To Matthew Morrison, a scholar who has been a brother in the field for years and for real, thank you. Your dissertation reading group at Columbia all those years ago helped get the conceptual and literary ball rolling, setting forth a momentum that culminates with this book. To friends and peers who have read parts of this project or have just been sources of commiseration and support along the way, I got this done with your help and I sincerely thank you: Nijah Cunningham, Adom Getachew, Shay Harris, Jarvis McInnis, Fredara Hadley, Jessica Holmes, Heidi Lee, Cisco Bradley, Michelle Lou, Jeff Treviño, Ifrah Magan, Imani Owens, Elliot Powell, Nathaniel Sloan, Brandi T. Summers, Therí Pickens, and Bryant Terry.

Thank you to the Institute for Citizens and Scholars for their funding and support via their Career Enhancement Fellowship, which funded a crucial six-month sabbatical leave in 2020–2021, during a global pandemic, that allowed me to complete the book manuscript. A special shout-out to my fellow CEF fellows who, through our periodical check-ins and invaluable positive reinforcement, gave me the endurance and grit to get through the writing process; your valuable feedback on earlier drafts has contributed to whatever strengths this text has. Thank you, Amaka Okechukwu, Crystal Donkor, Aria S. Halliday, Maria Regina Firmino-Castillo, Ester Trujillo, and Renee Hudson.

To the homies and fam whose indelible spirit, care, friendship, and support made not only writing the book but living more bearable, thank you: Esther de Rothschild, Gaia Earthpeace, Michael Nikil Saval, Shannon Garrison, Anjali Kamat, Miling Yan Harrington, Josué Guesnerth Perea, Pablo José López Oro, Charles Reynoso, Ayanna Legros, Raquel Casilla, Miguel Luciano, Zaire Dizney, Sam K. Roberts, Yamila Sterling, and Don Ramon.

A special shoutout to Ms. Novella Ford and the Schomburg Center for Research in Black Culture—an institution worth its weight in gold. Thank you to the staff in the manuscripts and photos divisions for chaperoning me and my requests during those long hours there.

To the instructors and my peers at the LaGuardia High School for Music, Art, and the Performing Arts who helped me find myself; to my professors at Hunter College—Ruth DeFord Kotecha, Anthony Browne, Poundie

Burstein, the late Richard Burke, Barbara Hampton, Shafer Mahoney—and the resources of the City University of New York, including the Graduate Center; to the Mellon Mays Undergraduate Fellowship, Cally Waite, and the Social Science Research Council: thank you for the support and community you've provided me and many others over the years. The Institute for the Recruitment of Teachers, and my cohort and subsequent friends made there, *ayo*. Thank you to the Music Department at Stanford University, and the faculty, staff, and student cohort that provided a foundation for my professional career in academia—Debbie Barney, Velda Williams, Nette Worthey, Mario Champagne, Karol Berger, Jesse Rodin, Heather Hadlock, Murray Low (and the band), Herb Myers, Eleanor Selfridge-Field, Ericka Bratton, and Stanford's School of Humanities and Sciences and the Columbia University exchange scholars fellowship. Thank you to Susan Muscarella, Anthony Brown, and Jaz Sawyer of the Jazz Conservatory in Berkeley, California, where I had the pleasure of teaching many years ago.

A mis queridos tío y tía Juan Flores and Miriam Jiménez-Román, mentores insustituibles. Es un dolor profundo saber que, aunque ustedes habrían sido los más satisfecho por esta victoria, no estamos juntos para celebrarla. Aunque no pueda hablarles en este plano, sigo recibiendo con claridad y confianza su presencia, amor, y apoyo, y lo devuelvo incesablemente. And to the late Phoebe Jacobs, who plucked me from my high school jazz band and fortified me with age-old wisdom and advice on how to navigate the professional world, I recall the warm hugs, our lunch meetings in your apartment (always a turkey sandwich and fresh orange juice from Dean & Deluca), and your recollections of legends: Louis Armstrong, Duke Ellington, Ella Fitzgerald, Sarah Vaughan. Thank you for explaining to me the difference between a salad fork and a dinner fork and, more important, for having absolutely no doubt that I would "make it."

To Laetiçia Emmanuel, Yusha Marie-Sorzano, Rachael "RaeRae" McLaren, Brian Chipman, Megan "Mega" Sheila Vie Jenkins, Beatrice "Bebe" Anderson, Juliette "Julie-Jewels" Jones, Jamar Roberts, Tanwi Nandini Islam, Mojo Talantikite, Tristan Ivory, Fatima Jihada, Susie Kuo, Michael Charles Collett, Sebastián Calderón Bentín, Toby Lee, Shani Adess, Danny Deferrari, Zachariah Mamphilly, Renauld Clarke, Justino, Laura, and Jared Rodríguez, Carolyn Pincus, and Gabriel Vann-Landingham Dunn, thank you. Love you.

Benjamin Piekut has been a trusted friend and steward of this project through its various stages, high and low. Thanks for all the stoic and reliable advice which, I hope, will continue to pay dividends even beyond this. Michael E. Veal has been a warm friend and fount of musical knowledge and cultural currents since before this project was a book; thank you, Mike, for inviting me into your living musical spaces across all these many years. Thank you, Fumi Okiji, friend and admired thinker.

I am certain that there are names that I've left out that deserve a shout-out, so I extend this acknowledgment and thanks to the folks that have given me the time, knowledge, encouragement, and means to attempt and complete such an ambitious and surely imperfect project.

A mi familia—Jennifer, Veronica, and Eric Paredes, Melissa and Nelson Cardona, Christian Mateo Paredes Barchus, Mia Spain, Julissa Paredes, Mary Western, Tony and Kristina Western, Jenise Pérez, Tony Ortiz, Miguel Omar Pérez, Anastasia Román and Skylar Pineiro, Paul Maniaci, Osvaldo and Grace Román, Chorok, Sooji, and MJ Yoon—*con todo mi amor*. Donald Trammel, John Johnson, and Walter Williams, thank you for seeing me through the years. To the Coleman family—Aunt Dorette, Aunt Bunny, Uncle Rick, and Cousin Kev—thank you for your endless love and support. I hope I represented that small sliver of our family history well in the book's introduction.

This book is dedicated to the memory of few special people in my life. Two of those are my late paternal grandmother, Mildred Coleman, and maternal grandmother, Cristina Rodríguez—two very special women whose strength, resolve, character, and spirits I try carry with me each day.

To my indomitable sister Taina, I couldn't have asked for a better sibling and friend. My beautiful nieces Esperanza and Rosaria, I love you madly. Mica, you're a first-round draft pick to our family's roster.

To my beloved mother, María Cristina Román, there is no me without you. I am profoundly thankful for you, your selflessness, and the divinity that you brought to your love, parenting, and care. To my beloved late father, Earl R. Coleman—Pops—this book is dedicated to you. I thank you for your many lessons, the intellectual history and culture exposure that you prioritized for my sister and me, and for the deep care that you showed to and for me, even if it wasn't articulated verbally. I thank you for your most enduring gift, one that was passed down to me as it was to you: music.

And finally, I thank my wife and ride-or-die, Jeannie Joon Kwon. I think we *both* didn't know what to expect from this book's completion process. For the past five years you have tolerated and supported me through long, word-less nights at the computer, moments of administrative and tenure-related stress and despair, the low lows, mid mids, and the occasional and highly coveted milestone victories with unabated love and good humor. You read some portions of this work and gave me your thoughts, heard me tell the same stories more than a few times over, and only you would ever get the joke: *do you even know free jazz*? Thank you for keeping me going, and I'm happy to know that our love is indeed an experiment in collective improvisation.

Selected Discography

These entries include LPs and commercially available (and streaming) recordings referenced in the text. Dates refer to when the recording was released commercially.

Albert Ayler. *Something Different!!!!!!* Bird Notes BNL p 1, 1963.

Albert Ayler. *Spirits.* Debut deb-146, 1964.

Paul Bley, Ornette Coleman, Don Cherry, Charlie Haden, and Billy Higgins. *The Fabulous Paul Bley Quintet.* America Records AM6120, 1971 (recorded 1958).

Dave Brubeck. *Dave Brubeck Plays and Plays.* Fantasy 3259, 1958.

Dave Brubeck Quartet. *À la Mode.* Fantasy 3301, 1960.

Dave Brubeck Quartet. *Bernstein Plays Brubeck Plays Bernstein.* Columbia CS 8257, 1960.

Dave Brubeck Quartet. *Jazz at the College of the Pacific.* Fantasy 3-13, 1954.

John Cage. *Sonatas and Interludes for Prepared Piano.* Dial Records 19, 1951.

Ornette Coleman. *Change of the Century.* Atlantic Records 1327, 1959.

Ornette Coleman. *Something Else!!!!* Contemporary Records C3551, 1958.

Ornette Coleman. *Tomorrow Is the Question! The New Music of Ornette Coleman.* Contemporary Records S-7569, 1959.

Ornette Coleman. *Town Hall, 1962.* ESP-Disk, 1965.

Ornette Coleman Double Quartet. *Free Jazz: A Collective Improvisation.* Atlantic, 1961.

Ornette Coleman, Paul Bley, Don Cherry, Charlie Haden, and Billy Higgins. *Live at the Hilcrest Club 1958.* Inner City, 1976.

John Coltrane. *Ascension.* Edition I and II. Impulse! AS-95, 1966.

John Coltrane. *Crescent.* Impulse! A66, 1964.

John Coltrane. *"Live" at the Village Vanguard.* Impulse! A-10, 1962.

John Coltrane. *The Other Village Vanguard Tapes.* ABC Impulse! AS9325, 1977.

John Coltrane and Don Cherry. *The Avant-Garde.* Atlantic SD1451, 1966 (recorded 1960).

Gil Evans Orchestra. *Into the Hot,* Impulse! A-9, 1962.

Miles Davis. *The Complete Live at the Plugged Nickel 1965.* Columbia 10022 3211, 1995 (recorded 1965).

Miles Davis. *Miles in Tokyo.* Columbia CK 93596, 2005 (recorded 1964).

Eric Dolphy. *Out There.* New Jazz 8252, 1961.

Joe Harriott. *Free Form.* Jazzland JLP 49, 1960.

Andrew Hill. *Smokestack.* Blue Note BLP 4160, 1966.

Yusef Lateef. *Eastern Sounds.* Prestige/Moodsville MV22, 1962.

Yusef Lateef. *Jazz Mood.* Savoy MG 12103, 1957.

Yusef Lateef. *Prayer to the East.* Savoy MG 12117, 1957.

Modern Jazz Quartet/John Lewis. *The Modern Jazz Society Presents a Concert of Contemporary Music.* Norgran MG N 1040-A, 1955.

Freddie Redd Quartet with Jackie McLean. *The Music from "The Connection."* Blue Note BLP 4027, 1960.

Sonny Rollins. *Our Man in Jazz.* RCA-Victor 2612, 1963.

Sonny Rollins Quartet with Don Cherry. *Complete Live at the Village Gate 1962.* Solar Records 4569959, 2015.

Archie Shepp. *Fire Music.* Impulse! AS-86, 1965.

Sun Ra. *The Futuristic Sounds of Sun Ra*. Savoy Records, MG 12169, 1962.

Cecil Taylor. *Jazz Advance*. Transition TRLP19, 1957.

Cecil Taylor. *Jumpin' Punkins*. Candid CS 9013, 1986.

Cecil Taylor. *Live at the Café Montmartre*. Debut deb-138, 1962.

Cecil Taylor. *The World of Cecil Taylor*. Candid CJM 8006, 1961.

Cecil Taylor. *Unit Structures*. Blue Note BST 84237, 1966.

Cecil Taylor Quartet. *Looking Ahead*. Contemporary Records S7562, 1958.

Cecil Taylor and Buell Neidlinger. *The Complete Candid Recordings of Cecil Taylor and Buell Neidlinger*. Mosaic Records MR6-127/MD4127, 1989 (recorded 1961).

Tony (Anthony) Williams. *Life Time*. Blue Note BST 84180, 1964.

Appendix

Free Jazz: A Collective Improvisation, Atlantic SD 1364, recorded 1960					
0:00–0:21	0:22–5:10	5:11–5:39	5:40–9:42	9:43–10:05	10:06–19:34
<ul><li>[A^1] opening ensemble heterophonic "unison" (*tutti*), with circle of fourths outlined by Charlie Haden (Right Channel [RC])</li><li>[A^2] homophonic "unison" above drum activity</li></ul>	<ul><li>[B^1] **Eric Dolphy's (RC) solo**</li><li>[B^2] heterophonic riffs by horns at 0:39; occasional interjections until full ensemble is present at 1:54; episodes of riffs interspersed until end of solo</li><li>pulse maintained by Haden (RC) with another separate pulse implied by Ed Blackwell (Left Channel [LC]); same configuration for each subsequent horn soloist</li><li>Scott LaFaro (LC) and Blackwell (RC) improvise freely</li></ul>	<ul><li>[A^2] homophonic "unison" in horns; rhythm section approximates, especially Haden (RC)</li></ul>	<ul><li>[B^1] **Freddie Hubbard's (RC) solo**</li><li>Hubbard occasionally aligns with Haden's (RC) pulse</li><li>[B^2] collective heterophonic riffs at 6:30</li><li>Hubbard's solo continues without riffs at 7:06</li><li>collective riffs resume at 7:38</li></ul>	<ul><li>[A^2] homophonic "unison"</li><li>[A$^{3\,a\,+\,b}$] monophonic "unison" melody in the horns with (a) and (b) phrases; bassists and drummers approximate melody or play independently</li></ul>	<ul><li>[B^1] **Ornette Coleman's (LC) solo**</li><li>strong pulse in Haden's bassline, which Coleman and Billy Higgins follow</li><li>[B^2] "shout chorus" riffs played by other wind instruments throughout Coleman's solo</li><li>LaFaro (LC) switches from pizzicato to arco at 14:06; back at pizz. by 16:23</li></ul>
"First Take," *Twins*, Atlantic 1588, recorded 1960 (released 1971)					
0:00–0:20	0:21–2:28	2:29–2:54	2:55–4:48	4:49–5:10	5:11–8:26
<ul><li>[A^1]</li><li>[A^2]</li></ul>	<ul><li>[B^1] **Dolphy's (RC) solo**</li><li>[B^2] collective heterophonic riffs behind Dolphy begin almost immediately</li><li>pulse is initially dispersed but Haden (RC) and Higgins (LC) eventually settle into their own</li><li>LaFaro (LC) and Blackwell (RC) improvise freely</li></ul>	<ul><li>[A^2→A^1]</li><li>episode ends with held note "unison"</li></ul>	<ul><li>[B^1] **Hubbard's (RC) solo**</li><li>[B^2] collective heterophonic riffs at 3:28</li><li>ensemble heterophony overtakes Hubbard's solo</li></ul>	<ul><li>[A^2]</li><li>[A$^{3\,a\,+\,b}$]</li></ul>	<ul><li>[B^1] **Coleman's (LC) solo**</li><li>[B^2] riffs at 6:13</li><li>Remaining horns sustain long notes behind Coleman at 8:14</li></ul>

			Free Jazz, cont.		
19:35–19:45	19:46–25:20	25:21–25:25	25:26–29:50	29:51–29:59	30:00–33:46
• [A$^{3\,a\,+\,b}$] monophonic "unison" returns, carried by horns while the drummers and bassists continue improvising	• [B^1] **Don Cherry's (LC) solo** • [B^2] collective riffs at 20:36; Dolphy and then Hubbard (RC) have moments of exchange with Cherry • Coleman (LC), Dolphy, and Hubbard (RC) resume exchange behind Cherry at 24:04; Coleman and Dolphy rise above the texture with their dialog at 24:44	• [A$^{3\,b}$] latter half of monophonic "unison" (the bluesy "b" phrase)	• [B^1] **Haden (RC) begins his solo** with an ostinato motif • LaFaro (LC) walks a bassline; drums play lightly, in support • Haden (RC) begins tremolo at 27:33; both bassists play with tremolo by 28:00 • the pulse, marked lightly by drums, dissolves • bassists exchange motif in harmonics starting at 28:51	• [A^2] loud "unison" note marks transition between soloists	• [B^1] **LaFaro (LC) solos** • Haden (RC) accompanies LaFaro with previous harmonics motif and then a pedal/double-stop figure which, by 30:34, transforms into a guitar-like dialog between bassists • LaFaro resumes his more independent solo at 31:57 while Haden walks

			"First Take," cont.		
8:27–8:36	8:37–10:03	10:04–10:08	10:09–11:44	11:45–11:50	11:51–12:58
• [A$^{3\,a\,+\,b}$]	• [B^1] **Cherry's (LC) solo** • [B^2] collective riffs at 9:06	• [A$^{3\,b}$]	• [B^1] **Haden (RC) begins his solo** with a tremolo motif • LaFaro (LC) enters shortly thereafter; walks at 10:37 • Higgins (LC) plays shimmery ride cymbal and "drops bombs" on kick drum; Blackwell (RC) interjects occasionally on snare drum and toms	• [A^2] loud "unison" note transition	• [B^1] **LaFaro (LC) solos**, starting with tremolo motif • dialogic exchange emerges between the two bassists; drummers play supportively throughout

Free Jazz, cont.				
33:47–33:59	34:00–35:17	35:18–35:25	35:26–36:32	36:33–37:03
• [A^1 → A^2] frenetic heterophonic episode concludes with a homophonic "unison"	• [B^1] **Blackwell (RC) begins solo on toms** with a march-like figure • Higgins (LC) implies a pulse on bell of cymbal	• [A^2] loud "unison" note marks transition between soloists	• [B^1] **Higgins (LC) solos** on cymbals, gradually incorporating more drums, while Blackwell (RC) maintains swung pulse, engaging in dialog with Higgins on snare and kick drum	• [A^1] heterophonic passage much like the opening • [A^2] closing homophonic "unison"

"First Take," cont.				
12:59–13:09	13:10–15:02	15:03–15:11	15:12–16:27	16:27–16:55
• [A^1 → A^2]	• [B^1] **Blackwell (RC) freely improvises on toms** • Higgins (LC) plays supportively, in dialog with Blackwell	• [A^2] loud "unison" note marks transition between soloists	• [B^1] **Higgins (LC) solos** while Blackwell (RC) maintains a pulse	• [A^1 → A^2] closing "unison" note

Notes

Preface

1. Examples include Ornette Coleman's 1960 LP *Change of the Century*; singer Sam Cook's 1964 song "A Change Is Gonna Come"; Amiri Baraka's 1966 essay "The Changing Same (R&B and the New Black Music)," discussed at length in this book's Interlude; the revolutionary Detroit 'zine *Change*, established in 1965 for "sympathetic people, those who <u>listen</u> to the new music & find it of essential use to themselves," in print for only a year, edited by John Sinclair and Charles Moore at the Artists' Workshop Press.
2. Hollie I. West, "The Miles Davis Rhythm Mode," *Washington Post*, September 28, 1969.

Opening: "Free" Jazz

1. "Jazz Artist Coming to Taft Friday, November 17—Coleman to Offer Own Opus," *Cincinnati Enquirer*, November 5, 1961, 103.
2. "Jazz Concert," *Cincinnati Enquirer*, November 17, 1961, 10.
3. "Jazz Concert Canceled in Fight over Fine Print," *Cincinnati Post & Times Star*, November 18, 1961, 3.
4. "Free Jazz Hits Cincinnati Snag," *Down Beat* 29, no. 2 (January 18, 1962): 16–17.
5. I discuss this genealogy and its significance in "Heterophony," a book chapter in *Insurgent Music Theory Terminology and Critical Methods for Antiracist Music Studies*, ed. Jade Conlee and Tatiana Koike (University of Michigan Press, 2026).
6. Martin Williams, "Rehearsing with Ornette," *Metronome* 78, no. 12 (December 1961): 19, 39–40.
7. Amiri Baraka (LeRoi Jones), "The Jazz Avant Garde," *Metronome* 78, no. 9 (September 1961): 9–12, 39.
8. Baraka's 1963 essay "Jazz and the White Critic," published in *Down Beat* magazine, made him jazz criticism's bête noire at a time when color-blind ideals and "objective" notated music analyses were upheld as the norm by a white critical majority. See Baraka's *Black Music: Essays by LeRoi Jones (Amiri Baraka)* (New York: Akashic Books, 1967), 15–26.
9. As I discuss in Chapter 4, publisher Taylor Castell's open letter published in the opening pages of *Sounds & Fury* 2, no. 2 (April 1966) makes the *new thing*'s departure in modern jazz—and Baraka's role in that discourse—a matter of culpability in their choice to expand the magazine's focus beyond jazz. It begins "Some Thoughts on Publishing, or . . . Yes, LeRoi, There Is a White Power Structure."

10. See Eric Porter, "'Dizzy Atmosphere': The Challenge of Bebop," in *What Is This Thing Called Jazz? African American Musicians as Artists, Critics, and Activists* (University of California Press, 2002), 83–100.

11. See John Gennari, *Blowin' Hot and Cool: Jazz and Its Critics* (University of Chicago Press, 2006), especially 165–206 and 251–298.

12. Scott DeVeaux, *The Birth of Bebop: A Social and Musical History* (University of California Press, 1997), especially 167–169.

13. See Leonard Feather, *Inside Bebop* [later *Inside Jazz*] (J. J. Robbins & Sons, 1949) as a source of the creation of modern jazz's anti-commercialism myth.

14. Patrick Burke, *Come in and Hear the Truth: Jazz and Race on 52nd Street* (University of Chicago Press, 2008).

15. Guthrie Ramsey, *Race Music: Black Cultures from Bebop to Hip-Hop* (University of California Press, 2003), 96. The quote is drawn from Nat Shapiro and Nat Hentoff's edited volume of musicians' first-person narratives *Hear Me Talkin' to Ya': The Story of Jazz by the Men Who Made It* (Rinehart, 1955).

16. Guthrie Ramsey Jr., *Who Hears Here? On Black Music, Pasts and Present* (University of California Press, 2022).

17. Ekkehard Jost, *Free Jazz* (Da Capo Press, 1975). See especially 8–16 for a summary of Jost's scope and methods.

18. Sylvia Wynter, "Rethinking 'Aesthetics': Notes towards a Deciphering Practice," in *Ex-iles: Essays on Caribbean Cinema*, ed. Mbye Cham (Africa World Press, 1992), 238–279.

19. Sun Ra, "The Shadow of Tomorrow" from the Myth Science Arkestra's *Angels and Demons at Play* (Saturn Research 9956-2-0/Saturn LP 407), initially released between 1963 and 1967, rereleased by ABC Impulse! (AS-9245) with the full poem printed on the inner recto sleeve.

Chapter 1: Shapes of Jazz to Come

1. Marshall W. Stearns, *The Story of Jazz* (Oxford University Press, 1956), 282.

2. Ibid., 256.

3. Ibid., 260, 281.

4. Ibid., 307.

5. Mario Dunkel, "Marshall Winslow Stearns and the Politics of Jazz Historiography," *American Music* 30, no. 4 (Winter 2012): 493–494.

6. Ingrid Monson, *Freedom Sounds: Civil Rights Call Out to Jazz and Africa* (Oxford University Press, 2007), 288–293.

7. Renato Poggioli, *The Theory of the Avant-Garde*, trans. Gerald Fitzgerald (Belknap Press of Harvard University, 1962), 216.

8. Jochen Schulte-Sasse, "Foreword: Theory of Modernism versus Theory of the Avant-Garde" in Peter Bürger, *Theory of the Avant-Garde*, trans. Michael Shaw (University of Minnesota Press, 1984), vii–xxxix.

9. Poggioli sees this shallow art as a relic of an era's *modernism* and as something that will pass in relevance with time, whereas a modern art is permanently significant for its precedence even beyond its day: "The wiser historians and critics know, moreover, that unoriginal work, the mediocre or *manque*, reveals the spirit of its own times in a sharp and direct way

precisely because it remains a document and not [like modern art] a monument" (*Theory of the Avant-Garde*, 216).

10. John Tasker Howard and James Lyon, *Modern Music: A Popular Guide to Greater Musical Enjoyment*, revised ed. (Mentor Books; New American Library, 1958), 10.

11. Bruno Latour, *We Have Never Been Modern*, trans. Catherine Porter (Harvard University Press, 1993), 97–99.

12. Carol Oja, *Making Music Modern: New York in the 1920s* (Oxford University Press, 2000), 4.

13. See Barry Ulanov, *A History of Jazz in America* (Viking Press, 1952), 273–274.

14. Leonard Feather, *Inside Be-Bop* (J. J. Robbins & Sons, 1949), 1.

15. Allen Forte and Paul Hindemith, "Paul Hindemith's Contribution to Music Theory in the United States," *Journal of Music Theory* 42, no. 1 (Spring 1998): 1–14.

16. Arnold Schoenberg, *Harmonielehre/Theory of Harmony,* trans. Roy E. Carter (University of California Press, 2011), 10–11, quote on 400.

17. Oja, *Making Music Modern*, 326.

18. For a deeper discussion of Paul Whiteman's influence on the "elevation" of jazz in American culture and his reception in the black press, see Christi Jay Wells, "'The Ace of His Race': Paul Whiteman's Early Reception in the Black Press," *Jazz and Culture* 1, no. 1 (January 2008): 77–103.

19. Andre Millard, *America on Record: A History of Recorded Sound* (Cambridge University Press, 2005), 199–200.

20. Lawrence R. Samuel, *Brought to You By: Postwar Television Advertising and the American Dream* (University of Texas Press, 2001), 87–89.

21. Becky Conekin, "Fashioning the Playboy: Messages of Style and Masculinity in the Pages of *Playboy* Magazine, 1953–1963," *Fashion Theory* 4, no. 4 (2000): 447–466.

22. Andrew Mall, "Concentration, Diversity, and Consequence: Privileging Independent over Major Labels," *Popular Music* 37, no. 3 (2018): 449–451.

23. Nat Hentoff, "Modern Jazz Quartet," *High Fidelity* 5, no. 1 (March 1955): 36–38, 102–104, 106, 108.

24. Wolfram Knauer, "John Lewis," in *Grove Music Online*, accessed August 16, 2022, https://www-oxfordmusiconline-com.proxy.library.nyu.edu/grovemusic/view/10.1093/gmo/9781561592630.001.0001/omo-9781561592630-e-1002257573. It was during this stay in Paris in 1948 that Lewis penned his popular "Afternoon in Paris."

25. Gunther Schuller, *Gunther Schuller: A Life in Pursuit of Music and Beauty* (Boydell & Brewer; University of Rochester Press, 2011), 351–353, 372–375.

26. Christopher Coady, *John Lewis and the Challenge of "Real" Black Music* (University of Michigan Press, 2016), 73.

27. Hentoff, "Modern Jazz Quartet," 37.

28. Ibid., 36–38. Hentoff cites the *San Francisco Chronicle* as the source of the Gleason quote but gives no further attribution.

29. Coady, *John Lewis*, 127.

30. Schuller, *Gunther Schuller*, 457.

31. Christopher Coady expands on this: "Indeed, throughout this historic period Lewis can be seen to have reinvented hegemonic conventions through the clever deployment of vernacular devices—a composition approach ripe for double-voiced analysis. This musical play often began with the evocation of Western art music, usually through a combination of the use of straight rhythmic time, melodies devoid of blues sonorities, fanfares, composed counterpoint, and composition titles referring to European form (or simply

to European locales). These expectations were then teased in a myriad of ways, including the introduction of blues sonorities into composed counterpoint, the use of improvised counterpoint, the use of improvisation to meet relevant Western art music criteria in the exposition and episode sections of 'fugues,' and the reinterpretation of formal strictures implied by multimovement formats on the basis of folk conventions." Coady argues that Lewis's interpolations of vernacular music in "classical" forms loosened the strictures of, or "vernacularized," the latter (*John Lewis*, 115–116).

32. Musicologist Brigid Cohen theorizes the "third space" represented by the series of improvisation sessions led by French émigré composer Edgard Varèse at the Greenwich House in downtown Manhattan. These sessions, Cohen argues, in their mix of musicians and musical traditions are best understood as a third, liminal cultural space between jazz and classical music defined by its "ambivalent and transient cultural crossings that play out across an uneven playing field of power." See Cohen, "Enigmas of the Third Space: Mingus and Varèse at the Greenwich House, 1957," *Journal of the American Musicological Society* 71, no. 1 (Spring 2018): 155–211.

33. Schuller, *Gunther Schuller*, 57–58.

34. Monson, *Freedom Sounds*, 80–84.

35. Schuller, *Gunther Schuller*, 461.

36. Ibid., 462.

37. Ibid., 487–489. Freddie Hubbard attended the summer school in 1960.

38. Carissa Kowalski Dougherty, "The Coloring of Jazz: Race and Record Cover Design in American Jazz, 1950–1970," *Athanor* 24 (2006): 57–58.

39. A. B. Spellman, *Four Jazz Lives* (University of Michigan Press, 2004), xx.

40. Dave Brubeck, "Biography," accessed June 10, 2024, http://davebrubeck.com/biography.

41. Kelsey A. K. Klotz, "Dave Brubeck's Southern Strategy," *Daedalus* 148, no. 2 (2019), 53–54.

42. Dave Brubeck Quartet, *The Dave Brubeck Quartet*, Fantasy 3-7, 1952.

43. John Tynan, "Focus on Paul Horn," *Down Beat* 28, no. 4 (February 16, 1961): 17.

44. Todd Decker, *Who Should Sing Ol' Man River? The Lives of American Song* (Oxford University Press, 2015), 147.

45. Klotz, "Dave Brubeck's Southern Strategy," 158.

46. Denis Daniels, "Royal Ice Cream Sit-in," *NCpedia*, North Carolina Department of Natural and Cultural Resources, accessed September 21, 2020, https://www.ncpedia.org/royal-ice-cream-sit-in.

47. Cindy Loman, "The Story behind the Iconic Photo of Greensboro Sit-ins That the World Almost Didn't See," *Winston-Salem Journal*, January 30, 2021, https://journalnow.com/news/local/the-story-behind-the-iconic-photo-of-greensboro-sit-ins-that-the-world-almost-didnt/article_6833e64d-2839-5adc-a378-bb7ee8e87fa8.html.

48. The number of students joining the protests each day is specified on the Student Nonviolent Coordinating Committee digital gateway site, accessed September 21, 2020, https://snccdigital.org/.

49. Loman 2021.

50. Steve Smith, "Bill Smith, Master of Two Musical Worlds, Is Dead at 93," *New York Times*, March 21, 2020, https://www.nytimes.com/2020/03/21/arts/music/bill-smith-dead.html.

51. Ibid.

52. Klotz, "Dave Brubeck's Southern Strategy," 53.

53. Peter Keepnews, "Yusef Lateef, Innovative Jazz Saxophonist and Flutist, Dies at 93," *New York Times*, December 24, 2013, https://www.nytimes.com/2013/12/25/arts/music/yusef-lateef-innovative-jazz-saxophonist-and-flutist-dies-at-93.html.

54. Malcolm X, who quickly became the Nation's most recognizable spokesperson outside of the organization after meeting the founder, Elijah Muhammad, in 1952, was first made an assistant minister in Detroit, then helped establish the Nation's mosque in Boston and expanded Philadelphia's before being appointed the minister of Harlem's Temple No. 7 in 1954.

55. Marc Myers, "Interview: Yusef Lateef," *Jazz Wax*, February 7, 2008, https://www.jazzwax.com/2008/02/yusef-lateef-pa.html.

56. See James Holt, "Culture Catch: Yusef Lateef R.I.P. (February 1920–December 23, 2013)," in *Yusef Lateef: A Reader*, unpublished collected edition, which features an extensive interview with Lateef conducted by Steve Holtje that was published in a shortened and, according to the author, distorted form in *The Wire* 16, no. 164 (October 1997): 42–46. See also Ingrid Monson, "Yusef Lateef's Autophysiopsychic Quest," *Dædalus, the Journal of the American Academy of Arts & Sciences* 148, no. 2 (2019): 106.

57. Edward E. Curtis IV, "African-American Islamization Reconsidered: Black History Narratives and Muslim Identity," *Journal of the American Academy of Religion* 73, no. 3 (September 2005): 659–684.

58. Sohail Daulatzai, *Black Star, Crescent Moon: The Muslim International and Black Freedom beyond America* (University of Minnesota Press, 2012), 22–23. Daulatzai's use of the term "counter-citizenship" in relation to Black American Muslims is derived from Melani McAlister's *Epic Encounters: Culture, Media, and U.S. Interest in the Middle East since 1945* (University of California Press, 2005).

59. The practice of Islam in West Africa dates to the eighth century CE, and West African Muslims were enslaved and brought to the Americas. Margari Hill, "The Spread of Islam in West Africa: Containment, Mixing, and Reform from the Eighth to the Twentieth Century," *Stanford SPICE Digest*, Freeman Spogli Institute for International Studies, Spring 2009, https://spice.fsi.stanford.edu/docs/the_spread_of_islam_in_west_africa_containment_mixing_and_reform_from_the_eighth_to_the_twentieth_century.

60. Edwin E. Caverley, "Mohammad, Seal of the Prophets?," *Muslim World* 26, no. 1 (1936): 79–82.

61. Richard Brent Turner notes that Sunni orthodoxy believed that Ahmad assumed this pacifist stance to accommodate the British by discouraging violent anticolonial insurrection and religious conflict, which would allow the British to broker relationships with Indian Christians and a rising Hindu majority and provide the Ahmadis with protection. Turner, *Islam in the African American Experience* (Indiana University Press, 1997), 109–114.

62. Ibid., 117. See also Vivek Bald, *Bengali Harlem and the Lost Histories of South Asian America* (Harvard University Press, 2013).

63. Ibid., 119.

64. Ibid., 134.

65. The album uses the spellings "argol" and "rabat" for the instrument. The spellings in the text follow the English-language ethnomusicological convention. For descriptions and the regional varieties of these instruments, see Johnny Farraj and Sami Abu Shumays, *Inside Arabic Music: Arabic Maqam Performance and Theory in the 20th Century* (Oxford University Press, 2019), 30–31.

66. Myers, "Interview: Yusef Lateef."

67. Farraj and Shumays, *Inside Arabic Music*, 31.

68. Arnold Shaw, *The Jazz Age: Popular Music in the 1920's* (Oxford University Press, 1987), 111.

69. Harry B. Smith, Francis Wheeler, and Ted Snyder, "The Sheik of Araby" (Mills Music, 1921).

70. Samuel Scurry, "Orientalism in American Cinema: Providing an Historical and Geographical Context for Post-Colonial Theory" (Master's thesis, Clemson University, 2010), 15–26.

71. "Les Mille et une nuit," ca. 1301–1400, Arabe 3609-3611, Département des Manuscrits, Bibliothèque nationale de France, https://gallica.bnf.fr/ark:/12148/btv1b8433372b.

72. Monica L. Miller uses "social semiotic" in the context of black dandyism at the turn of the twentieth century across the African diaspora. The dandy's unique sartorial style and racialized bodies promoted a charged discursive dialectic between themselves and the viewer by virtue of their "knowing and telling cultural phenomena" in performativity. I am applying the same understanding of the term in relation to Lateef's "Afro-Asiatic" performance. Monica L. Miller, *Slaves to Fashion: Black Dandyism and the Styling of Black Diasporic Identity* (Duke University Press, 2009), 6–9.

73. Yusef Lateef, *Eastern Sounds*, liner notes by Joe Goldberg, Prestige/Moodville MV22, 1961.

74. Curtis, "African-American Islamization Reconsidered," 663–664.

75. The thirteenth-century Baghdadi musician and theorist Ṣafī al-Dīn al-Urmawī's treatise *Kitāb al-adwār* (*Book of Cycles*) is one historical source responsible for codifying Islamic music theory. Though there is no archival evidence linking Ahmadi musical instruction to al-Dīn's treatise, its array of scales may have filtered into Lateef's musical investigations partially inspired by his religious practice and, more generally, from the "Arabic"-sounding scale formulae deployed in popular music. See Owen Wright et al., "Arab Music," *Grove Music Online*, accessed November 2, 2020, https://doi-org.proxy.library.nyu.edu/10.1093/gmo/9781561592630.article.24284. For a more comprehensive study, see Farraj and Shumays, *Inside Arabic Music*, especially 4–5.

76. Monson, "Yusef Lateef's Autophysiopsychic Quest," 109–110.

77. Leonard L. Brown, writing on Coltrane's early years in Philadelphia, notes that his musical apprenticeship there happened in the "conservatory of the community," an "on-the-job training within the contexts of club settings, ballrooms, the black musicians' union, people's living rooms, and numerous jam sessions, as well as practice sessions with fellow musicians." See Leonard L. Brown, ed., *John Coltrane and Black America's Quest for Freedom: Spirituality and the Music* (Oxford University Press, 2010), 7, and specifically "Conversation with Yusef Lateef," 193, for source of the block quote.

78. Monson, "Yusef Lateef's Autophysiopsychic Quest," 110.

Chapter 2: Free to Not Make Sense

1. Manny Albam, "Education in Jazz—Advertisement for the Berklee School of Music," *Down Beat*, December 24, 1959, 6.

2. The jazz program at the Berklee School (now Berklee College) of Music had its roots in the curriculum designed by Lawrence Berk, the school's founder, for the Schillinger House, which he also founded. The Schillinger House was a college-level school for professional and preprofessional musicians intent on working in popular music and included classes in harmony that revolved around the theories of Joseph Schillinger, a Russian-born mathematician and theorist who proposed intervallic formulas for understanding and building scalar pitch collections and modulations based on intervallic symmetries, like the three-tonic system of major thirds that forms the basis of John Coltrane's "Giant Steps." Berk's

mission was to provide practical training and instruction led by experienced professional musicians with a focus on contemporary music. See Lee Berk, "The Jazz School: Berklee at 25," *Music Journal* 28, no. 8 (October 1970): 29; Ted Pease, "The Schillinger/Berklee Connection," Berklee, September 1, 2000, https://www.berklee.edu/berklee-today/fall-2000/The-Schillinger.

3. John Clellon Holmes, "The Golden Age," *Esquire* 51, no. 1 (January 1959): 100–102.

4. "A question often asked of me is why I play a plastic alto. I bought it originally because I needed a new horn badly, and I felt I could not afford a new brass instrument. The plastic horn is less expensive, and I said to myself 'Better a new horn than one that leaks.' After living with the plastic horn, I felt it begin to take on my emotion. The tine is breathier than the brass instrument, but I came to like the sound, and I found the flow of music to be more compact. I don't intend ever to buy another brass horn. On this plastic horn I feel as if I am continually creating my own sound." Ornette Coleman, *Change of the Century*, liner notes written by Gary Kramer, Atlantic SD1327, 1959.

5. Ornette Coleman, *The Shape of Jazz to Come*, liner notes by Martin Williams, Atlantic SD1317, 1959.

6. John S. Wilson, "Program of Jazz Offered Here: Town Hall Concert Includes Several New Groups and Well Known Performers," *New York Times*, November 30, 1959, 26.

7. John Mehegan, "Chords and Discords—The Question of Ornette Coleman," *Down Beat*, December 24, 1959, 6.

8. "The Controversial Mr. Coleman," *Down Beat*, November 26, 1959, 17.

9. "Strictly Ad-Lib," *Down Beat* 26, no. 24 (November 26, 1959): 66; "Strictly Ad-Lib," *Down Beat* 26, no. 26 (December 24, 1959): 12.

10. George Hoefer, "The Hot Box," *Down Beat* 27, no. 2 (January 21, 1960): 42.

11. "Not to Be Missed," *Harper's Bazaar* 93, no. 2978 (January 1960): 126. In her biography of Coleman, Maria Golia notes that he won the *Down Beat* critic poll's "Alto Saxophone New Star" category in August 1958, a year prior, and this recognition introduced him to the magazine's international readership. Golia also covers the myriad vexed reactions established musicians had to the Coleman group's Five Spot premiere. See Golia, *Ornette Coleman: The Territory and the Adventure* (Reaktion Books, 2020), 100, 114–119.

12. My definition of "heterophony" here is distinct from the standard ethno/musicological definition. I explain the genealogy—and misappropriation—of the term in Kwami Coleman, "*Free Jazz* and the 'New Thing': Aesthetics, Identity, and Texture, 1960–66," *Journal of Musicology* 38, no. 3 (Summer 2021): 261–295. Here, I define heterophony as the dense and opaque sound of decentralized simultaneity, in contrast to hierarchical polyphonic configurations.

13. "Caught in the Act," *Down Beat* 27, no. 9 (April 28, 1960): 81; "Caught in the Act," *Down Beat* 27, no. 10 (May 12, 1960): 47. See also David Lee, *The Battle of the Five Spot: Ornette and the New York Jazz Field* (Mercury Press, 2000), 14–18.

14. Leonard Feather, "The Blindfold Test—Ornette Coleman," *Down Beat* 27, no. 1 (January 7, 1960): 39.

15. In his liner notes for the 1959 album *Change of the Century*—his second album for Atlantic Records, recorded in Los Angeles—which he dictated to writer Gary Kramer, Coleman explains the music in his characteristically recondite way: "When our group plays, before we start out to play, we do not have any idea what the end result will be. Each player is free to contribute what he feels in the music at any given moment. We do not begin with a

preconceived notion as to what kind of effect we will achieve. When we record, sometimes I can hardly believe that what I hear when the tape is played back to me, is the playing of my group. I am so busy and absorbed when I play that I am nor [*sic*] aware of what I'm doing at the time I'm doing it. . . . Many people apparently don't trust their reactions to art or to music unless there is a verbal *explanation* for it. In music, the only thing that matters is whether you *feel* it or not."

16. Michael Frayn, "Miscellany in Birdland—At the House of Gone Sounds," *Manchester Observer*, December 12, 1959, 3. This quote was reprinted by Nat Hentoff in his 1961 *Esquire* profile of Coleman, where he identifies the unnamed critic as Kenneth Tynan.

17. Golia, *Ornette Coleman*, 82–87.

18. John Litweiler, *Ornette Coleman: A Harmolodic Life* (William Murrow, 1992), 29–31. See also A. B. Spellman, *Four Jazz Lives* (University of Michigan Press, 2004), 89.

19. Howard Mandel, *Miles, Ornette, and Cecil: Jazz beyond Jazz* (Routledge, 2008), 189.

20. Nat Hentoff, "Ornette Coleman: The Biggest Noise in Jazz," *Esquire*, March 1961, 84.

21. Coleman recounted to Hentoff how his self-education via a concert-pitch instructional manual as a teenager led to this misunderstanding: "He misinterpreted an instruction book he'd bought and believed the low C on his horn was the A in the book. Finally, when he joined a church band, the leader said scornfully, 'Look at this boy. Playing the instrument wrong for two years. He'll never be a saxophone player' " (ibid., 84).

22. This quote appears in Litweiler, *Ornette Coleman*, 94, without citation, and a source could not be found. Litweiler also includes an excerpt from Schuller's introduction to Ornette Coleman, *A Collection of the Compositions of Ornette Coleman*, ed. Schuller (MJQ Music, 1961), 2, where he writes, "We believe it precisely because Mr. Coleman was not 'handicapped' by conventional music education that he has been able to make his unique contribution to contemporary music."

23. Hentoff, "Ornette Coleman," 82–87.

24. Hentoff explains, "Ornette's concern with pitch is part of the dominant characteristic of his work—his conviction that the way the line is going and the pitches in which the notes of the line are played should primarily determine the harmonic progressions. He is not too far, in this broad sense, from certain contemporary classical composers who, rather than start a piece with a fixed tonality, prefer to let the melody lines create the harmonies. As always with Ornette, the source of his theory and practice in this area is his search for 'human' sounds in the music. . . . Similarly, he prefers changing rhythm patters instead of a repetitive, steady beat. 'Rhythm patterns,' he continues, 'should be more or less like natural breathing patterns. I would like the rhythm section to be as free as I'm trying to get, but very few players, rhythm or horns, can do this yet.' " Ornette Coleman, *Something Else!!!! The Music of Ornette Coleman*, liner notes by Nat Hentoff, Contemporary S7551, 1958.

25. Ibid.

26. Nat Hentoff, "The New Jazz—Black, Angry, and Hard to Understand," *New York Times*, December 25, 1966, 37–38.

27. Hentoff, liner notes for Coleman, *Something Else!!!!*

28. Martin Williams, speaking to George Russell in a conversation printed in the *Jazz Review*, credits Gerry Mulligan with dropping the piano from his group to play in a way less determined by (vertical) chords. Both Williams and Russell, however, believed that Mulligan's playing remained "conservative harmonically." See George Russell and Martin Williams, "Ornette Coleman and Tonality," *Jazz Review* 3, no. 5 (June 1960): 6–10, quote on 7. This point is also picked up by A. B. Spellman, whose interview with Coleman is interpolated into a more general profile of the artist in *Four Jazz Lives*, 129.

29. Coleman's next commercial release featuring a pianist in the ensemble is *New and Old Gospel,* recorded for Blue Note in March 1967. He also worked with a trio of bass and drums and organized several double quartet projects, first with an ensemble mirroring his own (*Free Jazz*), then with a string quartet (his 1962 Town Hall concert) and a woodwind quartet (*The Music of O.C.*).

30. Martin Williams, "Ornette Coleman—by Quincy Jones, Martin Williams, Hsio Wen Shih," in *Jazz Panorama: From the Pages of* The Jazz Review, ed. Martin Williams (Crowell-Collier Press, 1962), 284.

31. Hentoff, "Ornette Coleman," 84.

32. Gary Donaldson, *The First Modern Campaign: Kennedy, Nixon, and the Election of 1960* (Rowman & Littlefield, 2007), 39–41.

33. Ibid., viii–ix.

34. Daniel Patrick Moynihan, *The Negro Family: The Case for National Action* (Washington, DC: Office of Policy Planning and Research, U.S. Department of Labor, March 1965), ii.

35. Susan Greenbaum, *Blaming the Poor: The Long Shadow of the Moynihan Report on Cruel Images about Poverty* (Rutgers University Press, 2015), 20.

36. Moynihan, *The Negro Family,* 5–14.

37. Max Ascoli, "Editorial—This Liberal Magazine," *The Reporter,* April 21, 1955, 12–13.

38. Greenbaum, *Blaming the Poor,* 5.

39. Nathan Glazer and Daniel Patrick Moynihan, *Beyond the Melting Pot: The Negroes, Puerto Ricans, Jews, Italians, and Irish of New York City* (MIT Press, 1963), 6–9.

40. Ibid., 1, 11–12.

41. Ibid., 17.

42. "To what does one assimilate in modern America? The 'American' in abstract does not exist, though some sections of the country, such as the Far West, come closer to realizing him than does New York City. . . . There is also, in New York, a nonethnic city. There are the fields that draw talent from all over the country and all over the world. There are the areas, such as Greenwich Village, where those so collected congregate. On Broadway, in the radio and television industry, in the art world, in all the spheres of culture, mass or high, one finds the same mixture that one finds in every country. Those involved in these intense and absorbing pursuits would find the city described in these pages strange" (ibid., 20).

43. Ibid., 71.

44. Ibid., 77.

45. Ibid., 84.

46. Greenbaum, *Blaming the Poor,* 5.

47. Jean P. Le Blanc, "Jazz: The Happy Sound Is Dying," *Esquire,* April 1, 1962, 74–77, 144.

48. Max Roach and Abbey Lincoln, "Max and Abbey Pan 'Esquire' Story on Decadence of Cool," *Amsterdam News,* April 14, 1962, 47.

49. Robin D. G. Kelley, *Thelonious Monk: The Life and Times of an American Original* (New York: Free Press, 2009), 206.

50. La Marr Jurelle Bruce, *How to Go Mad without Losing Your Mind: Madness and Black Radical Creativity* (Duke University Press, 2021), 6.

51. George E. Lewis, *A Power Stronger Than Itself: The AACM and American Experimental Music* (University of Chicago Press, 2008), xxxviii.

52. Philip Brian Harper, *Abstractionist Aesthetics: Artistic Form and Social Critique in African American Culture* (New York University Press, 2015), 12.

53. Ibid., 97–106. Baraka reprinted the album review in his book *Black Music: Essays by LeRoi Jones (Amiri Baraka)* (Akashic Books, 1967).

54. Glissant, *Poetics of Relation*, 189–194.

55. Ibid., 190.

56. Ibid., 192.

57. Ornette Coleman, *Change of the Century*, liner notes by Ornette Coleman and Gary Kramer, Atlantic SD1327, 1959.

58. John S. Wilson, "Music: A Third Stream of Sound: Schuller Conducts at Circle in the Square: Classical and Jazz Techniques Fused," *New York Times*, May 17, 1960, 44.

59. Gunther Schuller, "Third Stream," *Saturday Review of Literature*, May 13, 1961, reprinted in *Musings: The Musical Worlds of Gunther Schuller* (Oxford University Press, 1986), 114–118.

60. Baraka, *Black Music*, 11.

61. Martin Williams and George Russell, "Ornette Coleman and Tonality," *Jazz Review* 3, no. 5 (June 1960): 7.

62. Russell makes an almost philosophical distinction between two schools of musical modernism, consisting of musicians who are "atonalists" (who "don't believe in the tonal center") and those who are "pan-tonalists" (musicians who "believe in a tonal center but . . . believe that all chords, all scales are relative to that tonal center"). Later in the conversation, confusingly, he substitutes "pan-modal" for "pan-tonal." He clarifies by saying, "The fact that Ornette has liberated himself from tonal centers has a metric implication because since all tonalities are relative to each other, it doesn't really matter where he is in this tune. . . . Pan-tonal jazz is here" (ibid., 8–9).

63. Ibid., 10.

64. Coleman, "*Free Jazz* and the 'New Thing.' "

65. Pete Welding and John Tynan, "Record Reviews—Double View of a Double Quartet," *Down Beat* 29, no. 2 (January 18, 1962): 28.

66. Ibid.

67. Ibid.

68. The composer Olly Wilson theorized the "heterogeneous sound ideal" as being a fundamental conceptual approach that valued timbral and textural diversity in Afro-diasporic music traditions in the United States and beyond. See Olly Wilson, "The Heterogeneous Sound Ideal in African American Music," in *New Perspectives on Music: Essays in Honor of Eileen Southern*, ed. Josephine Wright and Samuel A. Floyd Jr. (Harmonie Park Press, 1992), 327–338.

69. Miles Davis's criticism of Coleman in his autobiography is well known. See Miles Davis and Quincy Troupe, *Miles: The Autobiography* (Simon & Schuster, 1989), 250–251. However, in a 1961 article for *Esquire*, Davis makes two divergent comments on Coleman's music: positive ("I like Ornette . . . because he doesn't play clichés") and negative ("Just listen to what he writes and how he plays. If you're talking psychologically the man is all screwed up inside") (quoted in Hentoff, "Ornette Coleman," 82, 87), which suggests a conflicted or ambivalent opinion on Coleman's music the year *Free Jazz* was released.

70. Ornette Coleman, *Free Jazz: A Collective Improvisation by the Ornette Coleman Double Quartet*, Atlantic 1364, 1960.

71. Gunther Schuller remarked that Coleman would often eschew notated or dictated parameters in performance and would invite the other musicians to do the same. See the preface to *A Collection of the Compositions of Ornette Coleman*, ed. and transcribed by Gunther Schuller (MJQ Music, 1961), 2–4. Martin Williams observed in 1961 that one of Coleman's new pieces was "written out on a slip of manuscript paper" but he plays or sings the musicians' parts, or dictates instructions, rather than have them read a score. See Martin Williams, "Rehearsing with Ornette," *Metronome*, December 1961, 19.

72. Gunther Schuller, "Sonny Rollins and the Challenge of Thematic Improvisation," *Jazz Review* 1, no. 1 (November 1958): 6–9, 21. Jazz scholars point to Schuller's article, which argues for Rollins's smart soloing on "Blue 7," as the first in-depth (positivist) analysis of improvisational logic vis-à-vis musical form. See Benjamin Givan, "Gunther Schuller and the Challenge of Sonny Rollins: Stylistic Context, Intentionality, and Jazz Analysis," *Journal of the American Musicological Society* 67 (2014): 167–237.

73. Charry locates the "aesthetic of musical freedom" achieved by Coleman's ensemble in the areas of timbre, intonation, melodic construction, an adherence or divergence from tonality, a steady pulse or free meter, and the design of the composition with regard to a departure from the conventional twelve- and thirty-two-bar forms of the blues and popular song, respectively. Eric Charry, "Freedom and Form in Ornette Coleman's Early Atlantic Recordings," *Annual Review of Jazz Studies* 97 (1998): 262.

74. Ibid., 265.

75. Amiri Baraka (LeRoi Jones), "The Jazz Avant Garde," *Metronome* 78, no. 9 (September 1961): 9–10.

76. Ibid., 11.

77. Ibid., 12.

78. I could not find a single authoritative source for this attribution, but several music writers (including an editor for Apple Music, who wrote liner notes for the streaming version of the album) allege this to be the case. The titles are "W.R.U." (*Wit and Its Relation to Unconscious*, 1905), "T & T" (*Totem & Taboo: Resemblances between the Psychic Lives of Savages and Neurotics*, 1913), "C & D" (*Civilization and Its Discontents*, 1930), and "R.P.D.D." (*Relation of the Poet to Day Dreaming*, 1908). See Syd Fablo et al. "The Shape of Jazz to Come: A Guide to the Music of Ornette Coleman," *Rock Salted*, March 24, 2018, http://rocksalted. com/2018/03/the-shape-of-jazz-to-come-a-guide-to-the-music-of-ornette-coleman/.

79. Coleman recalled an incident to Spellman that occurred while they were performing at the Five Spot Café in 1961: "One night we were playing at the Five Spot and he [bassist Jimmy Garrison] got fairly emotionally upset, cussed us out and said there wasn't a fucking thing happening with the music, you know, we were all full of shit and everything and for us all to stop and let him start playing. You know, like we're playing our ass off and the Five Spot is packed and he says, 'Stop this goddam music, ain't a fucking thing happening, what do you Negroes think you're doing? You going crazy, I mean it's nothing, you know, nothing's happening, what are you doing? I mean let me have it, I know what's happening.' All this, right in the middle of the Five Spot. And so we all stopped and he didn't play a note, so we all picked it back up from where he broke in, you know. [This] . . . has to do with a person's inferior feeling of what he thinks he's been left out of. Like, 'I know I can play the bass and yet you guys are doing something I don't know how to fit what I'm doing with.' . . . So when Jimmy called me up a couple of weeks later and said, 'Well, Ornette, Coltrane called me up with this gig and I want to take it with him,' I said, 'Well go ahead, Jimmy. If you see a chance to better yourself, to make more money playing something you feel is right, then go ahead, because that's what it's all about.'" Spellman, *Four Jazz Lives*, 144–145.

80. Ibid., 128–129, quote on 150.

81. Ibid., 138–139.

82. Ibid., 134–135; Litweiler, *Ornette Coleman*, 104.

83. See Tom Lord's discographic notes under the artist entry "Ornette Coleman," https://lordi sco-com.proxy.library.nyu.edu/tjd/MusicianDetail?mid=6702.

84. Spellman specifies that the concert consisted of the Izenson piece, the string quartet, and one piece for the r-and-b band with the trio combined (*Four Jazz Lives*, 134–135). Litweiler

writes that the unreleased piece "Taurus" was Izenzon's original (*Ornette Coleman*, 104). Bill Coss, reviewing the concert for *Down Beat*, lists the piece as "Opus D." Bill Coss, "Caught in the Act—Ornette Coleman, Town Hall," *Down Beat* 30 no. 3 (January 31, 1963): 32.

85. Spellman, *Four Jazz Lives*, 135.
86. Coss, "Caught in the Act," 32.
87. Spellman, *Four Jazz Lives*, 149.
88. Ibid., 129–131.
89. Litweiler reprints a quote from an interview with Coleman by John Morthland, in a 1984 issue of *High Fidelity*, where he tells of his encounter with NBC-TV news anchors Chet Huntley and David Brinkley: "[They] came to the Five Spot and asked me, 'Can you read?' And I said, 'Only the newspaper,' because even when I told people I could do things like read music, it never helped me. So after that, write-ups always picked up on that quote. I made an album with Gunther Schuller called 'Abstraction,' and the liner notes said that I didn't know how to read or notate my own music. And all the time I had been in the studio sightreading *his* music! I realized that my image was sort of 'corn-pone musician,' this illiterate guy who just plays, so I started writing classical music. I still think of myself as basically a composer who does some performing." John Morthland, "Backbeat—Roots and Branches," *High Fidelity* 34, no. 10 (October 1984): 114; reprinted in edited form in Litweiler, *Ornette Coleman*, 104.

Chapter 3: Interlude: Points of Departure

1. Ben Ratliff, "Paul Bley, Adventurous Jazz Pianist, Dies at 83," *New York Times,* January 5, 2016, https://www.nytimes.com/2016/01/06/arts/music/paul-bley-adventurous-jazz-pianist-dies-at-83.html.
2. Paul Bley, Ornette Coleman, Don Cherry, Charlie Haden, and Billy Higgins, *Live at the Hilcrest Club 1958*, Inner City IC1004 (USA), 1976. An additional four pieces/tracks were released as Ornette Coleman, *Coleman Classics Vol. 1*, Improvising Artists Inc. 37.38.51 (USA), 1977.
3. Michael Bruce Cogswell, "Melodic Organization in Four Solos by Ornette Coleman" (MM thesis, University of North Texas, 1989), 16–19.
4. Ornette Coleman, *Change of the Century*, Atlantic SD1327, 1959.
5. Pete Welding, "Record Reviews—Joe Harriott, FREE FORM," *Down Beat* 29, no. 1 (January 4, 1962): 26, 28.
6. George E. Lewis, *A Power Stronger Than Itself: The AACM and American Experimental Music* (University of Chicago Press, 2008), 27.
7. Ibid., 28.
8. Ben Ratliff, "Andrew Hill: One Man's Lifelong Search for the Melody in Rhythm, *New York Times*, February 24, 2006, https://www.nytimes.com/2006/02/24/arts/music/andrew-hill-one-mans-lifelong-search-for-the-melody-in-rhythm.html.
9. Ibid.
10. Andrew Hill alleged that Blue Note held his recordings in their vaults, and maybe even lost one, in a colorful interview with Bob Rusch for *Cadence* magazine in 1976 (pp. 3–4). Pianist and music scholar James Gordon Williams, in his chapter on Hill, recounts Amiri Baraka's

belief that Blue Note purposefully delayed the release of Hill's albums in the late 1960s to punish him for his politics and engagement with Baraka's Black Arts Repertory Theatre/School. See James Gordon Williams, *Crossing The Bar Lines: The Politics and Practices of Black Musical Space* (University of Mississippi Press, 2021), 134–135.

11. Leonard Feather, "Andrew Hill/Blindfold Test," *Down Beat* 32, no. 2 (January 14, 1965): 30.

12. Andrew Hill, *Smokestack,* liner notes, Blue Note BLP 4160, 1963.

13. Eric Dolphy, *Out There,* liner notes by Joe Goldberg, New Jazz NJ-8252, 1960.

14. Clay Downham, "Eric Dolphy's Out: An Inquiry into George Russell's *Lydian Chromatic Concept,* the Music of Eric Dolphy, and Playing Outside" (MA thesis, University of Colorado, Boulder, 2018), 39, 40, 74.

15. Writers used many epithets to try to describe this new-sounding jazz, including "new thing," "new wave," "action music," "fire music," "out jazz," "energy jazz," "free jazz," and "post bop." Some of these, like "free jazz," "out jazz," and "fire music," are taken from album titles (Ornette Coleman, Eric Dolphy, and Archie Shepp, respectively).

16. Allen Z. Kronzek, "Back to the Woodshed: Bobby Hutcherson," *Down Beat* 33, no. 5 (March 10, 1966): 17.

17. George Hoefer, "Caught in the Act—Bill Dixon–Archie Shepp, Judson Hall, New York City," *Down Beat* 30, no. 7 (March 14, 1963): 36.

18. Cedric Robinson, *Black Marxism: The Making of the Black Radical Tradition,* 3rd ed., revised and updated (University of North Carolina Press, 2020), 3–4, 167–240.

19. Ibid., 170.

20. Manning Marable, *Race, Reform, Rebellion: The Second Reconstruction and Beyond in Black America, 1945–2006,* 3rd ed. (University of Mississippi Press, 2007), 62.

21. Amiri Baraka, *Blues People: The Negro Experience in White America and the Music That Developed from It* (William Morrow; Quill Paperbacks, 1963), 233.

22. Ingrid Monson, *Freedom Sounds: Civil Rights Calls Out to Jazz and Africa* (Oxford University Press, 2007), 175–178.

23. Abbey Lincoln, interview by Sally Plaxson, December 17–18, 1996, transcript, 30, Archives Center, National Museum of American History, Smithsonian Institution, Washington, DC.

24. Fred Moten, *In the Break: The Aesthetics of the Black Radical Tradition* (University of Minnesota Press, 2003), 22.

25. Daphne Brooks, *Bodies in Dissent: Spectacular Performances of Race and Freedom, 1850–1910* (Duke University Press, 2003), 6.

26. Moten, *In the Break,* 129.

27. Daphne Brooks, "Nina Simone's Triple Play," *Callaloo* 34, no. 1 (2011): 179–180, 182–187.

28. Amiri Baraka, *Black Music* (Da Capo Press, 1968), 180.

29. Ibid., 187–188, 199.

30. Ibid., 198.

31. A. B. Spellman, interview by author, November 11, 2020.

32. Amiri Baraka, *The Autobiography of LeRoi Jones* (Lawrence Hill Books, 1997), 261.

33. George Lewis quotes this illustrative passage in Baraka's autobiography: "We knew the music was hip and new and out beyond anything anyone downtown was doing, in music, painting, poetry, dance, or whatever the fuck. And we felt, I know I did, that we were linked to that music that Trane and Ornette and C. T., Shepp and Dolphy and the others, were making, so the old white arrogance and elitism of Europe as Center Art was stupid on its face" (ibid., 261, quoted in Lewis, *A Power Stronger Than Itself,* 43).

34. Jon Panish, *The Color of Jazz: Race and Representation in Postwar American Culture* (University of Mississippi Press, 1997), 61.

35. Smethurst elaborates: "The usual demarcation of the beginning of the Black Arts Movement (BAM) has often been the creation of [the Black Arts Repertory Theatre/School] in Harlem in 1965, following Baraka's migration uptown to Harlem after the murder of Malcolm X at the Audubon Ballroom in New York City. This certainly is a plausible beginning, especially since any event marking the advent of a cultural movement (or any movement) is always an arbitrary marker. Even in terms of Baraka, one might cite a variety of possible beginnings for his rupture with the interracial bohemia of lower Manhattan, either symbolically and/or actually, and his entry into a new sort of black radicalism that was only embryonic before. Such markers include his involvement in the proto–Black Power group On Guard for Freedom, his participation in the 1961 demonstration outside the United Nations building protesting the murder of Patrice Lumumba with the complicity of the Kennedy Administration that many African American radicals saw as marking a new stage of black militancy, the writing and performance of *Dutchman*, the publication of *The Dead Lecturer*, and so on." James Smethurst, *Brick City Vanguard: Amiri Baraka, Black Music, Black Modernity* (University of Massachusetts Press, 2020), 106–107.

36. I base this on Smethurst's perceptive summary of Baraka's creative and political objectives around the time he wrote "The Changing Same": "Interestingly, as Baraka moved into his Black Arts phase, particularly that portion of his Black Arts career most influenced by Maulana Karenga and his Kawaida philosophy, myth in many respects superseded history as it has been generally understood (e.g., an account of what 'really' happened) or stood in for history. Perhaps another way to put it is that, anticipating much later black speculative fiction/science fiction/fantasy, Baraka posited that history is always myth, always about power, and that black interests and black self-determination require myths that are about the understanding of basic social relations and social identity, about black self-determination and development, rather than a record of true events as such. In this view, decisions about what events and causes of events are significant and what are not are always subjective, partial, and closely correlated with social interests, be they national, racial, class, or gender" (ibid., 165).

37. Baraka, *Black Music*, 193–194.

38. Valerie Wilmer, *As Serious as Your Life: John Coltrane and Beyond* (Serpent's Tail, 1992), 98.

39. See Jeff Schwartz's online book *Albert Ayler: His Life and Music*, which compiles excerpts from interviews with Ayler and those close to him: https://web.archive.org/web/2017011 9070000/http://www.reocities.com/jeff_l_schwartz/chpt1.html. A general, compiled biography which also mentions these sources and influences is on the tribute website https:// www.ayler.co.uk/. See also Richard Koloda, *Holy Ghost: The Life and Death of Free Jazz Pioneer Albert Ayler* (Jawbone Press, 2022), especially 32–44.

40. Wilmer, *As Serious as Your Life*, 94.

41. The audio of this broadcast was commercially released as Albert Ayler's *Holy Ghost* box set, Revenant—RVN 213.

42. Benjamin Piekut, *Henry Cow: The World Is a Problem* (Duke University Press, 2019), 387–388.

43. Ibid., 400.

44. Albert Ayler, *Spirits*, liner notes, Debut DEB-146, 1964.

Chapter 4: Sound and Fury

1. Gunther Schuller, "Thelonious Monk at Town Hall," *Jazz Review* 2, no. 5 (June 1959): 6–8.

2. Dom Cerulli, "Review—Cecil Taylor, *Jazz Advance*," *Down Beat* 24, no. 7 (April 4, 1957): 37–38.

3. For a detailed account of Taylor's studies at New England Conservatory, see Allan Chase's excellent blogpost "Cecil Taylor's Education and Student Writings," October 13, 2019, https://allan-chase.com/2019/10/13/cecil-taylors-education-student-writings-and-some-thoughts-on-his-relationship-to-contemporary-classical-music/.

4. A. B. Spellman quotes Taylor's recollection that said faculty member called his music "mood music," which was "okay as long as it's not [Duke Ellington's] 'Mood Indigo.'" From that point onward, Taylor remembers, he took it upon himself to "be black if for no other reason than that they thought that black was bad." A. B. Spellman, *Four Jazz Lives* (University of Michigan Press, 1966/2004), 54–55.

5. Zita Carno, "Review—Cecil Taylor, *Hard Driving Jazz*," *Jazz Review* 2, no. 11 (December 1959): 34.

6. Ted White, "Review in Depth—Cecil Taylor: The Danger of Style," *Metronome* 78, no. 9 (September 1961): 36–37.

7. Spellman, *Four Jazz Lives*, 29.

8. George E. Lewis expounds upon the de facto segregation of white and black musical experimentalists in "Improvised Music after 1950: Afrological and Eurological Perspectives," originally published in *Black Music Research Journal* 16, no. 1 (1996): 91–122.

9. "Special: The 1957 International Jazz Critics Poll," *Down Beat* 24, no. 17 (August 22, 1957): 14.

10. See Eunmi Shim, *Lennie Tristano: His Life in Music* (University of Michigan Press, 2007), 106–110.

11. Cerulli, "Review—Cecil Taylor, *Jazz Advance*," 37; Ralph Gleason, "Jazz Piano: A History," *Down Beat* 24, no. 22 (October 31, 1957): 16. For more on Tristano and his recognition and praise by critics and musicians, see Ingrid Monson, *Freedom Sounds: Civil Rights Call Out to Jazz and Africa* (Oxford University Press, 2007), 88–92, and Eunmi Kim's dissertation, "Lennie Tristano (1919–1978): His Life, Music, and Teaching" (University of Illinois–Urbana Champagne, 1999), 501–522.

12. Schuller, "Thelonious Monk at Town Hall," 8.

13. George J. Boughton, "Soviet-Cuban Relations, 1956–1960," *Journal of Interamerican Studies and World Affairs* 16, no. 4 (November 1974): 436.

14. Ironically, Monk is depicted as a French resistance fighter—possibly an homage to his friend and patron the Baroness Pannonica de Koenigswarter—on the cover of his 1968 Columbia LP *Underground*.

15. *Jazz Advance* was recorded by the label Transition in Boston. The title of the Newport album is *The Gigi Gryce–Donald Byrd Jazz Laboratory and the Cecil Taylor Quartet at Newport*, released by Verve Records (Verve MG V-8238) in 1958.

16. Gunther Schuller, "Reviews: Recordings—Cecil Taylor: *Jazz Advance*, Transition 19, and Cecil Taylor, *Quartet at Newport*, Verve MG V-8238," *Jazz Review* 2, no. 1 (January 1959): 28.

17. Ibid., 30–31.

18. Whitney Balliett, "Jazz Records–Abstract (Continued)," *New Yorker*, October 28, 1961, 164–165.

19. Martin Williams, "Extended Improvisation and Form: Some Solutions," *Jazz Review* 1, no. 2 (December 1958): 13–15, 49.

20. Andrew Bartlett, in a groundbreaking 1995 article, provides a close reading of the poetic liner notes Taylor wrote for his 1966 Blue Note LP *Unit Structures* which also function as a manifesto of the composer/pianist's sound and ensemble concepts. Andrew Bartlett, "Cecil Taylor, Identity Energy, and the Avant-Garde African American Body," *Perspectives in New Music* 33, nos. 1–2 (Winter–Summer 1995): 274–293. See also Cecil Taylor, *Unit Structures*, Blue Note BST 84237, 1966. Ekkehard Jost discusses sound energy as a component and function in Taylor's playing in *Free Jazz* (Da Capo Press, 1994), 69–78.

21. Valerie Wilmer, *As Serious as Your Life: John Coltrane and Beyond* (Serpent's Tail, 1992), 51.

22. Spellman, *Four Jazz Lives*, 51–52.

23. In William Thompson's liner notes to *Love for Sale* (1959) he notes that Taylor's original "Little Lees/Louise" is dedicated to "his number one fan and gifted personal representative, Louise Thompson, formerly with New York's avant-garde Living Theatre." Note also that John Cage had a relationship with Living Theatre directors Julian Beck and Judith Malina. See Sara Haefeli, *John Cage: A Research and Information Guide* (Routledge, 2018). Details on Taylor's extramusical influences are from Bill Coss, "Cecil Taylor's Struggle for Existence: Portrait of the Artist as a Coiled Spring," *Down Beat* 28, no. 22 (October 26, 1961): 19–21.

24. For a detailed account of Taylor's method from a later collaborator and band member, see Taylor Ho Bynum, "Forty-Four Thoughts for Cecil Taylor: A Literary Improvisation," *The Baffler*, February 22, 2022, http://thebaffler.com/latest/44-thoughts-for-cecil-taylor-ho-bynum, and Bynum, "Visceral and Cathartic Joy: An Appreciation of Cecil Taylor," *Point of Departure*, June 2018, http://pointofdeparture.org/archives/PoD-63/PoD63Taylor.html.

25. Liner notes to *The Complete Candid Recordings of Cecil Taylor and Buell Neidlinger*, Mosaic MR6-127.

26. Cecil Taylor Quartet, *Looking Ahead*, Contemporary Records S7562, 1958.

27. Spellman, *Four Jazz Lives*, 56.

28. Amiri Baraka, "Review—*The World of Cecil Taylor*," *Metronome* 78, no. 5 (May 1961): 36–37.

29. Amiri Baraka, "The Jazz Avant-garde," *Metronome* 78, no. 9 (September 1961): 9–12, 39.

30. Spellman, *Four Jazz Lives*, 5.

31. Nat Hentoff quotes Taylor in the liner notes of *Looking Ahead* (1958): "Everything I've lived, I am. . . . I am not afraid of European influences. The point is to use them—as Ellington did—as part of my life as an American Negro." The quote is from Spellman, *Four Jazz Lives*, 28.

32. Spellman, *Four Jazz Lives*, 5, 28.

33. The *Chicago Defender*, a black newspaper, notified its readers of an upcoming performance of Harry Belafonte's folk troupe, the Belafonte Folk Singers, who were on a sixty-five-city tour of the United States. "Considered the first 'reparatory choral group' in America, the Singers will offer a diversified program, including works of Grieg, Bartok, and Schubert based on native folk tunes, as well as folk music from around the world, with particular emphasis on American Negro Spirituals." "Belafonte Singers on Tour," *Defender Daily*, September 28, 1960, A21.

34. Two examples from 1961 are Coss, "Cecil Taylor's Struggle for Existence" and Frank Kofsky, "Review: *The World of Cecil Taylor*," *Down Beat* 28, no. 7 (March 30, 1961): 40–41.

35. Coss, "Cecil Taylor's Struggle for Existence," 20–21. Taylor tells Spellman, "It was Lawrence Brown [a trombone player who played in Ellington's band for almost four decades] who said to me that a piano player is like a whole orchestra" (Spellman, *Four Jazz Lives*, 53).

36. Ramsey Burt, *Judson Dance Theater: Performative Traces* (Routledge, 2006), 128.

37. Spellman, *Four Jazz Lives*, 37.

38. Ibid., 36.

39. Spellman writes, "The contemporary American composer John Cage recently criticized modern jazz for using regular intervals and for being based too much on the emotions. When asked to comment on this, Cecil said: 'He doesn't have the right to make any comment about jazz, nor would Stravinsky have any right to make evaluations about jazz, because they don't know the tradition that jazz came out of. I've spent years in school learning about European music and its traditions, but these cats don't know a thing about Harlem except that it's there. Right away, when they talk about music they talk in terms of what music is to them. They never subject themselves to, like, what are Louis Armstrong's criteria for beauty, and until they do that, then I'm not interested in what they have to say. Because they simply don't recognize the criteria'" (ibid., 34, 36).

40. Ibid., 38, 40.

41. Nat Hentoff, "The Persistent Challenge of Cecil Taylor," *Down Beat* 32, no. 5 (February 25, 1965): 17.

42. Spellman, *Four Jazz Lives*, 43–44.

43. Hentoff, "The Persistent Challenge of Cecil Taylor," 40.

44. Spellman, *Four Jazz Lives*, 44–45.

45. Ibid., 45.

46. Ibid., 45–46.

47. Nat Hentoff, "Cecil Taylor: Prophet of the New Jazz Radicals," *Status* 1, no. 2 (November 1965): 44.

48. Spellman, *Four Jazz Lives*, 9.

49. Neidlinger elaborates on the difficulty of holding together a group playing such abstract music: "Trying to make a living playing with Cecil is absolutely unbelievable, because there is no economic advantage to playing music like that. It's completely unsalable in the nightclubs because if there's one thing they hate to see it's a bunch of people sitting around openmouthed with their brains absolutely paralyzed by the music, unable to call for the waiter. They want to sell drinks. But when Cecil's playing, people are likely to tell the waiter to shut up and be still. . . . We used to run into this all the time at the Five Spot. For some reason, I guess because I'm white, the owners considered me, like, the one to talk to whenever there was trouble. We'd be playing along for an hour or so and I'd get the old radio signal—the hand across the throat. Cut 'em off! Cut 'em off! . . . But you can't. If Igor Stravinsky was sitting down writing, you wouldn't all of the sudden run in and say, 'Stop it Igor! Like, we want to sell a few drinks!' It's about the same thing. You can't tell Cecil to stop" (ibid., 8).

50. Ibid., 17.

51. That Western Europe's audiences were more receptive and seemingly less racist comes up in the testimonies of many postwar black American musicians. Those positive touring experiences inspired many, like Kenny Clarke, Bud Powell, and Dexter Gordon, to expatriate. For more, see Tyler Stovall, *Paris Noir: African Americans in the City of Light* (Houghton Mifflin, 1996); Rashida Braggs, *Jazz Diasporas: Race, Music, and Migration in Post–World War II Paris* (University of California Press, 2016).

52. Spellman, *Four Jazz Lives*, 25.
53. For a detailed account of the "October Revolution," see Benjamin Piekut, *Experimentalism Otherwise: The New York Avant-Garde and Its Limits* (University of California Press, 2011), 102–139.
54. Spellman recounts the unfortunate egging of an unnamed group by members of a Harlem audience in the outdoor concert series that Baraka's Black Arts group organized in the summer of 1965 (*Four Jazz Lives*, 17).
55. Ibid., 21–22.
56. Ibid., 48–49.
57. Coss, "Cecil Taylor's Struggle for Existence," 20–21.
58. Ibid., 20.
59. Spellman, *Four Jazz Lives*, 14–15.
60. Ira Gitler, liner notes to Freddie Redd Quartet, *The Music from "The Connection,"* Blue Note ST-84027. Recorded February 15, 1960.
61. "Strictly Ad Lib" column, *Down Beat* 28, no. 2 (January 19, 1961): 10. See also Marvin Carlson, "A Concise Introduction to the Living Theatre," Digital Theatre + DT+ Fundamentals, accessed June 2, 2025, https://edu-digitaltheatreplus-com.proxy.library. nyu.edu/content/guides/the-living-theatre?utm_campaign=share-feature.
62. This album has been alternately released as *New York City R&B* and *Jumpin' Punkins*.
63. Cecil Taylor and Buell Neidlinger, *New York City R&B*, liner notes by Nat Hentoff, Doxy ACV2106, 1961.
64. Nat Hentoff liner notes on Taylor and Neidlinger, *New York City R&B*.
65. Spellman, *Four Jazz Lives*, 11–12.
66. Ibid., 43–44.
67. Ibid., 44.
68. Hentoff, "The Persistent Challenge of Cecil Taylor," 18.
69. David Grundy discusses Taylor's poetic work from this period in "'Everything That You Do': On the Poetry of Cecil Taylor," *Chicago Review* 62, no. 4 (2019), https://www.chicag oreview.org/david-grundy-everything-that-you-do-on-the-poetry-of-cecil-taylor/.
70. Don Heckman, "Way Out There," *Down Beat Music '63*, 8th Yearbook (1963): 48.
71. Whitney Balliett, "Musical Events—Jazz Concerts," *New Yorker*, January 11, 1964, 92–94.
72. See Matt Weston's website, http://www.mattweston.com/cecilpanel.html. According to Weston in an email to author, May 25, 2021, the original tape on which the discussion was captured was partially recorded over, and the subsequent transcript (which was originally published in a 1964 edition of Bennington's literary journal *Silo*) contains only a fragment of the panel conversation.
73. John J. Desmond, *Jazz—The Experimenters*, USA, 1965, Library of Congress, Music Division.

Chapter 5: Anti Jazz, Anti Music

1. "Malcolm Scores U.S. and Kennedy," *New York Times*, December 2, 1963, 21.
2. In his eulogy, made at El-Shabazz's funeral at the Faith Temple of God in Harlem, actor Ossie Davis remembered him this way:

> "Malcolm had stopped being a 'Negro' years ago.

"It had become too small, too puny, too puny, too weak a word for him. Malcolm was bigger than that. Malcolm had become an Afro-American and he wanted—so desperately—that we, that all of his people, would become Afro-Americans too. . . .

"They will say that he is of hate—a fanatic, a racist—who can only bring evil to the cause for which you struggle!

"And we will answer and say unto them: Did you ever talk to Brother Malcolm? Did you ever touch, or have him smile at you? Did you ever really listen to him? Did he ever do a mean thing? Was he ever himself associated with violence or any public disturbance? For if you did you would know him. And if you knew him you would know why we must honor him: Malcolm was our manhood, our living, black manhood! This was his meaning to his people. And in honoring him we honor the best in ourselves. . . .

"However much we may have differed with him—or with each other about him and his value as a man—let his going from us serve only to bring us together now. Consigning these mortal remains to earth, the common mother of all, secure in the knowledge that what we place in the ground is no more now a man—but a seed—which, after the winter of discontent, will come forth again to meet us. And we will know him then for what he was and is—a Prince—our own black shining Prince!—who didn't hesitate to die, because he loved us so." (Ossie Davis, "Our Shining Black Prince," in *Malcolm X: The Man and His Times*, ed. John Henrik Clarke [Africa World Press, 1990], xi–xiii)

3. Gunther Schuller, "Sonny Rollins and the Challenge of Thematic Improvisation," *Jazz Review* 1, no. 1 (November 1958): 6–11, 21. For a critique of Schuller's article, see Benjamin Givan, "Gunther Schuller and the Challenge of Sonny Rollins: Stylistic Context, Intentionality, and Jazz Analysis," *Journal of the American Musicological Society* 67, no. 1 (Spring 2014): 167–237.

4. The Sonny Rollins Collection at the Schomburg Library, New York Public Library contains a wealth of Rollins's methodical, philosophical, and spiritual journaling from the 1950s onward. Since my research and writing of this chapter, these have been compiled, edited, and published by Sam V. H. Reese in *The Notebooks of Sonny Rollins* (New York Review Books, 2024).

5. "For two years, only rumors are available. The most often heard these days are about his playing daily on the Williamsburg Bridge. Then, beginning in the summer of 1961, there occurred a half-dozen reports that the artist was ending his retirement. These reports prove true in November." Bill Coss, "The Return of Sonny Rollins," *Down Beat* 29, no. 1 (January 4, 1962): 13.

6. "Jimmy Smith Signs with Verve—And How!," *Down Beat* 30, no. 7 (March 14, 1963): 12.

7. Dan Morgenstern., "'Live' at the Village Gate," *ASCAP Jazz Notes*, no. 6 (October 1962): 2. Recordings of the other nights at the Gate were available for some time as bootlegs circulating on the internet. They are now commercially released as *Sonny Rollins Quartet with Don Cherry—Complete Live at the Village Gate 1962*, Solar Records 4569959, 2015.

8. On an undated lined white looseleaf Rollins wrote, "<u>Tone row</u> improvisation by the bass. CHROMATIC IMPROVISATION. Intuitive relation of the solos to the bass." Sonny Rollins, Schomburg SC MG 898, Box 4, fl. 4.2–4.4.

9. On a white lined looseleaf dated March 2, 1963, Rollins wrote "Orange—E; Red—A; Blue—Ab; Green—D; Yellow—F#; Violet—E♭ < according to Don Cherry" (ibid.).

10. Ibid.

11. Sonny Rollins, SC MG 898, Box 20, fl. 20.1.

12. Pete Welding, "Review—Sonny Rollins, *Our Man in Jazz*," *Down Beat* 30, no. 8 (March 28, 1963): 30, 32.

13. Reader Richard Thompson critiqued Welding's review in a letter published in the "Chords and Discords" column: "Could this be the same man who rated a similar Ornette Coleman effort five stars? Can one who finds Rollins & Co. 'boring' find Coleman's noise 'very exciting'? . . . As for this 'grip of the new thing,' anyone who has listened closely to Rollins knows that this music is merely an extension of what he has been doing ever since he appeared on the scene." *Down Beat* 30, no. 11 (May 9, 1963): 5.

14. Ekkehard Jost, *Free Jazz* (Da Capo Press, 1975/1994), 139.

15. Rollins kept up this experimentation with yet another group of relatively younger *new thing* musicians at Birdland, bassist Henry Grimes and drummer Charles Moffett, who recorded with Taylor and Coleman, respectively. "Strictly Ad Lib," *Down Beat* 30, no. 13 (June 6, 1963): 10. *Down Beat* misprints Moffett's name as "Clarence."

16. Ibid.

17. John Litweiler, in his biography of Coleman, credits Rollins with being a catalyst for Coltrane's explorations of free playing. See John Litweiler, *Ornette Coleman: A Harmolodic Life* (William Morrow, 1992), 125.

18. Bill Coss, "The Newport Jazz Festival," *Metronome* 75, no. 9 (September 1958): 14.

19. John Tynan, "Take 5," *Down Beat* 28, no. 24 (November 23, 1961): 40.

20. Whitney Balliett, "Anti-Music," in *Such Sweet Thunder* (MacDonald, 1968), 46.

21. For research works on this topic, see Lewis Porter's *John Coltrane: His Life and Music* (University of Michigan Press, 1998), especially 262–292; Ashley Kahn, *A Love Supreme: The Story of John Coltrane's Signature Album* (Viking, 2002); Leonard L. Brown, ed., *John Coltrane and Black America's Quest for Freedom: Spirituality and the Music* (Oxford University Press, 2010). The 2017 documentary *Chasing Trane: The John Coltrane Documentary*, directed by John Scheinfeld, emphasizes Coltrane's spiritual quest. The Saint John Coltrane African Orthodox Church (http://coltranechurch.org) of San Francisco holds a *Love Supreme* meditation on the first Sunday of every month in addition to its weekly 11 a.m. mass (as of this writing); for more on the church, see Nicholas Louis Baham III, *The Coltrane Church: Apostles of Sound, Agents of Social Justice* (McFarland, 2015).

22. Todd S. Jenkins discusses the delayed 1967 release date in *Free Jazz and Free Improvisation* (Greenwood Press, 2004), 1:lxvii.

23. John Coltrane and Don Cherry, *The Avant-Garde*, liner notes by A. B. Spellman, Atlantic SD1451, 1960.

24. Coltrane had worked with Monk extensively in 1957, including a six-month residency at the Five Spot Café with Monk's quartet (featuring Wilbur Ware on bass and Frankie Dunlop on drums, replaced by Shadow Wilson) starting in July. See Robin D. G. Kelley, *Thelonious Monk: The Life and Times of an American Original* (Free Press, 2009), 229–235.

25. Author's interview with Reggie Workman, March 11, 2012.

26. Spellman says that Heath was on Coleman's first album, *Something Else!!!* (1958), where the two tunes were first recorded, but this is an error. Heath participated in Coleman's second commercial release, *Tomorrow Is the Question!*, recorded in Los Angeles in January 1959.

27. Matthew Warnock, "McCoy Tyner Interview: A Life in Jazz," *Guitar International*, October 21, 2009, http://guitarinternational.com/2009/10/21/mccoy/.

28. "*The Black Scholar* Interviews McCoy Tyner," *Black Scholar* 2, no. 2 (October 1970): 44.

29. See Frank Kofsky, *John Coltrane and the Jazz Revolution of the 1960s* (Pathfinder, 1998); Philippe Carles and Jean-Louis Comolli, *Free Jazz Black Power*, trans. Grégory Pierrot (University of Mississippi Press, 1971); Valerie Wilmer, *As Serious as Your Life: John Coltrane and Beyond* (Serpent's Tail, 1992); Lewis Porter, *John Coltrane: His Life and Music* (University of Michigan Press, 1998); Ben Ratliff, *Coltrane: The Story of a Sound* (Farrar, Straus and Giroux, 2007); Leonard Brown, ed., *John Coltrane and Black America's Quest for Freedom: Spirituality and the Music* (Oxford University Press, 2010). See also Chris DeVito et al., *The John Coltrane Reference*, ed. Lewis Porter (Routledge, 2008).

30. John Coltrane, *The Other Village Vanguard Tapes*, ABC Impulse! AS9325, was released in 1977 and is now available on the *Coltrane—The Complete 1961 Village Vanguard Recordings* CD box set. Abdul-Malik's instrument is mislabeled "oud" on the LP.

31. Archie Shepp, interview with the author, September 19, 2020.

32. "*The Black Scholar* Interviews McCoy Tyner," 44–45.

33. The order of solos on both performances (on Part/Side One and on Part/Side Two) are John Coltrane, Dewey Johnson, Pharoah Sanders, Freddie Hubbard, and Marion Brown; John Tchicai, McCoy Tyner, Art Davis, Jimmy Garrison, and (only on Part I) Elvin Jones.

34. "*The Black Scholar* Interviews McCoy Tyner," 45.

35. John S. Wilson, "Jazz and the Anarchy of the Avant-garde," *New York Times*, April 24, 1966, X23.

36. Bill Mathieu, "Spotlight Review—Avante-Garde [*sic*] Summit—John Coltrane, *Ascension*," *Down Beat* 33, no. 9 (May 5, 1966): 25.

37. An ad printed in the *Chicago Daily Defender* on Wednesday, November 10, 1965 (p. 10) lists Davis's dates as November 24–December 6, but an ad from Monday, December 6 (p. 12) reads, "Trumpet star Miles Davis and his quintet are scheduled to bow into Old Town's Plugged Nickel on N. Wells tonight for a five day engagement ending Dec. 10. Other members of the group are Tony Williams, drums; Wayne Shorter, tenor sax; Herbie Hancock, piano; and Ron Carter, bass."

38. John Szwed, *So What: The Life of Miles Davis* (Simon & Schuster, 2002), 254–255.

39. The original American commercial release, *Miles Davis—Cookin' at the Plugged Nickel*, Columbia CJ 40645, was released on CD in 1987 and contains the first set of December 22 and "Milestones" from the third set of December 23. The box set *Miles Davis—The Complete Live at the Plugged Nickel 1965*, Columbia CXK 66955, was released in 1995. Columbia's Japanese division released selections from the two nights on LP in 1976.

40. Michelle Mercer, *Footprints: The Life and Work of Wayne Shorter* (Penguin, 2007), 109.

41. Ibid.

42. Hancock speaking on *Miles Ahead*, Mark Obenhaus, dir., Obenhaus Films, 1986.

43. Garrett Michaelsen, "Making 'Anti-Music': Divergent Interactional Strategies in the Miles Davis Quintet's *Complete Live at the Plugged Nickel*," *Music Theory Online* 25, no. 3 (September 2019), https://www.mtosmt.org/issues/mto.19.25.3/mto.19.25.3.michaelsen.html.

44. Music theorist Keith Waters discusses this phenomenon in the context of *hypermeter*, or larger, superstructural groupings of the song form's most basic units (i.e., a four-beat bar). In other words, when playing a thirty-two-bar tune, musicians can "feel" the passage of eight-bar units since they are each a symmetrical quarter of the overall length of the form. Hypermeter, for the musicians in Davis's quartet, was an intuited point of reference in free

improvisation grounded by a steady pulse. Keith Waters, *The Studio Recordings of the Miles Davis Quintet: 1965–68* (Oxford University Press, 2011), 64–73.

45. Anthony Williams, *Life Time*, Blue Note BST 84180, 1964. The remaining tracks on *Life Time*—"Memory" and "Barb's Song to the Wizard"—were recorded on a second day with a new quartet consisting of vibist/marimbaist Bobby Hutcherson, bassist Ron Carter, and pianist Herbie Hancock, and they also contain extended periods of free, heterophonic improvisation.

46. The extant recordings of the Japanese tour include the quintet's performances in Hibiya Yagai Ongaku-do Hall (July 12) and Kōsei Nenkin Hall (July 14) in Tokyo and Maruyama Ongaku-do Hall (July 15) in Kyoto. *Miles in Tokyo* captures the quintet's performance in Tokyo's Kōsei Nenkin Kaikan Hall.

47. Sam Rivers, quoted by Nat Hentoff in his liner notes to Rivers's 1964 LP *Fuchsia Swing Song* (Blue Note BLP4184). *Miles in Tokyo* was first released by CBS/Sony Japan (SONX-60064-R) in 1969.

48. Michaelsen in "Making 'Anti-Music'" describes the impetus behind Davis's hiring of these younger musicians as stemming from his desire for "discomfort . . . which in turn would provoke change after his comparatively fallow period of the early 1960," a trope taken up by Davis's biographers of this period.

49. Nat Shapiro, "Heralding 'the New Thing' in Music," *Status* 2, no. 6 (October 1966): 61–62.

50. Nat Hentoff, "The New Jazz—Black, Angry, and Hard to Understand," *New York Times*, December 26, 1966, A10, A38.

51. Don Heckman, "What's Next for Jazz?," *Down Beat's Music '65*, 10th Yearbook (1965): 32–34.

52. For an example of this rarified view of music as art, which has been the governing assumption in the field of musicology since its inception, see Peter Kivy, *The Music Alone: Philosophical Reflections on the Purely Musical Experience* (Cornell University Press, 1990). For a critique of this aesthetic epistemology and one of its most influential promulgators, Theodor Adorno, see Fumi Okiji, *Jazz as Critique: Adorno and Black Expression Revisited* (Stanford University Press, 2018).

53. For more on the particularly Germanic Eurocentrism of academic music in the United States, see David Josephson, "The German Musical Exile and the Course of American Musicology," *Current Musicology*, nos. 79–80 (April 2005): 9–53.

54. LeRoi Jones [Amiri Baraka], "Voice from the Avant-garde: Archie Shepp," *Down Beat* 32, no. 1 (January 14, 1965): 18–20, 36; Archie Shepp, "An Artist Speaks Bluntly," *Down Beat* 32, no. 26 (December 16, 1965): 11, 42.

55. Jones, "Voice from the Avant-garde," 18, 20.

56. Ibid., 36.

57. Bill Coss, "Lennie Tristano Speaks Out," *Down Beat* 29, no. 30 (December 6, 1962): 20–21.

58. Jones, "Voice from the Avant-garde," 36.

59. Shepp, "An Artist Speaks Bluntly," 11.

60. "Le Roi Jones, the Negro poet-playwright who has recently made a point of outraging white liberals by a total attack on their world and values, also happens to be one of the leading critics taking up 'The New Thing' as a valid artistic statement, perhaps the only one now possible in jazz. Jones is joined in the defense by such jazz critics as Don Heckman and Martin Williams." Herm Schoenfeld, "Jazz Mugged by 'New Thing,'" *Variety* 238, no. 8 (April 24, 1965): 49.

61. Don Heckman's articles in volume 32 of *Down Beat* are "Inside Ornette Coleman—Part 1," no. 19 (September 9, 1965): 13–15; "Notation and the Jazz Composer," no. 20 (September 23, 1965): 24–25; and "Inside Ornette Coleman—Part 2," no. 23 (December 16, 1965): 20–21.

62. Leonard Feather, "Feather's Nest," *Down Beat* 32, no. 20 (September 23, 1965): 44, and "Feathers Nest: A Plea for Less Critical Infighting, More Attention to the Music Itself," *Down Beat* 32, no. 26 (December 16, 1965): 13.

63. Whitney Balliett, "Jazz Concerts — Charge!," *New Yorker*, March 20, 1965, 175–176.

64. Francis Newton [Eric Hobsbawm], "New Thing," *New Statesman*, May 28, 1965, 855.

65. Ralph Berton, "Editorial," *Sounds & Fury* 2, no. 2 (April 1966): 39.

66. "The Division's strength is built on its ability both to market successfully its popular and classical catalog—the largest in existence—and to introduce new trends. **Teen-Age Market.** This market is the most important single growth area for the industry, and during the year Columbia Records served it with particular success." Columbia Broadcasting System, Inc., "1965 Annual Report to the Shareholders," 31. Ann Arbor: ProQuest Historical Annual Reports, https://about.proquest.com/en/products-services/pq_hist_annual_repts/.

67. Dan Morgenstern et al., "The Jazz Avant-garde: Pro and Con—A Discussion," *Down Beat's Music '65*, 10th Yearbook (1965): 89, 94–95.

68. Ibid., 95.

69. See Katherine A. Bussard and Kristen Gresh, eds., *Life Magazine and the Power of Photography* (Princeton University Art Museum, 2020).

70. Morgenstern et al., "The Jazz Avant-garde," 92, 95.

71. Ibid., 95.

72. Newton [Hobsbawm], "New Thing," 855.

Closing: Black Power

1. Don Heckman, "Breakthrough '66," *Down Beat's Music 66*, 11th Yearbook (1967): 14–15.

2. Ibid., 16–17.

3. Ibid., 17.

4. Amiri Baraka, "The Changing Same (R&B and the New Black Music)," in *Black Music* (Da Capo Press, 1967), 185.

5. Taylor Castell, "Publisher's Page," *Sounds & Fury* 2, no. 2 (April 1966): n.p.; Ralph Burton, "Those in Favor," *Sounds & Fury* 2, no. 2 (April 1966): 39.

6. Bruce Cook, "Jazz—The Introverted New Jazz Style May Not Be Relevant Today," *Chicago Tribune*, May 7, 1967, 60.

7. Nat Hentoff, "The Life Perspectives of the New Jazz," *Down Beat Music* 12 (1967): 23.

8. Alain Corneau, "Marion Brown: Black, Brown and Free," *Jazz Magazine*, no. 133 (August 1966): 27–33.

9. Philippe Carles and Jean-Louis Comolli, *Free Jazz/Black Power*, trans. Grégory Pierrot (University of Mississippi Press, 2015), 12–13.

10. Steve Lehman, "I Love You with an Asterisk: African-American Experimental Music and the French Jazz Press, 1970–1980," *Critical Studies in Improvisation/Études critiques en improvisation* 1, no. 2 (2005): 38–53.

11. Drott lists musicians Sonny Murray, Marion Brown, Anthony Braxton, Steve Lacy, Noah Howard, Frank Wright, Alan Silva, Steve Potts, and the Art Ensemble of Chicago as having "decamped" to Paris starting in the late 1960s. Paris had been a haven for African American artists since the First World War, with James Reese Europe and the Harlem Hellfighters 369th Infantry Regiment. See Eric Drott, "Free Jazz and the French Critic," *Journal of the American Musicological Society* 61, no. 3 (2008): 542.

12. See Ingrid Monson, *Freedom Sounds: Civil Rights Call Out to Jazz and Africa* (Oxford University Press, 2007); Benjamin Piekut, *Experimentalism Otherwise: The New York Avant-Garde and Its Limits* (University of California Press, 2011).

13. Jayne Cortez, *Somewhere in Advance of Nowhere* (Serpent's Tail; High Risk Books, 1996), quoted in Robin D. G. Kelley's *Freedom Dreams: The Black Radical Imagination* (Beacon Press, 2002), xii.

14. See Nina Kraus, *Of Sound Mind: How Our Brain Constructs a Meaningful Sonic World* (MIT Press, 2021) for a general introduction. A general overview of the positive effects of sound and negative effects of noise on our nervous and immune systems is Andi Zhang et al., "The Immune System Can Hear Noise," *Frontiers in Immunology* 11 (2021), https://doi.org/10.3389/fimmu.2020.619189.

15. Jacques Attali, *Noise: The Political Economy of Music*, trans. Brian Massumi (University of Minnesota Press, 2009), 139.

16. Ibid., 6, 19.

17. Michael D. Anderson., "Saturn/El Saturn History," *Sun Ra Music Archive* (blog), accessed December 3, 2023, https://sunraarchive.yourwebsitespace.com/history_of_saturn_records.

18. John Szwed, *Space Is the Place: The Lives and Times of Sun Ra* (Duke University Press, 2020), 29.

19. The U.S. government's rocket program was headquartered in Huntsville, where Alabama A&M is located.

20. Szwed, *Space Is the Place*, 31–32.

21. Anderson, "Saturn/El Saturn History."

22. Szwed, *Space Is the Place*, 183–186.

23. Ibid., xviii.

24. Ibid., xxv.

Selected Bibliography

Anderson, Michael D. "Saturn/El Saturn History." *The Sun Ra Music Archive* (blog). Accessed December 3, 2023. https://sunraarchive.yourwebsitespace.com.

Anderson, Iain. *This Is Our Music: Free Jazz, the Sixties, and American Culture*. University of Pennsylvania Press, 2007.

Attali, Jacques. *Noise: The Political Economy of Music*. Translated by Brian Massumi. University of Minnesota Press, 2009.

Baham, Nicholas Louis, III. *The Coltrane Church: Apostles of Sound, Agents of Social Justice*. McFarland, 2015.

Bald, Vivek. *Bengali Harlem and the Lost Histories of South Asian America*. Harvard University Press, 2013.

Banes, Sally. "The Birth of the Judson Dance Theatre: 'A Concert of Dance' at Judson Church, July 6, 1962." *Dance Chronicle* 5, no. 2 (1982): 167–212.

Baraka, Amiri. *The Autobiography of LeRoi Jones*. Lawrence Hill Books, 1997.

Baraka, Amiri. *Black Music*. Da Capo Press, 1967.

Baraka, Amiri. *Black Music: Essays by LeRoi Jones (Amiri Baraka)*. Akashic Books, 1967.

Baraka, Amiri. *Blues People: The Negro Experience in White America and the Music That Developed from It*. William Morrow; Quill Paperbacks, 1963.

Baraka, Amiri. "The Changing Same (R&B and the New Black Music)." In *Black Music*. Da Capo Press, 1967.

Bartlett, Andrew. "Cecil Taylor, Identity Energy, and the Avant-Garde African American Body." *Perspectives in New Music* 33, nos. 1–2 (Winter–Summer 1995): 274–293.

Berk, Lee. "The Jazz School: Berklee at 25." *Music Journal* 28, no. 8 (October 1970): 29.

Berliner, Paul F., ed. *Thinking in Jazz: The Infinite Art of Improvisation*. University of Chicago Press, 1994.

Bierman, Benjamin. "Unlocking the Mysteries of the Second Miles Davis Quintet." *Journal of Jazz Studies* 7, no. 2 (Fall 2011): 258–265.

Boughton, George J. "Soviet-Cuban Relations, 1956–1960." *Journal of Interamerican Studies and World Affairs* 16, no. 4 (November 1974): 436–453.

Braggs, Rashida. *Jazz Diasporas: Race, Music, and Migration in Post–World War II Paris*. University of California Press, 2016.

Brooks, Daphne. *Bodies in Dissent: Spectacular Performances of Race and Freedom*. Duke University Press, 2003.

Brooks, Daphne. "Nina Simone's Triple Play." *Callaloo* 34, no. 1 (2011): 176–197.

Brown, Leonard L., ed. *John Coltrane and Black America's Quest for Freedom: Spirituality and the Music*. Oxford University Press, 2010.

Bruce, La Marr Jurelle. *How to Go Mad without Losing Your Mind: Madness and Black Radical Creativity*. Duke University Press, 2021.

Bürger, Peter. *Theory of the Avant-Garde*. Translated by Michael Shaw. University of Minnesota Press, 1984.

Burt, Ramsey. *Judson Dance Theater: Performative Traces*. Routledge, 2006.

Bussard, Katherine A., and Kristen Gresh, eds. *Life Magazine and the Power of Photography*. Princeton University Art Museum, 2020.

Carles, Philippe, and Jean-Louis Comolli. *Free Jazz Black Power*. Translated by Grégory Pierrot. University of Mississippi Press, 1971.

Caverley, Edwin E. "Mohammad, Seal of the Prophets?" *Muslim World* 26, no. 1 (1936): 79–82.

Charry, Eric. "Freedom and Form in Ornette Coleman's Early Atlantic Recordings." *Annual Review of Jazz Studies* 97 (1998): 261–294.

Chase, Allan. "Cecil Taylor's Education & Student Writings." *Allan Chase—Jazz Pedagogy, History & Improvisation* (blog), October 13, 2019.

Coady, Christopher. *John Lewis and the Challenge of "Real" Black Music*. University of Michigan Press, 2016.

Cogswell, Michael Bruce. "Melodic Organization in Four Solos by Ornette Coleman." Master's thesis, University of North Texas, 1989.

Clarke, John Henrik. *Malcolm X: The Man and His Times*. Africa World Press, 1990.

Cohen, Brigid. "Enigmas of the Third Space: Mingus and Varèse at the Greenwich House." *Journal of the American Musicological Society* 71, no. 1 (Spring 2018): 155–211.

Coleman, Kwami. "Free Jazz and the 'New Thing': Aesthetics, Identity, and Texture, 1960–1966." *Journal of Musicology* 38, no. 3 (Summer 2021): 261–295.

Coleman, Kwami. "The Second Quintet: Miles Davis, the Jazz Avant-Garde, and Change, 1959–68." Ph.D. diss., Stanford University, 2014.

Coleman, Ornette. *A Collection of the Compositions of Ornette Coleman*. Edited by Gunther Schuller. MJQ Music, 1961.

Conekin, Becky. "Fashioning the Playboy: Messages of Style and Masculinity in the Pages of Playboy Magazine, 1953–1963." *Fashion Theory* 4, no. 4 (2000): 447–466.

Cortez, Jayne. *Somewhere in Advance of Nowhere*. Serpent's Tail; High Risk Books, 1996.

Curtis, Edward E., IV. "African-American Islamization Reconsidered: Black History Narratives and Muslim Identity." *Journal of the American Academy of Religion* 73, no. 3 (September 2005): 659–684.

Daulatzai, Sohail. *Black Star, Crescent Moon: The Muslim International and Black Freedom beyond America*. University of Minnesota Press, 2012.

Davis, Miles, and Quincy Troupe. *Miles: The Autobiography*. Simon & Schuster, 1989.

Decker, Todd. *Who Should Sing Ol' Man River? The Lives of American Song*. Oxford University Press, 2015.

Deveaux, Scott. *The Birth of Bebop: A Social and Musical History*. University of California Press, 1997.

Deveaux, Scott. "Constructing the Jazz Tradition: Jazz Historiography." *Black American Literature Forum* 25, no. 3 (Fall 1991): 525–560.

DeVito, Chris, Yasuhiro Fujioka, Wolf Schmaler, and David Anthony Wild. *The John Coltrane Reference*. Edited by Lewis Porter. Routledge, 2013.

Donaldson, Gary. *The First Modern Campaign: Kennedy, Nixon, and the Election of 1960*. Rowman & Littlefield, 2007.

Dougherty, Carissa Kowalski. "The Coloring of Jazz: Race and Record Cover Design in American Jazz, 1950–1970." *Athanor* 24 (2006): 57–58.

Downham, Clay. "Eric Dolphy's Out: An Inquiry into George Russell's Lydian Chromatic Concept, the Music of Eric Dolphy, and Playing Outside." Master's thesis, University of Colorado, Boulder, 2018.

Drott, Eric. "Free Jazz and the French Critic." *Journal of the American Musicological Society* 61, no. 3 (2008): 541–582.

Dunkel, Mario. "Marshall Winslow Stearns and the Politics of Jazz Historiography." *American Music* 20, no. 4 (Winter 2012): 493–494.

Farraj, Johnny, and Sami Abu Shumays. *Inside Arabic Music: Arabic Maqam Performance and Theory in the 20th Century*. Oxford University Press, 2019.

Feather, Leonard. *The Encyclopedia of Jazz in the Sixties*. Horizon Press, 1966.

Feather, Leonard. *Inside Be-Bop*. J. J. Robbins & Sons, 1949.

Forte, Allen, and Paul Hindemith. "Paul Hindemith's Contribution to Music Theory in the United States." *Journal of Music Theory* 42, no. 1 (Spring 1998): 1–14.

Gennari, John. *Blowin' Hot and Cool: Jazz and Its Critics*. University of Chicago Press, 2006.

Gennari, John. "Jazz Criticism: Its Development and Ideologies." *Black American Literature Forum* 25, no. 3 (Autumn 1991): 449–523.

Gilroy, Paul. "Sounds Authentic: Black Music, Ethnicity, and the Challenge of a *Changing Same*." *Black Music Research Journal* 11, no. 2 (Autumn 1991): 111–136.

Givan, Benjamin. "Gunther Schuller and the Challenge of Sonny Rollins: Stylistic Context, Intentionality, and Jazz Analysis." *Journal of the American Musicological Society* 67 (2014): 167–237.

Glazer, Nathan, and Daniel Patrick Moynihan. *Beyond the Melting Pot: The Negroes, Puerto Ricans, Jews, Italians, and Irish of New York City*. MIT Press, 1963.

Glissant, Édouard. *Poetics of Relation*. University of Michigan Press, 1997.

Golia, Maria. *Ornette Coleman: The Territory and the Adventure*. Reaktion Books, 2020.

Gray, John. *Creative Improvised Music: An International Bibliography of the Jazz Avant-Garde, 1959–Present*. Black Music Reference Series, vol. 9. African Diasporic Press, 2019.

Greenbaum, Susan. *Blaming the Poor: The Long Shadow of the Moynihan Report on Cruel Images about Poverty*. Rutgers University Press, 2015.

Grundy, David. "'Everything That You Do': On the Poetry of Cecil Taylor." *Chicago Review* 64, no. 4 (2019): https://www.chicagoreview.org/david-grundy-everything-that-you-do-on-the-poetry-of-cecil-taylor/.

Haefeli, Sara. *John Cage: A Research and Information Guide*. Routledge, 2018.

Harper, Philip Brian. *Abstractionist Aesthetics: Artistic Form and Social Critique in African American Culture*. New York University Press, 2015.

Hill, Margari. "The Spread of Islam in West Africa: Containment, Mixing, and Reform from the Eighth to the Twentieth Century." *Stanford SPICE Digest*, Freeman Spogli Institute for International Studies, Spring 2009. https://spice.fsi.stanford.edu/docs/the_spread_of_islam_in_west_africa_containment_mixing_and_reform_from_the_eighth_to_the_twentieth_century.

Hodeir, André. "Letter of Evolutionism and the Role of Criticism." In *Towards Jazz*, translated by Noel Burch. Grove Press, 1962.

Howard, John Tasker, and James Lyon. *Modern Music: A Popular Guide to Greater Musical Enjoyment*. Mentor Books; New American Library, 1958.

Jenkins, Todd S. *Free Jazz and Free Improvisation*. Vol. 1. Greenwood Press, 2004.

Josephson, David. "The German Musical Exile and the Course of American Musicology." *Current Musicology*, nos. 79–80 (April 2005): 9–53.

Jost, Ekkehard. *Free Jazz*. Da Capo Press, 1975.

Kahn, Ashley. *A Love Supreme: The Story of John Coltrane's Signature Album*. Viking Press, 2002.

Kelley, Robin D. G. *Africa Speaks, American Answers: Modern Jazz in Revolutionary Times*. Harvard University Press, 2012.

Kelley, Robin D. G. "Dig They Freedom: Meditations on History and the Black Avant-Garde." *Lenox Avenue: A Journal of Interarts Inquiry* 3 (1997): 13–27.

Kelley, Robin D. G. *Freedom Dreams: The Black Radical Imagination*. Beacon Press, 2002.

Kelley, Robin D. G. "New Monastery: Monk and the Jazz Avant-Garde." *Black Music Research Journal* 19, no. 2 (Autumn 1999): 135–168.

Kelley, Robin D. G. *Thelonious Monk: The Life and Times of an American Original*. Free Press, 2009.

Kim, Eunmi. "Lennie Tristano (1919–1978): His Life, Music, and Teaching." PhD diss., University of Illinois, Urbana-Champagne, 1999.

Kivy, Peter. *The Music Alone: Philosophical Reflections on the Purely Musical Experience*. Cornell University Press, 1990.

Klotz, Kelsey A. K. "Dave Brubeck's Southern Strategy." *Daedalus* 148, no. 2 (2019): 52–66.

Knauer, Wolfram. "John Lewis." In *Grove Music Online*, edited by Deane Root, Philip V. Bohlman, Jonathan Cross, Tammy L. Kernodle, Honey Meconi, and John H. Roberts, *Oxford Music Online*. n.d. Accessed August 16, 2022. https://www-oxfordmusiconline-com. proxy.library.nyu.edu/grovemusic/view/10.1093/gmo/9781561592630.001.0001/omo-9781561592630-e-1002257573. Added "Oxford Music Online" as a possible resolution.

Kofsky, Frank. *John Coltrane and the Jazz Revolution of the 1960s*. Pathfinder, 1998.

Kraus, Nina. *Of Sound Mind: How Our Brain Constructs a Meaningful Sonic World*. MIT Press, 2021.

Latour, Bruno. *We Have Never Been Modern*. Translated by Catherine Porter. Harvard University Press, 1993.

Lee, David. *The Battle of the Five Spot: Ornette and the New York Jazz Field*. Mercury Press, 2000.

Lehman, Steve. "I Love You with an Asterisk: African-American Experimental Music and the French Jazz Press, 1970–1980." *Critical Studies in Improvisation/Études Critiques En Improvisation* 1, no. 2 (2005): 38–53.

Lewis, George E. "Improvised Music after 1950: Afrological and Eurological Perspectives." *Black Music Research Journal* 16, no. 1 (1996): 91–122.

Lewis, George E. *A Power Stronger Than Itself: The AACM and American Experimental Music*. University of Chicago Press, 2008.

Litweiler, John. *Ornette Coleman: A Harmolodic Life*. William Morrow, 1992.

Mall, Andrew. "Concentration, Diversity, and Consequence: Privileging Independent over Major Labels." *Popular Music* 37, no. 3 (2018): 444–465.

Mandel, Howard. *Miles, Ornette, and Cecil: Jazz Beyond Jazz*. Routledge, 2008.

Marable, Manning. *Race, Reform, Rebellion: The Second Reconstruction and Beyond in Black America, 1945–2006*. 3rd ed. University of Mississippi Press, 2007.

McAlister, Melani. *Epic Encounters: Culture, Media, and U.S. Interest in the Middle East since 1945*. University of California Press, 2005.

Mercer, Michelle. *Footprints: The Life and Work of Wayne Shorter*. Penguin, 2007.

Michaelsen, Garrett. "Making 'Anti-Music': Divergent Interactional Strategies in the Miles Davis Quintet's *Complete Live at the Plugged Nickel*." *Music Theory Online* 25, no. 3 (September 2019). https://mtosmt.org/ojs/index.php/mto/article/view/611.

Millard, Andre. *America on Record: A History of Recorded Sound*. Cambridge University Press, 2005.

Miller, Monica L. *Slaves to Fashion: Black Dandyism and the Styling of Black Diasporic Identity*. Duke University Press, 2009.

MJQ Music. *The Modern Jazz Quartet: The Legendary Profile*. MJQ Music, 1977.

Monson, Ingrid. *Freedom Sounds: Civil Rights Call Out to Jazz and Africa*. Oxford University Press, 2007.

Monson, Ingrid. "Hearing, Seeing, and Perpetual Agency." *Critical Inquiry* 34, no. S2 (Winter 2008): S36–S58.

Monson, Ingrid. "The Problem with White Hipness: Race, Gender, and Cultural Conceptions in Jazz Historical Discourse." *Journal of the American Musicological Society* 48, no. 3 (Autumn 1995): 396–422.

Monson, Ingrid. *Saying Something: Jazz Improvisation and Interaction*. University of Chicago Press, 1996.

Monson, Ingrid. "Yusef Lateef's Autophysiopsychic Quest." *Dædalus, the Journal of the American Academy of Arts & Sciences* 148, no. 2 (2019): 104–114.

Moten, Fred. "Blackness and Nothingness (Mysticism in the Flesh)." *South Atlantic Quarterly* 112, no. 4 (Fall 2013): 737–780.

Moten, Fred. *In the Break: The Aesthetics of the Black Radical Tradition*. University of Minnesota Press, 2003.

Oja, Carol. *Making Music Modern: New York in the 1920s.* Oxford University Press, 2000.

Okiji, Fumi. *Jazz as Critique: Adorno and Black Expression Revisited.* Stanford University Press, 2018.

O'Meally, Robert, Brent Hayes Edwards, and Farah Jasmine Griffin, eds. *Uptown Conversation: The New Jazz Studies.* Columbia University Press, 2004.

Panish, Jon. *The Color of Jazz: Race and Representation in Postwar American Culture.* University of Mississippi Press, 1997.

Pease, Ted. "The Schillinger/Berklee Connection." *Berklee Today,* September 1, 2000. https://www.berklee.edu/berklee-today/fall-2000/The-Schillinger.

Piekut, Benjamin. *Experimentalism Otherwise: The New York Avant-Garde and Its Limits.* University of California Press, 2011.

Piekut, Benjamin. *Henry Cow: The World Is a Problem.* Duke University Press, 2019.

Piekut, Benjamin. "Race, Community, and Conflict in the Jazz Composers Guild." *Jazz Perspectives* 3, no. 3 (December 2009): 191–231.

Poggioli, Renato. *The Theory of the Avant-Garde.* Translated by Gerald Fitzgerald. Belknap Press of Harvard University, 1962.

Porter, Lewis. *John Coltrane: His Life and Music.* University of Michigan Press, 1998.

Ramsey, Guthrie P., Jr. *Race Music: Black Cultures from Bebop to Hip-Hop.* University of California Press, 2003.

Ramsey, Guthrie P., Jr. *Who Hears Here? On Black Music, Pasts and Present.* University of California Press, 2022.

Rasula, Jed. "Jazz and American Modernism." In *The Cambridge Companion to American Modernism,* edited by Walter Kalaidjian. Cambridge University Press, 2005.

Rasula, Jed. "The Media of Memory: The Seductive Menace of Records in Jazz History." In *Jazz among the Discourses,* edited by Krin Gabbard. Duke University Press, 1995.

Ratliff, Ben. *Coltrane: The Story of a Sound.* Farrar, Straus and Giroux, 2007.

Reese, Sam V. H. *The Notebooks of Sonny Rollins.* New York Review of Books, 2024.

Robinson, Cedric. *Black Marxism: The Making of the Black Radical Tradition.* 3rd ed. Revised and updated. University of North Carolina Press, 2020.

Rubin, Joan Shelley. *Cultural Considerations: Essays on Readers, Writers, and Musicians in Postwar America.* University of Massachusetts Press, 2013.

Russell, George. *The Lydian Chromatic Concept of Tonal Organization (For All Instruments).* Concept, 1959.

Samuel, Lawrence R. *Brought to You By: Postwar Television Advertising and the American Dream.* University of Texas Press, 2001.

Schoenberg, Arnold. *Theory of Harmony.* Translated by Roy E. Carter. University of California Press, 2011.

Schuller, Gunther. *A Collection of the Compositions of Ornette Coleman.* MJQ Music, 1961.

Schuller, Gunther. *Gunther Schuller: A Life in Pursuit of Music and Beauty.* Boydell & Brewer; University of Rochester Press, 2011.

Schuller, Gunther. "Third Stream." In *Musings: The Musical Worlds of Gunther Schuller.* Oxford University Press, 1986.

Schwartz, Jeff. *Albert Ayler: His Life and Music.* 1992. https://web.archive.org/web/20161017170130/http://www.reocities.com/jeff_l_schwartz/ayler.html.

Scurry, Samuel. "Orientalism in American Cinema: Providing an Historical and Geographical Context for Post-Colonial Theory." Master's thesis, Clemson University, 2010.

Shaw, Arnold. *The Jazz Age: Popular Music in the 1920's.* Oxford University Press, 1987.

Shaw, Michael, trans. "Foreword: Theory of Modernism versus Theory of the Avant-Garde." In *Theory of the Avant-Garde.* University of Minnesota Press, 1984.

Smethurst, James. *Brick City Vanguard: Amiri Baraka, Black Music, Black Modernity.* University of Massachusetts Press, 2020.

Smethurst, James. "'Pat Your Foot and Turn the Corner': Amiri Baraka, the Black Arts Movement, and the Poetics of a Popular Avant-Garde." *African American Review* 37, nos. 2–3 (Summer–Autumn 2003): 261–270.

Spellman, A. B. *Four Jazz Lives*. University of Michigan Press, 1966.

Stearns, Marshall W. *The Story of Jazz*. Oxford University Press, 1956.

Stovall, Tyler. *Paris Noir: African Americans in the City of Light*. Houghton Mifflin, 1996.

Szwed, John. *So What: The Life of Miles Davis*. Simon & Schuster, 2002.

Szwed, John. *Space Is the Place: The Lives and Times of Sun Ra*. Duke University Press, 2020.

Turner, Richard Brent. *Islam in the African American Experience*. Indiana University Press, 1997.

Ulanov, Barry. *A History of Jazz in America*. Viking Press, 1952.

Waters, Keith. *The Studio Recordings of the Miles Davis Quintet: 1965–1968*. Oxford University Press, 2011.

Wells, Christi Jay. "'The Ace of His Race': Paul Whiteman's Early Reception in the Black Press." *Jazz and Culture* 1, no. 1 (January 2008): 77–103.

Williams, James Gordon. *Crossing the Bar Lines: The Politics and Practices of Black Musical Space*. University of Mississippi Press, 2021.

Williams, Martin. *The Jazz Tradition*. New and revised ed. Oxford University Press, 1983.

Williams, Martin. "Ornette Coleman—by Quincy Jones, Martin Williams, Hsio Wen Shih." In *Jazz Panorama: From the Pages of the Jazz Review*, edited by Martin Williams. New York: Crowell-Collier Press, 1962.

Wilmer, Valerie. *As Serious as Your Life: John Coltrane and Beyond*. Serpent's Tail, 1992.

Wilson, Olly. "The Heterogeneous Sound Ideal in African American Music." In *New Perspectives on Music: Essays in Honor of Eileen Southern*, edited by Josephine Wright and Samuel A. Floyd Jr. Harmonie Park Press, 1992.

Wynter, Sylvia. "On How We Mistook the Map for the Territory, and Re-Imprisoned Ourselves in Our Unbearable Wrongness of Being, of Désêtre: Black Studies toward the Human Project." In *Not Only the Master's Tools: African American Studies in Theory and Practice*, edited by Lewis R. Gordon and Jane Anna Gordon. Paradigm, 2006.

Wynter, Sylvia. "Rethinking 'Aesthetics': Notes towards a Deciphering Practice." In *Exiles: Essays on Caribbean Cinema*, edited by Mbye B. Cham. Africa World Press, 1992.

Zhang, Andi. "The Immune System Can Hear Noise." *Frontiers in Immunology* 11 (2021). https://doi.org/10.3389/fimmu.2020.619189.

Index

For the benefit of digital users, indexed terms that span two pages (e.g., 52–53) may, on occasion, appear on only one of those pages.

Printed in Dunstable, United Kingdom

85221343R00140